Routledge Revivals

Allomorphy in Inflexion

First published in 1987, this book broke new ground in research on inflectional morphology. Drawing on evidence from a wide variety of languages, it shows that this is not just a phenomenon left over from obsolete phonological processes but a subject deserving of respect in its own right. The book proposes constraints in three areas: (1) the organization of inflection class systems; (2) inflectional homonymy, or syncretism; (3) the direction of allomorphic conditioning.

Carstairs-McCarthy's notion of 'paradigm economy' revolutionized the study of inflection class systems but in its purest form, presented in this book, the hypothesis was too strong. In more recent works, the author has therefore argued that a version of it is an unexpected by-product of the brain's aptitude for handling multiple vocabularies. The study of *inflectional homonymy* was pioneered by Roman Jakobson as evidence for the structuring of morphosyntactic categories or feature sets (case, number, tense, mood and so on) but his approach differed from that of this book, whose radical suggestions fertilized much subsequent work on 'inflectional identity'. *The direction of conditioning*, first explored in this text, is debated actively within the Distributed Morphology framework popular within Chomskyan generative linguistics, despite disagreement with the Carstairs-McCarthy view that morphology is a domain of grammar entirely distinct from syntax. In *The Evolution of Morphology* (2010) the author takes these topics further, and also explains why stem alternation and affixation are importantly distinct as modes of inflectional expression.

Inflectional allomorphy is an apparently pointless complication exhibited by many languages. However, this book suggests reasons why it is, nevertheless, easy for the brain to handle. The work thus has important implications beyond language, extending into human cognition.

Allomorphy in Inflexion

Andrew Carstairs-McCarthy

First published in 1987
by Croom Helm Ltd

This edition first published in 2013 by Routledge
2 Park Square, Milton Park, Abingdon, Oxon, OX14 4RN

Simultaneously published in the USA and Canada
by Routledge
711 Third Avenue, New York, NY 10017

Routledge is an imprint of the Taylor & Francis Group, an informa business

© 1987 Andrew Carstairs-McCarthy

All rights reserved. No part of this book may be reprinted or reproduced or utilised in any form or by any electronic, mechanical, or other means, now known or hereafter invented, including photocopying and recording, or in any information storage or retrieval system, without permission in writing from the publishers.

Publisher's Note
The publisher has gone to great lengths to ensure the quality of this reprint but points out that some imperfections in the original copies may be apparent.

Disclaimer
The publisher has made every effort to trace copyright holders and welcomes correspondence from those they have been unable to contact.

A Library of Congress record exists under ISBN: 86032794

ISBN 13: 978-0-415-82504-7 (hbk)
ISBN 13: 978-0-203-69447-3 (ebk)

Allomorphy in Inflexion

Andrew Carstairs

CROOM HELM
London • New York • Sydney

© 1987 Andrew Carstairs
Croom Helm Ltd, Provident House,
Burrell Row, Beckenham, Kent BR3 1AT
Croom Helm Australia, 44-50 Waterloo Road,
North Ryde, 2113, New South Wales

British Library Cataloguing in Publication Data

Carstairs, Andrew
   Allomorphy in inflexion. — (Croom Helm
   Linguistics series)
   1. Grammar, Comparative and general —
   Morphology
   I. Title   II. Series
   415   P241

ISBN 0-7099-3483-1

Published in the USA by
Croom Helm
in association with Methuen, Inc.
29 West 35th Street
New York, NY 10001

Library of Congress Cataloging-in-Publication Data
Carstairs, Andrew Damerell.
   Allomorphy in inflexion.

   (Croom Helm Linguistics Series)
   Includes bibliographies.
   1. Grammar, comparative and general — Inflection.
   2. Morphophonemics. 3. German language — Inflection.
   I. Title. II. Series.
   P251.C37   1987   415   86-32794
   ISBN 0-7099-3483-1

Typeset in 10pt Times Roman by Leaper & Gard Ltd, Bristol, England
Printed and bound in Great Britain
by Billings & Sons Limited, Worcester.

To Jeremy

Contents

Preface and Acknowledgements   xiii
Abbreviations   xv

1. Introduction   1
   1.1 Aims and assumptions   1
   1.2 Method   7
   1.3 The one-to-one inflexional pattern and deviations from it   12
   1.4 Phonologically conditioned allomorphy and 'abstractness'   18
   Notes   21

2. The Status of Inflexional Paradigms   24
   2.1 Paradigms and allomorphy   24
   2.2 Recent views of the paradigm   26
   2.3 Prodigality and parsimony in inflexion   28
      2.3.1 Are inflexions distributed independently?   32
      2.3.2 The nonexistence of 'syntactic parsimony'   35
   Notes   40

3. The Paradigm Economy Principle   42
   3.1 A first formulation   42
      3.1.1 Some Hungarian, Zulu and Dyirbal evidence   42
      3.1.2 Definitions   47
      3.1.3 Consequences   52
   3.2 Revisions and refinements   56
      3.2.1 Prima facie counterevidence to the Paradigm Economy Principle   56
      3.2.2 The relevance of lexically determined morphosyntax and morphosemantics   59
      3.2.3 Macroparadigm uniqueness   70
      3.2.4 Slabs and paradigm mixture   77
   Notes   83

4.	Homonymy Within Paradigms		87
	4.1	Introduction: approaches to inflexional homonymy	87
	4.2	A general restriction on systematic homonymy	90
		4.2.1 The structure of the argument	90
		4.2.2 Systematic versus accidental homonymy	93
		4.2.3 The morphosyntactic status of systematic homonymy	102
		4.2.4 The data of the Appendix: a first observation	107
		4.2.5 A possible function for systematic homonymy	109
		4.2.6 Syncretism, take-over and the Systematic Homonymy Claim	114
		4.2.7 Consequences of the Systematic Homonymy Claim for language change	124
		4.2.8 The reliability of the Appendix	127
	4.3	Some individual homonymies	128
		4.3.1 Homonymy losses in Italian and Georgian	128
		4.3.2 An Arabic Case-homonymy and its implications	132
		4.3.3 Nominative–Accusative Neuter homonymies in Indo-European	137
	Notes		138
	Appendix to Chapter 4: A selection of inflexional homonymies		141
	Comments on the Appendix		144
5.	Syntagmatic Constraints on Allomorphy		147
	5.1	Inward and outward sensitivity	147
		5.1.1 Identifying pure sensitivity	147
		5.1.2 Pure inward sensitivity	152
		5.1.3 Peripherality and homonymy	162
		5.1.4 Outward sensitivity	165
		5.1.5 Zero realisations and morphosyntactic zeros	169
		5.1.6 A problem: inconstancy of sequence in realisation	175

		5.1.7	A second problem: phonological sensitivity outwards	179

       5.1.7 A second problem: phonological sensitivity outwards 179
       5.1.8 The Peripherality Constraint and Deviation III 188
  5.2 Peripherality and other constraints on allomorphy 195
       5.2.1 Adjacency 195
       5.2.2 The Elsewhere Condition 198
       5.2.3 The Mirror Principle 201
  Notes 203

6. Two Questions Concerning Stem Allomorphy 207
  6.1 Introduction: types of stem 207
  6.2 Stem allomorphy and the Peripherality Constraint 210
  6.3 Stem allomorphy and the Paradigm Economy Principle 221
  Notes 233

7. A Case Study: Paradigm Economy in German Nouns 234
  7.1 The facts and the problems 234
  7.2 German nominal macroparadigms 237
  7.3 The weak declension-types 241
  Notes 250
  Appendix to Chapter 7: Inflexional vacillation among German nouns of declension-type XIII (*Name*) 251

8. Next Steps 252
  Note 257

Bibliography 258
Indexes 266

Preface and Acknowledgements

This book began life as parts of a London University PhD thesis written between 1979 and 1981 (Carstairs 1981b; 1984b). In revising it for book publication, I have tried to take account of more recent relevant work, and have been encouraged by the continued growth of interest in morphology on the part of linguistic theorists, but I have not felt it necessary to alter my main proposals radically.

I have been taught linguistics over a number of years at Oxford, London, MIT and London again, and owe a great deal to people at all these places. But I would like to thank especially my supervisors at the School of Oriental and African Studies from 1979 to 1981, Theodora Bynon and Geoffrey Horrocks, who accepted the burden of overseeing work on what probably seemed an eccentric and unpromising topic and who encouraged me unstintingly throughout; and also Paul Kiparsky, who was my adviser during my first attempt to write a PhD thesis on inflexional morphology in 1971-72 and who made valuable comments on material underlying parts of this one.

I am grateful to several people for advice on particular languages: D.W. Arnott and Mary McIntosh (Fulfulde), Paddy Considine (Latin), Richard Hudson (Beja), A.K. Irvine (Arabic and Hebrew), R.H. Robins (Yurok), David Rycroft (Zulu) and Peter Sherwood (Hungarian). Naturally they are not responsible for any mistakes, nor for the conclusions which I draw from relevant facts. Mary McIntosh and David Rycroft were especially generous with their time and energy in discussing ideas on morphology in general and criticising drafts of various parts of the thesis. Other people who helped me with comments, criticisms or discussion at various stages are Waria Amin, C.E. Bazell, Bob Beard, Richard Coates, Wolfgang Dressler, Jim Harris, Steve Johnson, Fred Karlsson, Ruth Kempson, Koenraad Kuiper, Rochelle Lieber, Peter Matthews, Frans Plank, Martin Prior, N.J. Sims-Williams, Alan Sommerstein, Andy Spencer, Nigel Vincent, Wolfgang Wurzel, Arnold Zwicky, and an anonymous reader for Croom Helm.

I have presented papers based on earlier drafts of various chapters at seminars and conferences in Britain, Poland, New

Zealand and Australia. I owe a lot to the discussions which followed these presentations, and also to a series of seminars on morphology run by Dick Hudson at University College London in the summer of 1980.

The Leverhulme Trust, by their award of a Senior Studentship, made it financially possible for me to return to SOAS as a graduate student. More recently, the University of Canterbury (New Zealand) has provided a congenial working environment, financial help (Research Grant 573346), and subsidised conference leave to enable me to attend the Workshop on Natural Morphology held at the Societas Linguistica Europaea in Poznań, Poland, in August 1983. I am particularly grateful to Kate Trevella and Orma Shaw in the English Department for typing the long and difficult manuscript.

Finally, I would like to thank my flat-mates in London, Allen Morris and Hugh Haward, who put up with a lot of bad temper while I was working on the thesis, and Jeremy McCarthy in Christchurch, who has inspired the final revision.

Christchurch, New Zealand

Abbreviations

Abbreviations are used for the names of certain morpho-syntactic categories and properties, as follows:

AbG	Ablative, Genitive	L(oc)	Locative
Abl	Ablative	M(asc)	Masculine
A(cc)	Accusative	NAG	Nominative, Accusative, Genitive
Act	Active		
DAb	Dative, Ablative		
D(at)	Dative	N(eut)	Neuter
Decl	declension	N(om)	Nominative
Def	Definite	NVA	Nominative, Vocative, Accusative
Erg	Ergative		
F(em)	Feminine		
Fut	Future	Pass	Passive
G(en)	Genitive	Perf	Perfective
GL	Genitive, Locative	Pf	Perfective
IDAb	Instrumental, Dative, Ablative	Pl	Plural
		Poss	Possessive
Imper	Imperative	Pres	Present
Impf	Imperfective	Sg	Singular
Indef	Indefinite	Subj	Subject
Ind(ic)	Indicative	Subjunc	Subjunctive
Infin	Infinitive	Voc	Vocative
I(nstr)	Instrumental		

1

Introduction

1.1 AIMS AND ASSUMPTIONS

The aim of this book is to propose and defend certain generalisations about morphological behaviour. These generalisations are intended to be valid for all languages which exhibit morphological behaviour of the relevant kinds and are therefore, in that sense, claims about linguistic universals. They concern inflexional morphology, and more particularly the relationship between morphological 'expression' and 'content' (or 'signifiant' and 'signifié').

All languages relate sounds to meanings, and do so partly through attributing significance to the order of meaningful units smaller than the total utterance. The first of these remarks is quite banal. The second is somewhat less so; it is not logically necessary that a communication system for use by human beings should be 'articulated' (in Martinet's sense) at two levels, the phonological and the syntactic; but the fact that language is so articulated is one of the few elements of common ground among all serious students of language. It follows that the description of any language will involve a distinction between its phonology on the one hand and what we can loosely call its syntactic-semantic apparatus on the other. By no means all languages, however, display the sort of behaviour which in a traditional grammatical description of Greek or Latin is treated under the heading 'inflexional morphology'. It has, moreover, been notoriously difficult to arrive at a satisfactory general definition of the term 'word', designating the linguistic unit whose internal structure is the subject-matter of morphology. These are two of the reasons why some linguists have not merely neglected morphology as uninteresting but actually denied its existence as a distinct component of grammar altogether. The first assumption that I will make is that this is incorrect, and that in many languages one can identify grammatical units — 'words' — with an internal structure which differs more or less from that of sentences and which therefore cannot be described adequately by reference only to the rules of sentence structure or syntax. This assumption is scarcely controversial among generative grammarians today, since the 'lexicalist hypothesis' about word-formation has displaced the 'transformationalist hypothesis' (cf. Chomsky 1970; Scalise 1984); still, for arguments to back up the assumption, non-generativists and persistent sceptics can turn to Peter Matthews' work on morphology (e.g. Matthews 1974: 2-8).

I assume also Matthews' notions **morphosyntactic category** and **morphosyntactic property** (1972b: 161-2; 1974: 66, 136). Morphosyntactic properties are what inflexions express or realise, such as Masculine Gender, Past Tense or Accusative Case; I regard them as constituting the inflexional 'content' (as opposed to 'expression') referred to earlier. Morphosyntactic categories are classes of contrasting and mutually exclusive morphosyntactic properties, such as, in Latin, Gender, Tense and Case. Each category, together with the properties it contains, is applicable to one or more parts of speech or word-classes. I adopt here, as I do throughout, Matthews' practice of giving a capital initial letter to the names of morphosyntactic categories and properties. For brevity, I will often omit the word 'morphosyntactic', but all references to categories and properties should be understood as references to morphosyntactic ones unless I make it plain that I am using these terms in some other way. In particular, I will not use 'category' in the sense of 'word-class' or 'part of speech'.

The set of categories and properties relevant to one language is not necessarily the same as that relevant to the next. This could hardly be otherwise, given that there are 'isolating' languages which have no inflexion at all and consequently no morphosyntactic properties, according to my definition; that is, in an isolating language like Vietnamese, for example, verbal tenses (if they exist) must be purely syntactic or semantic and cannot be called morphosyntactic. The non-universality of categories and properties, in this sense, is so obvious as to be hardly worth mentioning. But it leads directly to a problem which is far from banal, namely: what are the criteria for identifying the morphosyntactic properties and categories relevant to a given language? My answer to this question resembles the answer that I will give to various other fundamental questions of definition. To arrive at a watertight set of criteria would involve discussion of, and decisions about, a number of problems quite far removed from the aim of this book, such as the handling of syntactic 'cooccurrence restrictions' in the widest sense (including concord and 'sequence of tenses'). But there are enough clear examples of inflexion, involving morphosyntactic properties that are fairly straightforwardly identifiable, to provide us with a core of material to begin our investigation. Refining the criteria to cope with the more controversial penumbra can wait until we know whether our study of the core material looks like yielding profitable results in the shape of interesting (i.e. readily falsifiable but nevertheless unfalsified) generalisations; and at that stage we can legitimately allow our provisional results to influence our decisions.

There is, however, one characteristic of morphosyntactic properties which we can regard as definitive straight away. If morphosyntactic properties are what inflexions realise, then a distinction between two properties which is never manifested in any distinction between inflected word-forms is impossible. One may, of course, want to recognise, even in an inflected language, syntactically relevant 'properties' or 'features' which are never expressed morphologically. 'Properties' of this kind will include, for example, many of Fillmore's (1968) 'cases', which are explicitly more abstract entities than the traditional morphological Cases of a language such as Latin. Under this heading, too, comes (for example) Dixon's (1972) distinction between instrumental and ergative 'cases' in Dyirbal. Dixon claims that there are good syntactic grounds for distinguishing these two 'cases'; but, since there is never any overt morphological distinction between them, we are not entitled to recognise here more than one *morpho*syntactic Case, any more than the syntactic distinction between the object of transitive verbs and the subject of embedded infinitival sentences in Latin justifies us in recognising more than one morphosyntactic property Accusative, which happens to be manifested by nouns in these two distinct syntactic contexts. A necessary condition, then, for a clear example of a morphosyntactic property is that it should have an overt inflexional manifestation in at least some members of the appropriate word-class.

The decision to concentrate on uncontroversial or 'core' instances of inflexion enables us largely to skirt around the issue of distinguishing between inflexion and derivation. This longstanding problem has been tackled by numerous recent writers on morphology (e.g. Matthews 1974; M. Allen 1979; Plank 1981; Anderson 1982; Scalise 1984), and, at first sight, it may seem imperative that I should circumscribe the subject-matter of this book by offering clear criteria for the distinction. But the fact that I do not do so is not a serious deficiency, precisely because none of the claims that I will put forward hinges on where one draws the line between inflexion and derivation, or even on acknowledging that there is a line to be drawn. In other words, none of my generalisations, as presented, depends crucially on excluding 'derivational' phenomena from its scope, and I leave open the possibility that these generalisations may be applicable to morphological behaviour which would traditionally be labelled 'derivational'.

That said, one can nevertheless identify a kind of spectrum of morphological behaviour with 'derivational' and 'inflexional' extremes. Most linguists will probably agree in calling a morphological process (of affixation, for example) 'inflexional' if it has all the following characteristics:

(a) it expresses a meaning (or realises a property) which all members of the relevant word-class can manifest (that is, the expression of that meaning is totally 'productive');
(b) it is in complementary distribution with some other process or processes which realise the same property (that is, allomorphy is involved);
(c) the property which it realises is one of a finite set (or 'category') of mutually exclusive properties, one of which must be manifested in every word-form belonging to the relevant word-class;
(d) it does not alter the word-class membership of the forms to which it applies;
(e) it is syntactically relevant in the sense that the property it realises is involved in quite precisely specifiable 'cooccurrence restrictions' with properties realised elsewhere in the sentence (for example, restrictions due to concord, government or 'sequence of tenses').

In contrast, most linguists will probably agree in calling a process 'derivational' if it has all the following characteristics:

(f) it is not fully productive (that is, there are some members of the relevant word-class to which it idiosyncratically fails to apply);
(g) no single property or 'meaning' can be associated with it;
(h) it alters the word-class membership of the forms to which it applies;
(i) it is not syntactically relevant in the sense of (e) (except insofar as characteristic (h) implies syntactic relevance).[1]

The traditional difficulty of demarcation arises from the fact that few morphological processes display all and only the characteristics (a)-(e) or (f)-(i) respectively, and many display some characteristics taken from both sets. For example, the process of affixing the 'agentive' suffix -*er* to verbs in English, which would traditionally be called 'derivational', does indeed have characteristics (h) and (i) but lacks characteristic (g) and would seem to possess characteristic (a). It may also lack characteristic (f), if we are prepared to accept in some contexts agent nouns in -*er* formed even from those verbs for which the usual corresponding agent noun has some other form (e.g. *cycle*, *type*). In contrast, the suffixation of -*e* to form the Plural of Afrikaans nouns, which would traditionally be called an inflexional process, does indeed have properties (a), (b) and (d), since all Afrikaans 'count nouns' (as one might expect) can form a Plural which is syntactically still a noun, but only some of them do so by adding -*e*; on the other hand, this process lacks characteristic (e), since, perhaps alone among Indo-European languages, Afrikaans has no 'Number concord' of any kind. 'Core' examples of inflexional morphology, I suggest, are ones which share most of characteristics (a)-(e) and lack most of characteristics (f)-(i). The great majority of the morphological examples which I will be discussing will be unequivocally inflexional in this sense; but, again, nothing in the claims and suggestions that I will be putting forward makes it vital that I should avoid straying occasionally towards the derivational end of the spectrum.

I have designated morphosyntactic properties as the basic units of morphological content. What about the basic units of morphological expression (the morphological 'signifiants')? In discussing the characteristics typical of the two ends of the morphological spectrum (inflexional and derivational), I referred to 'morphological processes' such as affixation which might 'realise' morphosyntactic properties. I will in fact generally refer to morphological 'significants' as **inflexional realisations** or **inflexional exponents**[2] of morphosyntactic properties, or sometimes simply as **inflexions**. These apparently rather cumbersome terms are chosen in preference to, for example, 'morpheme' or 'morph' because they seem appropriate cover terms not only for affixation but also for such processes as infixation, ablaut, consonantal alternation, tonal alternation and reduplication, all of which may play a part in inflexion. For example, in the English words *dogs*, I would say that the morphosyntactic property Plural is realised by (or has as its inflexional exponent) the suffix *-s* (or [z]), while in the word *men* it is realised by ablaut or, more specifically, the substitution of *-e-* for the Singular form's *-a-*. My definitions thus do not commit me to trying to identify a Plural 'morpheme' or 'morph' on the level of expression in a word-form such as *man*, where inflexion does not involve affixation. Another reason for avoiding the term 'morpheme' is purely practical; it has been used in so many different senses that its use here would carry too much risk of confusion and misunderstanding, even if I defined carefully at the outset the sense in which I intended to use it myself. To a lesser extent, this is also true of the term 'formative', which I likewise avoid.

The term 'allomorphy', which appears in the title of this book, is to be understood by reference to the more precise questions which I will be posing presently about the relationship between morphosyntactic properties and their exponents. To anticipate somewhat, I will be looking for evidence of constraints on certain deviations from the simplest conceivable pattern of exponence; and the deviations which I will have most to say about all involve the sort of behaviour that would traditionally be called 'allomorphic'. 'Constraints on allomorphy' is therefore a useful and relatively comprehensible shorthand for what, in my terminology, should more strictly be called 'constraints on deviation from the simplest conceivable pattern of relationship between morphosyntactic properties and their inflexional exponents'.

1.2 METHOD

My aim, as stated at the beginning of the introduction, is to propose and defend certain empirical generalisations about the relationship between morphosyntactic properties and their exponents. Any generalisation is a claim that certain things are so. But any empirical generalisation — that is, any generalisation which is not a tautology, or true by definition — carries with it too the claim that certain things which might have been so are, in fact, not so. Any serious attempt to generalise about actual morphological behaviour, therefore, commits us also to thinking about logically possible morphological behaviour — what might happen as well as what does. Establishing what actually happens in the inflexional morphology of some language is relatively much easier than establishing what happens in the syntax; the brute facts of inflexional morphology have been fully described, at least at the level of observational adequacy, for all the languages for which pedagogical grammar-books exist, and, when a linguistic field-worker goes to work on a hitherto undescribed language, one can be sure that the 200-page monograph that results will treat pretty fully the grammatical categories which are expressed by inflexion and the shapes of the inflexions which express them, even if the treatment of syntactic processes is sketchy. But the morphological theorist, just like the syntactic theorist, must always look beyond what actually happens. When looking at some array of morphological data (say, a verbal Person-Number-Tense paradigm), he must constantly exercise his imagination and ask not only 'What do we observe here?' but also 'What might we have expected to observe here, or what might conceivably have observed, that we do not observe?'.

The two words 'expected' and 'conceivably' are important. Of course, there is, in principle, an infinite range of morphological phenomena which logically might occur in a given language but which in fact do not; the linguist needs some method of distinguishing within this range those non-occurrences which are of potential theoretical interest (corresponding to the 'starred' sentences in a disquisition on syntax). To illustrate the sort of method that the morphologist must use, I will start by citing certain facts about non-occurrences, or 'observational gaps', in Latin inflexional morphology:

(101) No Latin noun has a Case ending seventeen syllables long.
(102) No Latin noun has an Accusative ending -*at*.
(103) In Latin, there are not two semantically arbitrary classes of nouns, one of which inflects for Number only and the other for Case only; rather, all 'count' nouns (except for a tiny group of indeclinables) inflect for both Number and Case.
(104) Latin has no Dual Number.
(105) In Latin, no noun expresses Plurality by means of ablaut.
(106) In Latin, no noun expresses Plurality by inverting the order of consonants in the stem (as if *dominus* (Nom Sg) 'lord' had a Nominative Plural '*nomidus*').

In deciding which of these facts are of linguistic interest and in what way, a linguist will draw upon his general knowledge of how morphology operates in a variety of languages. Faced with the range of facts cited in (101)-(106), most linguists would, I suggest, agree in allocating them to three broad categories as follows:

A. Facts of no interest: (101).
B. Accidental facts about Latin (i.e. facts not reflecting any wider linguistic generalisation): (102), (104), (105).
C. Facts possibly reflecting some general linguistic principle: (103), (106).

The grounds on which I assign these facts of Latin to one or another of the categories (A), (B) and (C) will certainly not be the same in detail as those which another linguist will advance if faced with the same task. He might even disagree with my actual categorisation of some fact, on the basis of a broader linguistic expertise than I possess. But any practising linguist would, I think, agree about the sort of evidence that is relevant to the categorisation, even if (as the recent history of linguistics makes likely) he has not devoted much attention to questions of inflexional morphology. I emphasise this probability of agreement about the status of various kinds of observational gap because it is what chiefly guarantees that, even starting with a relatively clean slate on the theory of inflexional morphology, we can nevertheless hope that the questions we ask are ones which other linguists will agree to be worthwhile, and the conclusions we reach will strike other linguists as at least close enough to the truth to deserve consideration and criticism.

The reasons for my decisions about the six Latin facts are:

(101′) Seventeen-syllable affixes would be intolerably cumbersome. The fact that neither Latin nor (so far as I know) any other language has any can be put down to the banal fact that human language is a communication system and that, in any communication system, features which unnecessarily slow down transmission will be avoided. One could imagine, perhaps, a communication medium so 'noisy', in the technical sense, that seventeen-syllable affixes, and the slowness they would entail, would nevertheless be necessary for the accurate understanding of messages received. But neither human speech nor writing is such a medium. This fact about Latin is thus outside the sphere of linguistics, just like (for example) the fact that probably no one has uttered a sentence 5,000 words long.[3]

(102′) The ending -*at* is a possible ending in Latin (cf. *am-ō* 'I love', *am-at* 'he loves'); moreover, there is no intrinsic reason why it should not function as an Accusative Singular ending, since at least one language (Hungarian) uses it (or, more exactly, an ending phonetically similar to it) to mark the Accusative (or, more exactly, a Case similar enough in function to the Latin Accusative to deserve the same label): cf. Hungarian *toll* 'pen', *tollat* 'pen (Accusative)'. The fact that Latin does not use this ending for this purpose can be explained in historical terms, but from the general linguistic point of view it is a pure accident.

(104′) Many languages, of course, have a Dual Number, including some within the Indo-European family whose morphological and (to a lesser extent) syntactic characteristics are quite similar to those of Latin, such as Sanskrit, ancient Greek and Slovenian, and it is clear that the Dual is an ancient feature of Indo-European. From our point of view, then, the absence of a Dual Number in Latin (apart from morphological vestiges in *duo* 'two', *ambō* 'both') should probably be regarded as an accident, although we ought not to rule out the possibility of eventually relating the disappearance of the Dual from Latin to some other respect in which Latin differs from those languages which retain it, in such a way that the Latin development will no longer seem arbitrary from the general linguistic point of view.

(105') Ablaut — grammatically conditioned stem or root vowel change — certainly functions as a mark of Plurality in some languages (cf. English *tooth/teeth*), and it operates in Latin to distinguish some verbal Perfective stems from the corresponding Imperfective[4] stems (e.g. *fēcī* 'I made' versus *faciō* 'I make'). The fact that ablaut is not used in Latin Plural formation may therefore seem accidental. But it is noticeable that not only ablaut but also reduplication and some other consonantal changes are exploited in Latin for distinguishing Perfective and Imperfective stems and for no other inflexional purpose (e.g. *rumpō* 'I break', *cadō* 'I fall' versus *rūpī* 'I broke', *cecidī* 'I fell'). We may therefore want to investigate whether there are any wider principles affecting how, in individual languages, particular morphological 'processes' (in Sapir's (1921) sense) are specialised for certain functions.[5]

(103') In a language which normally gives morphological expression to Number distinctions, it is quite possible for some nouns to be exceptions (for example, English *sheep, deer*). Similarly, in a language where nouns are generally marked for Case, it is quite possible for some nouns to be indeclinable — to maintain the same shape in all Cases (e.g. Russian *pal'to* '*overcoat*'). In Latin, it is true that all nouns and adjectives fail to distinguish Dative and Ablative Cases in the Plural and that all Neuters fail to distinguish the Nominative and Accusative Cases, either Singular or Plural; but, again, the category of Case is morphologically irrelevant only to a very few indeclinables (e.g. *nefas* 'wicked deed'). In none of these languages, however, do we find two distinct classes of nouns, each of which manifests one of the two morphosyntactic categories but not the other; rather, what the English, Russian and Latin examples all seem to suggest is that in each language there is a set of morphosyntactic categories applicable to all members of the class 'noun' and, failing the sort of semantic excuse that 'mass nouns' have, an individual noun may exceptionally ignore (or fail to express morphologically) one of these categories only if it ignores them all.[6] Here, therefore, is a non-occurrence in Latin which seems not to be accidental; in view of the similar non-occurrences in other languages, we are entitled to suspect a general linguistic constraint at work.

(106′) This fact is in some respects similar to fact (105), which I assigned to category (B). Fact (105) — Latin's failure to use ablaut to mark Plurality — was deemed accidental from the general linguistic point of view because ablaut is certainly exploited as a Plural marker in other languages, although we left open the possibility that deeper investigation might nevertheless reveal some general principle at work in Latin. Fact (106), on the other hand, is assigned to category (C) because there is, to my knowledge, no language in which grammatically-conditioned consonantal change takes the form of inversion of the order of the consonants in a root. There is no obvious reason why this should be so; languages tolerate quite radical deformations of the 'basic' form of the root, through infixing and ablaut affecting more than one syllable (the Semitic languages are notorious in this respect). But it seems as if there is a limit to the degree of root-deformation which is permissible for inflexional purposes and that, wherever precisely the limit is to be drawn, the imaginary Latin Plural '*nomidus*' for *dominus* would overstep it.[7]

By means of these Latin examples I have tried to demonstrate the legitimacy and usefulness, in morphological investigation, of paying attention to what might occur in individual languages but does not. I have listed certain facts about things which do not occur in the inflexional morphology of Latin, and I have suggested that two of these observational gaps (points (103) and (106)) stem not from Latin grammar in particular but from constraints on language in general — about the grammatical features which can be expressed morphologically and the morphological processes which can be used to express them. Moreover, I have suggested that most linguists would agree fairly readily about the wider significance of these two particular Latin 'non-facts'. So, thinking about what might happen in

Latin but does not has served a useful purpose in drawing our attention to two apparently general facts of morphological behaviour which we might otherwise have overlooked. Throughout this book, I will in similar fashion attach considerable importance to not only the actual morphological behaviour of various languages but also 'non-facts' or observational gaps in their behaviour. The gaps will be used to illustrate behaviour which not merely does not occur but could not, if my empirical generalisations are correct. By the same token, they will illustrate precisely what sort of behaviour we will need to discover in some actual language in order to weaken or undermine my generalisations. But, of course, the more vulnerable a generalisation is, the greater is its empirical content and the stronger the predictions which it entails.

1.3 THE ONE-TO-ONE INFLEXIONAL PATTERN AND DEVIATIONS FROM IT

In section 1.1, I announced the business of this book as being with the relationship between morphosyntactic properties and their inflexional exponents. The very length of the book implies that (at least in my view) this relationship is complex. What we need is a way of approaching this complexity which will help us to discover order in it, if there is any order to be discovered. A good approach, I suggest, is to ask what languages would be like if the relationship were not complex at all but quite simple — the simplest possible, in fact. We can then ask ourselves what sorts of deviation from this simple pattern are conceivable and proceed to investigate how many of the conceivable sorts of deviation (or combinations of them) occur in actual languages. If all conceivable varieties occur, then inflexional morphology is indeed just a conglomeration of language-particular idiosyncrasies, of little interest to the linguistic theorist. If, on the other hand, we find that there are some conceivable varieties of deviation from the one-to-one pattern which never seem to crop up, we can regard this as at least prima facie evidence for the existence of universal constraints on inflexional behaviour.

Deciding whether one state of affairs is 'simpler' than another may not be easy, of course; if we are using 'simplicity' in an everyday, non-technical sense, appeal to it may seem to amount to an appeal to personal taste, supported perhaps by aesthetic criteria but still with an irremediably subjective element. Fortunately, however, everyone will surely agree about the simplest imaginable relationship between inflexional content and expression: perfect one-to-one pairing between morphosyntactic properties on the one hand and their inflexional exponents on the other. If all human languages behaved like this, scope for variety in inflexional patterning would be quite limited. It would of course be necessary to specify for individual languages what morphosyntactic properties were relevant and what the actual shapes of their exponents were. The arrangement of the exponents within words might also be to a large extent, or even overwhelmingly, language-particular. But it would not be necessary to cope with grammatically conditioned allomorphy, discontinuous morphs, 'portmanteau morphs', 'replacive morphs' or systematic homonymy. Moreoever, since syntax already exists as a component of grammar concerned with the arrangement, or order, of items within the sentence, the distinction between syntax and morphology might well seem otiose. 'Morphology' could just be a name for that branch of syntax concerned with the arrangement of items within words, rather than the arrangement of words themselves; and, insofar as the same principles governed both, we might conclude that there was no need at all to recognise 'morphology', even of this rather attenuated kind, as a separate component of grammar.

The idea of attributing a special status to the one-to-one pattern of inflexional realisation is not new. This is the pattern which would result from universal compliance with what has been called 'Humboldt's Universal' (Vennemann 1972: 183; G. Hudson 1980: 115), and, in the terminology of the 'Natural Morphology' developed by Dressler, Mayerthaler and others (cf. Mayerthaler 1981; 34-5), it exemplifies inflexional 'coding' which is both 'uniform' and 'transparent'. Our interest in the one-to-one pattern is different from that of these linguists, however. They are interested in it as a kind of ideal state towards which morphological systems allegedly tend, unless perturbed by phonological and other interference. For us, on the other hand, it constitutes the starting-point for consideration of other conceivable inflexional patterns. There is a difference of emphasis but no incompatibility between these interests. Morphological principles which operate to promote compliance with Humboldt's Universal may well exist alongside principles which limit the nature and extent of deviation from it. In this book, however, the focus will be on the latter.

Any deviation from consistent one-to-one pairing of exponents and properties must fall into one of two categories: it must involve either a many-to-one or a one-to-many relationship. Almost equally evidently, the well-known distinction between the two dimensions of linguistic structure, the paradigmatic and the syntagmatic, must be relevant here. Combining these two ideas, we can see that all logically possible instances of deviation from one-to-one patterning must fall into at least one of the following four classes:[8]

(107) **Deviation I:** One property to many exponents syntagmatically
(108) **Deviation II:** One to many paradigmatically
(109) **Deviation III:** Many to one syntagmatically
(110) **Deviation IV:** Many to one paradigmatically

For morphological theory, the interest of this classification lies in whether or not it helps to identify logically possible linguistic behaviour which is not actually observed in human languages. I will argue that it does, although somewhat indirectly.

The first question which arises, clearly, is whether all these types of deviation occur in actual human languages. The answer is yes. It is quite easy to find examples of each:

(111) *I: One to many syntagmatically*
This type involves what Matthews (1974) calls 'extended exponence'. The first example below is his.
 a. Ancient Attic Greek *elelykete* 'you (Pl) had loosed': superficially, at least, the Perfective Tense-Aspect is realised twice in this word-form, namely by the reduplicated prefix -*le*- and the suffix -*k*- on either side of the root -*ly*- 'loose'.
 b. Zulu: *úmfána (a)kágézi* 'the boy is not washing'. Comparing this with the corresponding Positive sentence *úmfána uyágeza* 'the boy is washing' and with other Present Tense forms of this and other verbs, we can find evidence for five-fold realisation of the property Negative, namely (1) the optional presence of the Negative prefix *a*-; (2) the absence of the prefix -*ya*-; (3) the replacement of *u*- by *ka*-

as the marker indicating concord with the subject *úmfána* 'the boy'; (4) the replacement of the low tone on the root -*gez*- 'wash' by a high tone; (5) the substitution of -*i* for the final -*a*.⁹

(112)   II: *One to many paradigmatically*
This deviation is exemplified in lexically or grammatically conditioned allomorphy. One could also characterise it as suppletion in inflexion (although the term 'suppletion' is more traditionally restricted to stem alternations, as in *go* versus *went*). A standard example is the English nominal property Plural, realised usually by -(*e*)*s* but also, for example, by -*en* in *oxen* and by vowel change in *teeth*, *men*, *mice*. Introducing a term which will recur frequently in later chapters, we can say that the realisation of Plural in English nouns is **sensitive** to the stem. Less hackneyed examples are:

a. The Zulu alternation, already mentioned, between *u*- and -*ka*- to mark verbal concord with a Singular subject belonging to the so-called Class 1 ('Class' here being a lexically determined, semantically more or less arbitrary grouping roughly analogous to Gender in Indo-European languages). The grammatical conditioning, as we have seen, involves the absence or presence of the property Negative.

b. In all Latin verbs, 2nd Person Singular Indicative Active is realised as a suffix -*istī* in the Present Tense of the Perfective Aspect but by a different suffix -*s* (with perhaps a preceding vowel) everywhere else.

c. In Hungarian, the usual mark of the property Plural in nouns is a -*k* suffix (generally with a preceding 'thematic' vowel or stem change or both), e.g. *dal* 'song', *dalok* 'songs'; *madár*¹⁰ 'bird', *madarak* 'birds'. But when the noun is also suffixally marked for possession, the -*k* suffix is replaced by one containing -*i*-, e.g. *dalod* 'your song', *dalaid* 'your songs'; *madarunk* 'our bird', *madaraink* 'our birds'.

(113)   III: *Many to one syntagmatically*
This type is exemplified in what Matthews (1974) calls 'cumulative' and 'overlapping' exponence; that is, instances where, in some word-form, more than one morphosyntactic property is realised in one

unsegmentable morph or morphological process. Behaviour of this kind is a hall-mark of 'fusional' languages, and Case and Number in Latin nouns furnish a standard example of cumulation. I will therefore give a couple of less obvious examples, deliberately chosen from languages generally labelled 'agglutinating':

a. In Turkish, Negation is usually expressed in verbs by a suffix -*me*- (in some phonological environments -*miy*-),[11] which is accompanied by stress on the preceding syllable, thus:

gelíyorum	'I am coming'	gélmiyorum	'I am not coming'
gelecék	'he will come'	gélmiyecek	'he will not come'
geldík	'we came'	gélmedik	'we did not come'

However, in the Present Aorist Tense, a different pattern emerges:

gelírim	'I come'	gelmém	'I do not come'
gelírsin	'you (Sg) come'	gelmézsin	etc.
gelír	'he/she comes'	gelméz	
gelíriz	'we come'	gélmeyiz	
gelírsiniz	'you come'	gelmézsiniz	
gelírlér	'they come'	gelmezlér	

Here, in contrast to the other Tenses, there is no clear consistent syntagmatic dividing-line between an element realising Negative and an element realising Aorist. It seems necessary to treat the element -*méz* in *gelméz* as realising the two properties simultaneously, along with 3rd Person.

b. In the Zulu example cited at (111 b), the element -*ka*-, as well as realising Class 1 concord, also helps to realise Negation inasmuch as it contrasts with a Positive prefix *u*-. Moreover, the comparison of the Active verb-form in *úmfána akágézi* 'the boy is not washing' with the Passive one in *úmfána akágezwá* 'the boy is not being washed' illustrates that the suffix -*i*, as well as realising Negation, also helps to realise Active, inasmuch as it does not appear in the Passive Form.

(114)   *IV: Many to one paradigmatically*
This is simply homonymy within inflexional paradigms, which will be discussed in Chapter 4.

Our aim, as I have said, is to identify the gap between what is logically possible in inflexional morphology and what is actually observed. The fact that examples can be found in natural languages of all these four logically possible types of deviation from one-to-one property-exponent pairing may seem to make the prospect of finding such a gap somewhat bleak. But pessimism is premature. We have so far considered individual property-exponent relationships in isolation. But such relationships do not exist in isolation. In languages other than those of the purest 'isolating' type, most 'morphs' (in the widest sense, including roots, affixes and morphological processes such as ablaut) either may or must occur in word-forms combined with some other morph; and 'units of content' (or 'signifiés') not only combine within words on the 'plane of content' but also contrast paradigmatically with other units of content which, when they are morphosyntactic properties, fall typically into relatively small, relatively clearly delimited closed classes — our 'morphosyntactic categories'. The combination of morphosyntactic properties belonging to different categories and the contrast between properties belonging to the same category are, in fact, part and parcel of Deviations III and IV respectively — that is, those deviations characterised at (113) and (114) as involving overlap (or cumulation) and homonymy. So there is still a wide territory in which to hunt for constraints on inflexional realisations, namely among the possible ways in which inflexional 'signes' can cooccur within word-forms and contrast within inflexional paradigms.

In Chapters 2 to 6 I will put forward various proposals about constraints on the two paradigmatic deviations — Deviations II and IV. In Chapters 2 and 3 I propose a constraint on Deviation II involving the number of inflexional paradigms (declensions and conjugations) into which the inflexional resources of a language may be organised; I call this the Paradigm Economy Principle. Chapter 4 is also concerned with paradigms, but this time with constraining Deviation IV as it affects them; the main proposal advanced there is the Systematic Homonymy Claim. In Chapter 5 I propose a further constraint on Deviation II (the Peripherality Constraint) involving syntagmatic rather than paradigmatic factors. Then in Chapter 6 I discuss how the Paradigm Economy Principle and the Peripherality Constraint interact with the phenomenon of stem allomorphy. Deviation I will scarcely be discussed at all in this book, though it is alluded to in connexion with the Elsewhere Condition in section 5.2.2. The other syntagmatic deviation, Deviation III, assumes considerable importance in my discussion of homonymy in Chapter 4 and also figures in section 5.1.8; but again I propose no constraints on it as such. These omissions are not meant to imply that Deviations I and III are unworthy of study in their own right, but II and IV provide more than enough material to occupy a single book.

1.4 PHONOLOGICALLY CONDITIONED ALLOMORPHY AND 'ABSTRACTNESS'

The one-to-many paradigmatic relationships between morphosyntactic properties and their realisations illustrated in (112) all involve what would traditionally be called lexically or grammatically conditioned allomorphy. But these traditional labels imply a contrast with another kind of allomorphy, namely that which is phonologically conditioned. We therefore need to be able to decide which instances of allomorphy are phonologically conditioned, it seems, in order to exclude them from our search for constraints on sensitivity of the specifically morphological kind. But how do we decide this? One answer which has been explicitly or implicitly given by some generative phonologists is: there is phonologically conditioned alternation between two phonetically different surface forms (in our present context, two phonetically distinct realisations of some morphosyntactic property) only if the two surface forms are phonologically related in the sense of being derivable by phonological rules from the same underlying phonological representation. Thus, for example, in Anderson's view (1974: Chapter 4), to establish that the [ɪz ~ z ~ s] alternation of the regular English Plural marker is phonologically conditioned involves identifying a single underlying phonological representation from which the three surface alternants are derived by phonological rules. For him, there are only two alternatives (1974: 54): 'we could describe these ... either as suppletive forms from a list, or as phonologically determined variants *of a single basic form* [my emphasis].'¹²

But the nature of underlying phonological representations is itself a matter of dispute. Since Kiparsky (1968a) first voiced doubts about the justification for some of the highly abstract underlying phonological representations propounded by Chomsky and Halle (1968) in their treatment of English, various attempts have been made to constrain the power of phonological rules within generative grammar. Scholars who have given the highest priority to this, perhaps, are the 'Natural Generative Phonologists' Vennemann, Hooper, Grover Hudson and their followers. Because they posit underlying phonological representations which are much less abstract than those possible within the Chomsky–Halle framework, much of the allomorphy that Chomsky and Halle account for by phonological rules has to be accounted for by rules of a different kind governing the distribution of distinct representations (that is, in the area which concerns us here, distinct inflexional realisations or 'spell-outs'). Indeed, G. Hudson (1975), supported by Hooper (1976), has gone to the extreme of claiming that all surface alternations, except those which can be assigned to very low-level 'natural' allophony rules, must be regarded as equally suppletive; so, for example, there is a suppletive relationship between the realisation of Plural not only in *dogs, geese* and *oxen* but also in *dogs, cats* and *horses*. The area of disagreement is therefore considerable (at least superficially), and the debate on phonological abstractness is by no means resolved, though owing to the recent upsurge of interest in nonlinear phonology it no longer occupies centre stage. When we investigate possible constraints on morphological sensitivity, must we be inescapably drawn into the debate?

The answer is no. On one point, all phonologists would agree: there exist distinct 'rival' realisations for some morphosyntactic properties in some languages which it is clearly impossible to relate phonologically, at least without an absurdly generous notion of what phonological rules can do. Rival realisations of this kind include -(*e*)*s*, -*en* and vowel change as inflexions for Plural in English nouns. Neither Anderson nor any other linguist, to my knowledge, has ever attempted to derive these all from a single representation at the underlying phonological level. These 'rival' alternants thus constitute a quite uncontroversial instance of suppletion in the sense of allomorphy which is conditioned purely lexically or grammatically, not phonologically. Moreover, to establish them as such it has not been necessary to commit ourselves to any view on phonological abstractness in genuinely controversial cases. So, to avoid having to take sides on the phonological issue, my policy throughout this book will be to base my arguments so far as possible on examples that are equally uncontroversial. My conclusions will therefore not presuppose a particular view of the suppletive or non-suppletive status of more controversial alternations, or of whether (as G. Hudson argues) all alternations should be regarded as suppletive. The logical connexion is, if anything, the other way round. My conclusions may, in principle, have a bearing on the phonological 'abstractness' question, in that if, for example, some restriction emerges on the way in which grammatical conditioning can operate in alternations which are quite clearly suppletive, it will be of interest to see whether 'borderline' alternations — ones where a single underlying phonological representation is possible but doubtful — obey the same restriction. If they do, and if alternations closer to the phonological end of the spectrum do not, we will have introduced a useful new tool for phonological analysis. On the other hand, if constraints established for uncontroversially suppletive allomorphy are found to hold right across the spectrum (an unlikely but conceivable outcome), then Grover Hudson's view of all alternations as suppletive will have received independent support which will be all the more valuable as coming from an investigation whose starting-point is explicitly non-phonological.

There is an important distinction to be drawn here. The fact that I am unwilling to take a stand on whether there is a single underlying phonological representation for the English Plural -(e)s does not mean that I am agnostic as to whether the alternation is phonologically conditioned or not. Clearly it is, in the sense that once we know that an English noun has a regular -(e)s Plural, we know on purely phonological grounds which of the three alternants to choose. I am thus quite ready, in appropriate circumstances, to treat an alternation as phonologically conditioned even if the postulation of a 'single basic form', in Anderson's words, is as problematic as it would be for the Plural markers in the English *foxes, oxen* and *geese*. Examples of the sort of alternation that I have in mind are listed in Table 1.1. Anderson's account of allomorphy would seem to commit him to finding a single basic underlying representation for each of these alternations, no matter what the cost in arbitrary-seeming 'minor' phonological rules. In keeping with my position of neutrality on phonological theory, I take no view on whether this is correct. The point I want to emphasise here is that one can recognise an alternation as phonologically conditioned without committing oneself about the underlying phonological representation of the alternants. This is important, because it will be crucial for my argument in more than one place to be able to distinguish between lexically, or grammatically, conditioned allomorphy (such as that between the Plural inflexions of *foxes*, *oxen* and *geese*) and phonologically conditioned allomorphy (as exemplified in Table 1.1, and as in English *foxes*, *dogs* and *cats*).

Table 1.1

Language	Morphosyntactic properties realised	Alternants	Phonological conditions
a. Hungarian	2nd Sg Indefinite Present Indicative (in normal conjungation)	-ol -(a)sz [-(ɒ)s]	after sibilants and affricates; elsewhere
b. Turkish	3rd Sg Possessive (on nouns)	-i -si	after consonants; after vowels
c. Turkish	Genitive (on nouns)	-in -nin	after consonants; after vowels
d. Fang (Guthrie 1956: 551)	Noun Class 5	a- dz-	before consonants; before vowels
e. Warlpiri (Dixon 1980: 306)	Ergative (on nouns)	-ngku -rlu	after 2-syllable stems; after stems of 3 or more syllables

NOTES

1. If all derivational morphology involves syntactic transformation (the 'transformationalist' position rejected by Chomsky (1970) in favour of a 'lexicalist' position), then all derivation will by definition be 'syntactically relevant' in one sense. But I am not concerned with that sense here.

2. For me, in contrast to Matthews, the terms 'realisation' and 'exponent' are merely stylistic variants.

3. This argument is similar to one used by Chomsky on various occasions in distinguishing between unacceptability judgements that are relevant to syntax and ones that are not.

4. I follow Matthews (1972b) (who in turn follows Meillet (1933)) in recognising a category of Aspect in Latin Verbs, e.g. Imperfective *amō* 'I love' versus Perfective *amāvī* 'I (have) loved'.

5. Lieber (1981: 311-17) has suggested that affixation differs from all non-affixal ('string dependent') morphological processes in such a way that only affixes ('morphemes') will tend to have a single meaning or function within a given language. The facts about reduplication and ablaut in Latin that I have just mentioned run counter to this; so does the fact that the single affix *-en* in German has a large number of distinct inflexional functions. But the idea that there can be differences of this kind between different processes seems worth exploring.

6. Superficially, this assertion seems to be endangered by the situation in Sogdian, where so-called 'heavy' and 'light' nominal stems seem to belong to quite distinct Case-systems (Sims-Williams 1982). But the very instability of this dual system, whose origin is clearly due to certain phonological innovations, points to its 'unnaturalness' in general linguistic terms.

7. 'Autosegmental morphology', as developed by McCarthy (1981) and others to provide a model for various nonaffixal or nonconcatenative morphological processes, would presumably explain the nonoccurrence of '*nomidus*' by invoking the provision that association lines linking autosegmental tiers may not cross.

8. My exhaustive four-fold classification of deviations from one-to-one patterning is, so far as I can tell, original. Bally (1944: 143-5) introduces a promising distinction between *dystaxie*, corresponding to my two syntagmatic deviations, and *polysémie*, corresponding to my paradigmatic ones; but his subsequent discussion, in terms of lexical rather than grammatical 'signes', is rather elementary and disappointing. Pike (1963) acknowledges syntagmatic many-to-one patterning as characteristic of what he calls 'ideal matrices' (or 'optimal matrices') in morphology, but he does not attempt to classify types of morphological patterning exhaustively. Anttila (1977: 56-7) discusses briefly 'polymorphy' and 'polysemy' as deviations from 'one meaning — one form', but his classification, like Pike's, is not exhaustive. Under polymorphy he includes allomorphic alternation (i.e. my Deviation II) as well as 'compounds, phrases' (i.e. presumably, Deviation I as it applies to words rather than inflexional realisations), and under polysemy he includes homophony (i.e. Deviation IV) as well as metaphor, metonymy and loan translation (!), but Deviation III seems to have no place in the scheme. It is notable that Bally's 'polysémie' and Anttila's 'polysemy' are by no means the same:

Deviation:	I	II	III	IV
Anttila	polymorphy?	polymorphy	?	polysemy
Bally	dystaxie	polysémie	dystaxie	polysémie

Wheeler's (1980) two Tendencies A and B, which he suggests may contribute to inflexional change by favouring ease of production and ease of perception respectively, correspond roughly to my paradigmatic Deviations IV and II respectively.

9. This example is based on material from Rycroft & Ngcobo (1979) and Doke (1973). Acute accents represent underlying high tones, according to Rycroft's analysis.

10. The acute accent indicates vowel length in Hungarian orthography.

11. For clarity, both here and in most Turkish examples cited in this book, I use only roots with front unrounded vowels and affixes in their unrounded front-vowel shape.

12. Compare also Hyman (1975: 13), discussing *go* versus *went* and *mouse* versus *mice*: 'In both these cases it is not possible to *derive one form from the other* by means of a general phonological rule. Such cases of irregular allomorphs (known as 'suppletion') therefore differ in a crucial way from the more regular allomorphs *derived by phonological rules* [my emphasis].' Kenstowicz & Kisseberth (1979) seem to hold the same view (see, for example, page 140 and their conclusion on page 196 about the 'morpheme alternant' theory of underlying representations). By contrast, Chomsky & Halle (1968) seem never to commit themselves so absolutely; and an examination of their sample of 'readjustment rules' for English (pages 238-9), whose function is to convert lexical representations into phonological representations, suggests that they are willing in principle to countenance the handling of some phonologically conditioned allomorphy by means of rules which do not belong to the phonological component. The Anderson–Hyman view is criticised by Linell (1979) and also (from a somewhat different point of view) by me (Carstairs 1981a).

2
The Status of Inflexional Paradigms

2.1 PARADIGMS AND ALLOMORPHY

Chapter 3 will be concerned with relationships between distinct inflexional paradigms, and Chapter 4 with relationships between the exponents of certain morphosyntactic properties within a single paradigm. The bulk of the present chapter is concerned with prima facie evidence for the importance of the inflexional paradigm as a theoretical notion. By way of introduction, however, we need to make explicit the relevance of the study of paradigms to the aims set out in Chapter 1.

I will not attempt at this stage a formal definition of the term 'inflexional paradigm'. Instead, in Table 2.1 I illustrate what I take to be four distinct Latin nominal paradigms by setting out the inflected forms of four Latin nouns:[1]

Table 2.1

Sg	Nom	dominus 'lord'	bellum 'war'	rēx 'king'	caput 'head'
	Voc	domine	bellum	rēx	caput
	Acc	dominum	bellum	rēgem	caput
	Gen	dominī	bellī	rēgis	capitis
	Dat	dominō	bellō	rēgī	capitī
	Abl	dominō	bellō	rēge	capite
Pl	Nom/Voc	dominī	bella	rēgēs	capita
	Acc	dominōs	bella	rēgēs	capita
	Gen	dominōrum	bellōrum	rēgum	capitum
	Dat/Abl	dominīs	bellīs	rēgibus	capitibus

In these paradigms, there is no one Case-Number combination (for short: no one Case) with the same exponent in all four paradigms. Precisely how many exponents there are for some

Cases will depend on how much of the surface allomorphy can be accounted for phonologically; but even a conservative estimate of the number of distinct inflexions (that is, one which attributes the largest possible role to phonology) must recognise at least two exponents for each Case, roughly as in Table 2.2.

Table 2.2

	Singular	Plural
Nom	-s, -m, -Ø	-ī, -s, -a
Voc	-e, -s, -m, -Ø	-ī, -s, -a
Acc	-m, -Ø	-s, -a
Gen	-ī, -is	-rum, -um
Dat	-ō, -ī	-īs, -bus
Abl	-ō, -e	-īs, -bus

The plethora of distinct inflexional paradigms in Latin is thus responsible for a widespread incidence of Deviation II (the multiple realisation of individual properties on the paradigmatic axis). It follows that any success we may have in establishing constraints on the organisation of inflexions into paradigms will contribute to the establishment of constraints on Deviation II also.

A second feature of the data in Table 2.1 is the incidence of Deviation IV (the shared realisation of distinct properties on the paradigmatic axis). In all Latin noun paradigms, Dative and Ablative share the same exponent in the Plural, and so do Nominative and Vocative. In addition, Table 2.1 exhibits homonymies that are lexically more restricted: for example, that of Dative and Ablative in the Singular of *dominus* and *bellum*, and that of Nominative and Accusative in both the Singular and the Plural of *bellum* and *caput*. Inflexional paradigms are therefore a suitable hunting ground for constraints on Deviation IV also. This is not to say that all instances of Deviation IV involve homonymy within paradigms. In Table 2.1 there are some homonymies which cut across paradigms: for example, -ī as the shared exponent of Genitive Singular for *dominus* and Dative Singular for *rēx*. Deviation IV, as defined, can even cut across word classes: for example, -*is* is the exponent not only of Gen Sg for the noun *rēx* but also that of 2nd Sg Active for the verb *reg*- 'rule', in certain morphosyntactic contexts. Similarly, English -*s* (/-s ~ -z ~ ɪz/) and German -*en* both appear as inflexions in more than one word-class. Conceivably, there could be constraints on Deviation IV which have nothing to do with inflexional paradigms, just as there are on Deviation II (as I will suggest in Chapter 5); but in this book I will be concerned only with paradigm-internal homonymies.

2.2 RECENT VIEWS OF THE PARADIGM

Inflexional paradigms are familiar to everyone who has studied Latin or Greek in the traditional post-Renaissance European fashion. Someone who knows only that style of linguistic description might well imagine that the notion 'paradigm' would be regarded as indispensable and central by any linguist describing any highly inflected language. But this is not so. In the framework for linguistic description presented by the American structuralist Zellig Harris, paradigms were scarcely mentioned at all (Harris 1951). Harris's contemporary Lounsbury, in his structuralist description of the morphology of the verb in the inflexionally highly complex Iroquoian language Oneida, recognised five 'paradigmatic classes' of verb base which differed according to their influence on the shape of preceding pronominal elements; but 'paradigms' in the sense of lists of inflected forms belonging to one word or lexeme were, for him, purely illustrative, or raw material for the main descriptive task of identifying morphemes and their alternants (Lounsbury 1953). European structuralists, too, mainly neglected the paradigm in favour of the newer concept 'morpheme' (or 'monème'), as lamented by Seiler (1966), although in Britain there was a move to take seriously the Word-and-Paradigm alternative sketched by Hockett (1954) to the dominant Item-and-Arrangement model of description (Robins 1959; Matthews 1972b).

Within generative grammar, the initial preoccupation with syntax and phonology provided little incentive to reconsider the status and function of paradigms. The generative approach to phonology did, moreover, seem at first to supply a motive for maintaining the structuralist exclusion of paradigms from linguistic theory, in that it was thought that a proper understanding of phonological organisation and phonological change obviated the need to invoke explicitly non-phonological factors such as 'paradigm pressure' or 'analogical levelling' to explain 'exceptions' to 'sound laws'. This attitude began to change in the light of the sort of fact pointed out by Wanner (1972) and J.W. Harris (1973) in Italian and Spanish: the fact that formal complexity in the operation of apparently well-motivated phonological rules (unexpected ordering, failure of application or both) may be associated with uniformity, or absence of allomorphy, in the inflexional paradigm thereby produced. Facts such as this led Kiparsky (1971; 1972) to postulate a principle of elimination of allomorphy in paradigms, to be included in the 'evaluation measure' for grammars alongside principles of formal simplicity and maximal transparency. Halle seemed to accept this view with equanimity when he stated (1973: 9): 'It is well known that paradigm pressure plays a potent role in the evolution of languages ... If paradigms can influence the evolution of language then there is every reason to expect that paradigms must appear as entities in their own right somewhere in the grammar.' This did not, however, lead to any significant increase of interest in the paradigm on the part of mainstream American generativists, and the term 'paradigm' does not even appear in the index of Scalise's (1984) state-of-the-art report on generative morphology. In her influential monograph *On the Organization of the Lexicon* (1981: 70), Lieber reverted to the view that inflexional paradigms have no theoretical significance, alleging that all inflexional differences within a given word-class are predictable on the basis of stem allomorphy;[2] and although Williams (1981: 266-73) offers a 'theory of paradigms', his main interest turns out to be not in inflexional contrasts within word-classes but rather in ways of grouping morphosyntactic properties so as to try to account for syncretisms (which we will discuss further in Chapter 4).

The most persuasive recent champion of the theoretical importance of paradigms and inflexion classes is Wurzel (1984), working within the framework of 'natural morphology' developed by Dressler (1977; 1985), Mayerthaler (1981) and others. Yet the emphasis that Wurzel places on the notions of inflexion class stability and productivity shows that for him, as for Halle, the main evidence for the existence of paradigms as 'entities in their own right' still has to do with language change. But this provokes a fairly obvious question: is there no substantive evidence of a purely synchronic kind? In other words, if the kind of problem posed by the Italian and Spanish verb paradigms did not exist, or if the sort of information that Wurzel invokes about German inflexional change were not available, would there no longer be any reason for postulating any non-phonological principles involving paradigms at work in morphology? To answer this, we need to consider what logical possibilities exist, both for synchronic morphological organisation and for morphological change. As soon as we do so, it becomes clear, as I hope to show, that only a few of the things which logically might happen in 'paradigms' are actually observed to happen. Assuming, then, that these gaps are not accidental, we have independent evidence that paradigms are more than mere lists of word-forms.[3]

2.3 PRODIGALITY AND PARSIMONY IN INFLEXION

The aim of this section is to draw attention to certain general characteristics of inflexional morphology which are in essence well known but whose implications for the status of inflexional paradigms have not been generally noticed. The section thus serves as an introduction to the more rigorous treatment of the paradigm and paradigm-related constraints in Chapter 3.

Let us consider a hypothetical language L in which nouns are inflected for two Numbers, Singular and Plural, and six Cases, and in which there is cumulative exponence of Case and Number — in other words, the realisation of Case and Number involves Deviation III. Suppose further that in L each Case–Number combination may be realised by more than one affix, thus:

Table 2.3

	Singular	Plural
Case 1	-s, -m, -ø	-i:, -s, -a
2	-e, -s, -m, -ø	-i:, -s, -a
3	-m, -ø	-s, -a
4	-i:, -is	-rum, -um
5	-o:, -i:	-i:s, -bus
6	-o:, -e	-i:s, -bus

There is no doubt that L is a possible human language; in fact, a comparison of Table 2.3 with Table 2.2 shows at once that L could in fact be Latin. We will assume further that, as in Latin, there is no hope of relating 'rival' affixes phonologically, so that

Deviation II is genuinely manifested in each Case.

We will consider now how these affixes in L might be distributed among the nouns to which they are affixed; for if in order to preserve L's status as a possible human language it turns out that we must impose limits on the freedom of distribution of these affixes, we will in effect be constructing a general hypothesis about morphological organisation. We will begin with the possibility implying the least restriction, namely the possibility that any noun may take all of the 29 affixes; that is, that every noun has three forms in free variation for the Case–Number combination Singular-1, two for Singular-3, and so on. Let us sum this up by saying that L has the **Free Distribution Characteristic**. With the Free Distribution Characteristic, a nominal stem *re:g-* 'king' in L (preserving the similarity to Latin!) will have two Singular-4 forms *re:gi:* and *re:gis*, and two Plural-5 forms *re:gi:s* and *re:gibus*; conversely, a form such as *re:gi:* will, out of context, be multiply ambiguous, interpretable as Singular-4, Singular-5, Plural-1 or Plural-2.

A priori, we might expect such a degree of ambiguity to be intolerable. But languages notoriously tolerate a great deal of ambiguity of different kinds at different levels, and attempts to specify limits to this toleration by reference to quasi-quantitative notions such as 'functional yield' have not produced particularly persuasive results.[4] Besides, there are, of course, numerous languages lacking any morphological distinction of Number or Case, in which the semantic function of such marking is fulfilled by other means; and why could not our language L too use such means to resolve any prima facie ambiguity resulting from the Free Distribution Characteristic? So there does not seem to be any general linguistic principle involving ambiguity which would rule out L, with the Free Distribution Characteristic, as a possible human language. Yet we are still entitled, I think, to feel uneasy. With the Free Distribution Characteristic L's inflexional morphology loses most of its resemblance to that of Latin. The question, then, is whether there are any languages at all in which, when two or more affixes (or other inflexional devices) are available to realise a given morphosyntactic property or combination of properties, all these affixes collocate freely with all stems of the relevant part of speech. This amounts to asking whether the fact that Latin does not have the Free Distribution Characteristic is an accidental fact about Latin or is attributable to some general linguistic constraint.

It is certainly true that, in some languages, a few stems display alternative inflexions for some morphosyntactic properties: for example, English *fish*, Plural *fish* or *fishes*; Latin *domus* 'house', Dative Singular *domō* or *domuī*; German *Wort* 'word', Plural *Worte* or *Wörter*; Hungarian *szomszéd* 'neighbour', Plural with 3rd Singular Possessive *szomszédai* or *szomszédjai* 'his/her neighbours'. In some languages, also, there are a few morphosyntactic 'slots' where for all members of the relevant part of speech there is more than one inflexional possibility: for example, the 3rd Plural Perfective Present Indicative in Latin of the 'Golden Age', which may end in *-ēre*, *-erunt* or *-ērunt* (e.g. *regō* 'I rule'; *rexēre*, *rexerunt* or *rexērunt* 'they have ruled'). Similarly, in Finnish practically all nouns have two or more alternative Genitive Plurals,[5] e.g. *peruna* 'potato', Gen Pl *perunoiden*, *perunoitten*, *perunojen*, *perunien* or *perunain*. But it is equally true that this variability is unusual, in the sense that in most inflected languages most if not all inflected words have only one form for each morphosyntactic slot. The lavish variety of Genitive Plural endings in Finnish may reflect the relatively recent origin of the standard Finnish literary language and its acceptance of features proper to a number of different local dialects, and there are certainly stylistic or 'register' differences between them: '... les génitifs pluriels en *-in* (*tyttöin* 'des jeunes filles'), construits sur le thème vocalique d'un grand nombre de noms, ont un accent plus solennel. ... En revanche, à la place des génitifs pluriels en *-den*, on trouve assez fréquemment *-tten* (*katseitten* 'des regards' à côté de *katseiden* 'id.', sur *katse* 'regard') qui semble à certains sujets plus naturel que la forme en *-d-* ...' (Sauvageot 1949: 85-6; cf. also Harms 1957). As for idiosyncratic doublets like *fish* and *fishes*, closer examination of most of them reveals that they are not complete synonyms in stable coexistence. Sometimes the two alternatives can be assigned to different dialects or 'registers' (for example, *fishes* has a rather Biblical ring to my ear, *fish* being the normal modern Plural form); sometimes one of the two is in retreat while the other is encroaching (for example, in Hungarian, Plural Possessive forms without *-j-*, such as *szomszédai*, are apparently less productive than, and losing ground to, those with *-j-* (Sauvageot 1971: 146-9, 314-16, 376)); sometimes the two forms have clearly distinct lexical meanings (for example, German *Worte* 'words in the context of an utterance' versus *Wörter* 'words out of context (e.g. as listed in a dictionary)').

The absence or rarity of genuine alternative forms compatible with the Free Distribution Characteristic is reflected in the traditional terminology of linguistic description and language teaching: '*The* Genitive Singular of Latin *rēx* 'king' is *rēgis*', '*The* Plural of Hungarian *fal* 'wall' is *falak*', and so on, where it is clearly presupposed that, with a given stem, a given combination of morphosyntactic properties will be realised in only one way. It is by no means logically necessary that this should be so. I have already remarked that language has at its disposal devices quite adequate to deal with any ambiguity that the Free Distribution Characteristic might engender. On the basis of the evidence so far presented, therefore, it seems legitimate to hypothesise, as a distinct constraint on inflexional morphology, that no language may possess the Free Distribution Characteristic. More precisely, we might name and formulate a hypothesis on the following lines:

(201) INFLEXIONAL PARSIMONY HYPOTHESIS
Even when there is more than one inflexional realisation available for a given combination of morphosyntactic properties, each stem must select only one of these realisations (unless, where two or more are selected, the overt contrast is associated with some semantic or stylistic function).

The name chosen for this hypothesis is intended to hint at an explanation for it. I suggest that there is at work in inflexional as well as derivational morphology a tendency to put overt differences to use, to assign them some function — not to let them go prodigally to waste, as it were. The existence of such a tendency in derivational morphology has been noted by Aronoff, who uses it to account for the phenomenon of 'blocking' (1976: 43-5, 60). In derivational morphology, the use to which overt differences are put is relatively obvious, namely the distinction of lexical meanings. Thus, in English, one seldom or never finds two nominal forms derived from the same verb which are exactly synonymous. Examples of the kind of meaning differentiation which can occur are:

(202) composer of music *versus* compositor of type
disposal of rubbish,   disposition of troops
      assets

preference for one alternative over another	preferment to a post (usually ecclesiastical)
requirement that a condition be met	requisition of property for official purposes

Looking at this tendency from another angle, we can say that a language will not tolerate the coexistence of two derived forms unless they can be put to distinct semantic uses. In inflexional morphology, potential breaches of parsimony arise wherever more than one inflexional resource is available for a single grammatical function. The Inflexional Parsimony Hypothesis predicts that such breaches will not occur, however; that is, that languages will not display the Free Distribution Characteristic. Overwhelmingly the most frequent way of ensuring this is by requiring that each stem display one and only one of the available realisations for each morphologically relevant combination of properties; thus in Latin, for example, we find that the Dative Plural ending *-īs* is the only one that can cooccur with the stem *domin-* 'lord', while *-ibus* is the only one that can cooccur with *rēg-* 'king'. Alternatively, where more than one realisation is available for some slot, either one of the variants will go out of use (as seems to be happening with Hungarian *szomszédai* in the face of *szomszédjai* 'his/her neighbours') or else the difference will be 'functionalised' by the assignment of different meanings or stylistic connotations (as with German *Worte* versus *Wörter*).

2.3.1 Are inflexions distributed independently?

If the Inflexional Parsimony Hypothesis is correct, it imposes a considerable restriction on the use which our hypothetical language L could make of the inflexional resources presented in Table 2.3. But is this restriction sufficient, or does the Hypothesis need to be supplemented or tightened further?

The Inflexional Parsimony Hypothesis requires that each stem must select only one affix for each Case–Number combination, but it says nothing about the relationship, if any, between the selections made by one stem for different combinations. For example, from the fact that a stem *domin-* 'lord' has Singular-4 *domini:* the Inflexional Parsimony Hypothesis predicts nothing about whether the Plural-5 form will be *domini:s* or *dominibus*, the two options which Table 2.3 seems to make available. Similarly, if we postulate a Singular-4 form *domini:*, the Inflexional Parsimony Hypothesis tells us nothing about whether the Singular-5 form will be *domini:* or *domino:*. Let us suppose that, from the point of view of the general constraints on morphological organisation, both alternatives are possible for both these examples and that there are in general no mutual restrictions linking the choice of one affix with that of another. This amounts to saying that it is possible in L for any noun stem (or, at least, any vowel-final one) to select any possible combination of the affixes listed in Table 2.3, provided only that, in accordance with the Inflexional Parsimony Hypothesis, it chooses only one for each of the twelve Case–Number combinations. Let us summarise this by saying that the Case–Number affixes of L have the **Independent Distribution Characteristic**. One can arrive at the total number of possible affix distribution patterns for L by multiplying together the number of affixes available for each morphosyntactic property-bundle; this yields $3 \times 4 \times 2^4 \times 3^2 \times 2^4 = 27{,}648$. Even if we regard Plural-1 and Plural-2 as 'really' a single Case for paradigmatic purposes in virtue of their identical exponence, and likewise Plural-5 and Plural-6, this reduces the total only by a factor of six (i.e. 3×2) to 4,608. Yet, needless to say, the actual language on which L is based, namely Latin, does not contain anything like 27,648 or even 4,608 actual patterns for Case–Number affixation. Instead, we find a vastly more limited range of declension patterns — traditionally five, although the exact number that needs to be recognised will depend partly on the nature and power of the (morpho)phonological rules which we postulate as operating on the underlying representations of the affixes. Is this degree of restriction in Latin accidental? Almost all linguists, I think, would agree that it is not: that is, that our hypothetical Latin-like language L would not be a possible human language if its nouns selected realisations for each combination of morphosyntactic properties independently.

An intuitively plausible reason for this is not hard to find — one which casts doubt on whether what we have discovered is a specifically linguistic fact at all. Let us consider what morphological information would have to be specified individually in the lexicon, or learnt individually by the native speaker, for each noun if L possessed the Independent Distribution Characteristic. Clearly, each noun in L would have to be learnt along with no less than twelve 'rules' specifying how each Number and Case combination was to be 'spelt'. If morphological theory has to be constrained so as to exclude such a possibility, it seems natural to explain this constraint by reference to the enormous burden that would be imposed on the memory by the need to learn twelve separate Case–Number rules along with each noun. Is the constraint then a linguistic one at all, strictly speaking? Earlier, when discussing techniques of argument in morphological theory, I suggested that the first of our list of six logical possibilities which did not occur in Latin — namely, the fact that no Latin noun has a Case ending seventeen syllables long — was probably best regarded as a fact of no linguistic interest, to be explained rather in terms of elementary properties of any communication system whatsoever. If the individual specification of affixes in a twelve-term Case–Number system is ruled out solely by virtue of human memory limitations, then is not what we have found merely a rather unsurprising consequence of certain facts about human psychology and neurology, and not a specifically linguistic fact at all? If so, then surely linguistic theory as such need not pay any attention to it.

It would be easy to get bogged down here in difficult questions about the relationship between the psychology of language and other branches of cognitive psychology. I would argue, however, that even if many generalisations about human language can be related to wider generalisations covering other aspects of human thought and behaviour too, the wider generalisations will seldom suffice by themselves to explain the relevant linguistic facts entirely. In other words, there will generally be subsidiary questions of a more specifically linguistic kind to do with how the general constraint in question is actually manifested, or complied with, in language.[6] In the present case, the specifically linguistic question is: how far does language go to reduce the potential burden imposed on the memory by an array of inflexional affixes such as Table 2.3? To put it another way, what is the most complex distribution of Case–Number affixes, from the point of view of the language-learner, that language permits? From the answer to this question we can expect some indication of the actual upper limit to the number of affix distribution patterns that nouns in L may choose, more or less reduced from the logical upper limit that we have already established by simple arithmetic at 27,648. How precise this indication will be will depend on how tightly languages are actually constrained in this respect.

Before we attempt an answer to this question, it is worth reminding ourselves that one of the main reasons for the recent reawakening of interest in the notion of the morphological paradigm was the unexpected way in which phonological rules seemed to apply or fail to apply in the generation of forms such as those of the Present Tense of regular Spanish verbs — unexpected, that is, from the point of view of classical generative phonology as expounded by Chomsky & Halle (1968). But such facts as we have so far uncovered in considering the possible distribution of Case–Number affixes in L already provide some confirmation which is quite independent of any phonological evidence. If we say that the Independent Distribution Characteristic is impossible in human language and that this impossibility is due in some sense to the burden which a language with the Characteristic would impose on the memory, we are saying in effect that in the nominal Case–Number system of a language such as L, entailment relations hold between the distributions of certain of the affixes, and that these entailment relations are such as to enable the speaker to learn at least part of the affix-pattern for at least some nouns *en bloc*, thereby reducing the number of Case–Number combinations for which the realisations must be learnt individually. Our argument therefore confirms the need to recognise 'paradigm structure conditions' of the kind posited independently by Wurzel (1984: 116) for Latin noun inflexion. I will, however, be suggesting in Chapter 3 that these conditions are in certain respects considerably tighter than Wurzel envisages.

2.3.2 The nonexistence of 'syntactic parsimony'

The Inflexional Parsimony Hypothesis eliminates a vast number of the logically possible ways in which our hypothetical language L could exploit the affixal resources tabulated in Table 2.3. But is this principle purely morphological? What analogues, if any, does the Inflexional Parsimony Hypothesis have in syntax? I will argue in this section that there is in fact no corresponding syntactic principle. This conclusion is not vital to the main thread of my argument; nevertheless, the question is of interest because, if my conclusion is correct, it highlights one fundamental difference between the morphological and the syntactic organisation of language. We can paraphrase the formulation of the Inflexional Parsimony Hypothesis at (201) by saying that two inflexions cannot be functionally identical (realising the same morphosyntactic property or properties) unless they are distributionally complementary (cooccurring with non-overlapping subsets of the appropriate word-class or part of speech). The question now is: is there any constraint comparable with this in syntax?

It is well known that there are distributional limitations on lexical items which go beyond what is implied by their being members of one or another part of speech. Within the framework of the standard theory of generative grammar, as expounded by Chomsky (1965), these distributional limitations are described in terms of 'strict subcategorization features' and 'selectional features' contained in lexical entries. Some of these limitations are very familiar and are shared by large numbers of lexical items, such as the limitation on intransitive verbs expressed by Chomsky's (1965) feature [+ ___ #]; others, of lesser scope, are more idiosyncratic, like the restrictions on some adjectives in English which bar them from appearing in attributive position (e.g. *ill*) or in predicative position (e.g. *late* in the sense of 'deceased'); compare the sentences of (203) with those of (204):

(203) a. *John is an ill man.
 b. *King George VI has been late for 27 years.[7]

(204) a. John is a sick man.
 b. King George VI has been dead for 27 years.

Other notoriously arbitrary distinctions in syntactic behaviour (that is, ones which are inexplicable semantically) between particular lexical items are illustrated by the ungrammaticality of (206) (in standard British English) in contrast to (205):

(205) a. He persuaded me to come.
 b. John is likely to leave.

(206) a. *He convinced me to come.
 b. *John is probable to leave.

But there is an important difference between the ungrammaticality of Latin *rēgī 'of the king' (Genitive Singular) on the one hand and that of (203) and (206) on the other. Both involve distributional limitations, in some sense, but only the first can be related directly to other, complementary, distributional limitations involving other stems and inflexions. An example of such a complementary limitation is the one which renders ungrammatical the word-form *dominis 'of the lord' (Genitive Singular). The two facts are complementary, because they both involve the selection of the 'wrong' Genitive Singular ending, to wit the one appropriate to the other. In virtue of the Inflexional Parsimony Hypothesis, inflexions appropriate to each Case–Number combination of Latin nouns are in complementary distribution over the whole range of noun stems, and one can identify unequivocally the 'rival' inflexions to which each one is strictly complementary. But words such as *ill, late, convince, probable* do not have strictly complementary rivals, as (207) shows:

(207) a. John is ill/sick.
 b. The dead/late king was succeeded by his daughter.
 c. He persuaded/convinced me that I should come.
 d. It is probable/likely that John will leave.

What sort of distributional limitation in syntax would, then, be directly comparable to that involving the Latin Genitive Singular inflexions? What we need to find is an example of some lexical item which is not only subject to apparently arbitrary distributional limitations, as are the adjectives *ill* and *late* (in the sense 'deceased'), but is also paired with some exactly synonymous lexical item (or set of lexical items) whose distribution is exactly complementary. This would be the situation if, for example, the noun *bucket* were barred from appearing in any noun phrase functioning as object of the verbs *give, steal, throw* and other 'strong' verbs, and the synonymous *pail* were barred from appearing anywhere else — were barred, that is, from appearing in any subject noun phrases, or in the objects of prepositions or 'weak' verbs such as *receive, drop, clean,* or in isolation. But this kind of syntactic complementarity between lexical items does not seem to occur. To return to our metaphor, syntax is prodigal with the overt difference between the synonymous items *bucket* and *pail* — it allows this difference to 'go to waste' in a way which morphology would not tolerate.

It is important to emphasise that the sort of syntactic complementarity just envisaged for *bucket* and *pail* is quite distinct from the familiar morphological phenomenon of suppletion. An objector might argue that it is purely by convention that the Present and Past Tense forms *go* and *went* in English, or *ferō* 'I carry' and *tulī* 'I carried' in Latin, are regarded as alternants of the same lexical item; we could equally well regard them, perhaps, as separate lexical items with peculiar limitations on their distribution. If so, are they not parallel to the imaginary *bucket* and *pail* example which, we claimed, was linguistically impossible? The answer is no. It is characteristic of suppletive pairs such as *ferō/tulī* and *go/went* that neither member displays a complete range of inflexions; rather, they divide the labour between them, and it is precisely because of the absence of forms such as *wending[8], *goed that *go* and *went* are classified as suppletive alternants rather than synonyms. But in our hypothetical *bucket/pail* situation, both can display the complete range of nominal inflexion — both can be inflected for Plural and Genitive,[9] since nothing in their mirror-image distribution prevents this. To put it another way, the choice between the suppletive alternants *go* and *went* is determined by aspects of their syntactic context which are morphologically relevant to ordinary non-suppletive verbs too, such as the presence or absence of the property Past; whereas the choice in our hypothetical situation between the 'alternants' *bucket* and *pail* is determined by factors which have no relevance, morphological or syntactic, to ordinary nouns at all.

A determined objector may yet find some ammunition in favour of 'syntactic parsimony' among those languages where some verbs are apparently subcategorised in quite complex ways according to whether or not they can occur with subjects or objects belonging to certain syntactically or semantically definable classes. Languages of this kind include Athapaskan languages such as Navajo and Cherokee, where semantic classes such as 'animate creature', 'round object', 'liquid' correlate with apparently distinct verbs with meanings such as 'throw', 'fall', 'lie' (Davidson, Elford & Hoijer 1963). Suppose that in such a language there are two verbs meaning 'hit', quite dissimilar in shape, one of which is used only with animate objects and the other only with inanimate objects (call them *hit*$_a$ and *hit*$_i$):

would this not constitute the sort of complementarity which I have claimed does not exist?

In answer to this, I would first point out that the objector's case fails if it can be shown that the language possesses a morphosyntactic category of Animacy, containing two properties Animate and Inanimate, for which verbs are inflected in agreement with their objects. As soon as that is established — if we find, for example, that all or most transitive verbs have two forms which alternate in the same way as hit_a and hit_i, and especially if most such paired forms are partially similar phonologically rather than being quite dissimilar in the way that hit_a and hit_i are (*ex hypothesi*) — then what we have in hit_a and hit_i is not an example of 'syntactic parsimony' but a straightforward example of morphological suppletion. But suppose these conditions are not fulfilled — suppose, for example, that only a few verbs can be paired like hit_a and hit_i, and there is no recurring difference in shape which can be identified as a regular inflectional exponent of an Animate–Inanimate distinction? If any language does exhibit this kind of behaviour, then certainly it would seem to provide an instance in syntax of the kind of parsimony that I have claimed to be peculiar to morphology. But, if such behaviour were found, it would still be worth examining it in the light of a somewhat weaker claim about syntactic parsimony than the one I have advanced so far: not that syntactic parsimony is impossible, but that it is inherently unstable.

What I am suggesting is that there might be a strong general preference for analysing the sort of distributional complementarity between synonyms that we have hypothesised for hit_a and hit_i in lexical rather than syntactic terms — for analysing them, in other words, not as separate lexical items with syntactically rather than morphosyntactically determined complementarity in distribution, but, instead, as suppletive alternants of the same lexical items, with the corollary that what determines the choice between them must be a morphosyntactic property ('Animate' or 'Inanimate') acquired by the verb through concord with its object, rather than simply some syntactic or semantic property of the object alone, unmediated by concord. This preference, if genuine, will have diachronic consequences. Inasmuch as morphosyntactic properties tend to apply to whole word-classes rather than arbitrary subsets of word-classes, we will expect to find all transitive verbs acquiring morphological marks of the Animate–Inanimate distinction; and, inasmuch as stem suppletion is the exception rather than rule in most inflexional systems, we will expect the suppletive alternations within the group of verbs in question to be replaced by predictable alternations involving some regular process, such as the addition of a particular affix. Alternatively, if such symptoms of 'morphologisation' are absent, we will predict that the instability will be resolved in the opposite direction — that the complementarity in distribution between hit_a and hit_i, and similar paired or grouped 'synonyms', will become less rigid, thus destroying the crucial characteristic of parsimony. The complementarity will be broken if, for example, we find that hit_i as well as hit_a can be used with animate objects, provided that the object is inert or passive in the manner of an inanimate object. As soon as we observe this kind of behaviour, we can no longer say that hit_a and hit_i are exactly synonymous, as *bucket* and *pail* are in our hypothetical version of English, or as the suppletive stems *go* and *wen-* are in actual English, because there will be a distinction in meaning between sentences such as 'John hit_a Bill' and 'John hit_i Bill': the latter will imply or presuppose that Bill is unconscious, while the former will not. And this sort of contrast does in fact seem to be possible in the Athapaskan languages, where Davidson *et al.* report (1963: 36): 'In Dogrib, as in the other [Athapaskan] languages, the same noun may be employed with different classificatory stems, so giving the noun a distinctive denotation. Thus: *łet'e* 'bread' plus the verb *niyeh ?a* 'I pick up a category I [solid, compact] object' yields the meaning 'I pick up a loaf of bread'. But *łet'e* plus the verb *niyehtši* 'I pick up an object of category V [flat, fabric(like)]' means 'I pick up a slice of bread'.' Provisionally then, it seems reasonable to claim that the Inflexional Parsimony Hypothesis cannot be related directly to any constraint independently needed in syntactic (as opposed to lexical and morphological) analysis.

NOTES

1. Throughout this book, Latin forms are presented in the normal orthography of the first century AD, supplemented by a distinction between *u* and *v* for [u] and [w] and by macrons to indicate long vowels. The other symbols can be taken as having roughly IPA values, except that *c, qu, x* represent [k], [kw], [ks] respectively. For standard

descriptions of Latin inflexion see Ernout (1953), Sommer (1948) and Leumann (1977).

2. Lieber bases this claim partly on German noun inflexion, as analysed by Wurzel (1970), relying particularly on the distinction (which he has since abandoned (Wurzel: 1984)) between inflexional affixes proper (*Flexive*) and stem-forming elements (*Stammbildungselemente*). However, Lieber's claim can only be made to work for German if the Plural -*s* of nouns such as *Uhu* 'screech-owl', *Auto* 'car' is treated as a stem-forming element, not an inflexion proper — an analysis which Lieber (1982: 39) wrongly attributes to Wurzel. If the Plural -*s* is an inflexion proper, as Wurzel in fact takes it, then *Uhu* and *Auto* have exactly the same stem allomorphy as the inflexionally distinct *Tag* 'day', *Boot* 'boat', namely none at all. Lieber's claim can no doubt be reconciled with quite a wide range of inflexional behaviour if inflexional affixes can fairly freely be assigned to the stem rather than the desinence, without independent justification (cf. 1982: 45, fn. 13), but then the empirical content of the claim is considerably reduced.

3. Interesting typological and psycholinguistic, as well as diachronic, evidence on the status of paradigms is offered by Bybee (1985). Her arguments are, however, quite independent of the ones I will be putting forward.

4. For discussion of the 'functional yield' ('realisierte strukturale Ausnützung', 'rendement fonctionnel') of phonological contrasts, see Mathesius (1931) and, especially, Martinet (1955). For criticism of functional yield as a factor in accounting for phonological changes or the lack of them, see Weinreich *et al.* (1968: 133-7) and King (1969: 200-1).

5. I am grateful to Paul Kiparsky for pointing this out.

6. A similar argument in respect of phonology in particular has been advanced by Anderson (1981).

7. (203b) is, of course, acceptable if 'late' is interpreted as 'unpunctual'.

8. *Wending* does, of course, occur as Present Participle of the obsolescent verb *wend*, which occurs now only in the phrase *wend one's way*, and which now has a Past form *wended* distinct from *went*. The important point, however, is that *wending* does not occur alongside *going* as an alternative Present Participle for *go*.

9. I ignore here the question whether the Genitive -'*s* is strictly a nominal inflexion or a noun-phrase clitic (on which see Janda (1980)).

3

The Paradigm Economy Principle

3.1 A FIRST FORMULATION

3.1.1 Some Hungarian, Zulu and Dyirbal evidence

I argued in Chapter 2 that a certain hypothetical Latin-like language L diverged inflexionally from actual Latin in such a way as to render it impossible as a natural language. The difference between Latin and L is that in L each noun's inflexion for each of the twelve Case–Number combinations in the paradigm is determined independently. L therefore has what we called the Independent Distribution Characteristic; and I suggested that no natural language possesses this characteristic. But, if inflexions are not in fact distributed independently, our task now is to determine the nature of the restrictions which govern the organisation of inflexional resources into paradigms. In the course of developing more concrete proposals on this, I will present further material from three languages unrelated to each other or to Latin (or, at most, only extremely distantly related): Hungarian, Zulu and Dyirbal. The presentation will at first be informal, and from now on I will deliberately avoid using the term 'paradigm' until I come to define it for the purpose of formulating a claim about 'paradigm economy'.

The Hungarian material involves the Indicative and Subjunctive Person–Number endings for the Present Tense in the absence of any definite 3rd-Person object (i.e. the Present Indefinite). Some Persons have, at first sight, as many as six distinct realisations, as shown in Table 3.1.[1]

THE PARADIGM ECONOMY PRINCIPLE

Table 3.1: Present Indefinite

	Indicative	Subjunctive
Sg 1	-ok, -ek, -ök, -om, -em, -öm	-ak, -ek, -am, -em
2	-(a)sz, -(e)sz, -ol, -el, -öl	-Ø, -ál, -él
3	-Ø, -ik	-on, -en, -ön, -ék
Pl 1	-unk, -ünk	-unk, -ünk
2	-(o)tok, -(e)tek, -(ö)tök	-atok, -etek
3	-(a)nak, -(e)nek	-anak, -enek

A sample of five verbs, all at first sight inflexionally distinct, is given in Table 3.2.

Table 3.2

Indicative					
	olvasni	ülni	enni	érteni	írni
	'to read'	'to sit'	'to eat'	'to understand'	'to write'
Sg 1	olvas-ok	ül-ök	esz-em	ért-ek	ír-ok
2	olvas-ol	ül-sz	esz-el	ért-esz	ír-sz
3	olvas	ül	esz-ik	ért	ír
Pl 1	olvas-unk	ül-ünk	esz-unk	ért-ünk	ír-unk
2	olvas-tok	ül-tök	esz-tek	ért-etek	ír-tok
3	olvas-nak	ül-nek	esz-nek	ért-enek	ír-nak
Subjunctive					
Sg 1	olvass-ak	ülj-ek	egy-em	értj-ek	írj-ak
2	olvass, olvass-ál	ülj, ülj-él	egy-él	értj, értj-él	írj, írj-ál
3	olvass-on	ülj-en	egy-ek	értj-en	írj-on
Pl 1	olvass-unk	ülj-ünk	egy-ünk	értj-ünk	írj-unk
2	olvass-atok	ülj-etek	egy-etek	értj-etek	írj-atok
3	olvass-anak	ülj-enek	egy-enek	értj-enek	írj-anak

In all these verbs a Subjunctive stem is distinguishable from an Indicative one; but our concern at present is with the Person–Number endings.

The total number of possible distribution patterns for these endings, assuming independence in distribution, is 276,480. Not surprisingly, the number of patterns actually found in Hungarian does not remotely approach that staggering total. The actual total we arrive at, however, will depend on certain decisions we make about what are to count as distinct inflexions. Superficially, for example, *ülni* and *érteni* differ inflexionally because they have different endings in 1 Sg, 2 Sg, 2

43

Pl and 3 Pl of the Indicative. But if we start from the assumption that they exhibit the same inflexional pattern, these differences turn out to be entirely predictable on phonological grounds: the 'mobile vowel' found in the endings of *értesz, értetek, értenek* occurs only with stems ending in clusters of two or more consonants or a long vowel plus -*t*; and the front rounded vowel in the endings of *ülök, ültök* occurs only with stems containing front rounded vowels. Superficially, also, *olvasni* and *írni* exhibit different patterns because of the Indicative 2 Sg forms *olvasol* versus *írsz*; but, again, if we assume that they belong to the same pattern, their allocation to the 'subpatterns' with -*sz* and -*ol* is predictable on the basis that -*ol* always occurs after sibilants and affricates and -(*a*)*sz* never does. It turns out on this basis that there are really only two patterns for Hungarian verb inflexion, which we can call the normal and the *ik* conjugations, each of which exists in a back-vowel and a front-vowel version. The back-vowel versions are as shown in Table 3.3. The front-vowel versions (which occur with most, but not all, front-vowel-stem verbs) have inflexions that are exactly analogous to the back-vowel ones, except that rounding harmony governs the choice between alternants with *e* and ö.

Our Zulu material concerns the noun Class agreement prefixes (or 'concords') that crop up in possessive constructions. Zulu, like other Bantu languages, has several noun 'Classes', similar to Genders; and, within the sentence, many attributive and predicative elements are required to agree with their subject or head noun by displaying a prefix generally related in shape to

Table 3.3: Present Indefinite

		Indicative: Normal	*ik*	Subjunctive: Normal	*ik*
Sg 1		-ok	-om	-ak	-am
	2	-ol *after sibilants*; -(a)sz *elsewhere*	-ol	-Ø (*brusquer*)[2] -ál (*politer*)	
	3	-Ø	-ik	-on	-ék
Pl 1		-unk		-unk	
	2	-(o)tok		-atok	
	3	-(a)nak		-anak	

the one on the noun itself. For example, in the possessive construction, where a nominal modifer (usually semantically a possessor or a locative expression) follows the head noun, it displays a prefix (the 'possessive concord') determined by the Class and Number of the head. In Tables 3.4 and 3.5 there are some examples, in which numerals identify Classes and possessive concords are italicised.[3] As can be seen, the possessive concords for both Class 9/10 Plural and Class 5/6 Singular have two shapes. In fact, the same is true of most concords, as shown in Table 3.6. Here we see fifteen morphosyntactic property-bundles, all but one of which can be realised by two distinct inflexions. The maximum number of distinct inflexional patterns which Zulu nouns could logically exhibit, if inflexional distribution were completely free, is thus $2^{14} = 16,384$. The actual number of distinct inflexional patterns that we observe, however, is just two, as set out in Table 3.7.

Consider now the nominal Case-inflexions of the Australian language Dyirbal, as described by Dixon (1972). For two Cases, the Ergative and Simple Genitive, there is more than one inflexional exponent available (Dixon 1972: 42) as set out in Table 3.8. This yields a mathematical maximum of eight ($1 \times 4 \times 2$) distinct inflexional patterns for Dyirbal nouns. And certainly quite a few of these possibilities are instantiated, as

Table 3.4

a.	i.	kwaZulu 15-Zulu '(in) Zululand'	ii.	izin-tombi 9/10 Pl-girl 'the girls in Zululand'	*za*-kwa-Zulu *9/10 Pl*-15-Zulu
b.	i.	-ka-thisha 1a/2a Sg-teacher 'the teacher'	ii.	izin-tombi 'the teacher's girls'	*zi*-ka-thisha *9/10 Pl*-1a/2a Sg-teacher

Table 3.5

a.	i.	um-ntwana 1/2 Sg-child 'the child'	ii.	i-qanda 5/6 Sg-egg 'the child's egg'	*lo*m-ntwana (</la-um-ntwana/)[4] *5/6 Sg*-1/2 Sg-child
b.	i.	-ka-dokotela 1a/2a Sg-doctor 'the doctor'	ii.	i-qanda 'the doctor's egg'	*li*-ka-dokotela *5/6 Sg*-1a/2a Sg-doctor

Table 3.6

	Singular	Plural
1/2, 1a/2a	wa-, Ø	ba-
3/4	wa-, Ø	ya-, Ø
5/6	la-, li-	a-, Ø
7/8	sa-, si-	za-, zi-
9/10	ya-, Ø	za-, zi-
11/10	lwa-, lu-	za-, zi-
14	ba-, bu-	ba-, bu-
15	kwa-, ku-[5]	

Table 3.7

		Nominal modifier of:			
		(a) Class 1a/2a Singular:		(b) all other Class–Number combinations:	
		Sg	Pl	Sg	Pl
Head noun of Class:	1/2, 1a/2a	wa-	ba-	Ø	ba-
	3/4	wa-	ya-	Ø	Ø
	5/6	la-	a-	li-	Ø
	7/8	sa-	za-	si-	zi-
	9/10	ya-	za-	Ø	zi-
	11/10	lwa-	za-	lu-	zi-
	14	ba-	ba-	bu-	bu-
	15	kwa-		ku-	

illustrated in Table 3.9. At first sight, then, we must recognise at least five distinct distribution patterns for the noun inflexions of Dyirbal. It turns out, however, that this distribution is entirely phonologically determined. As Dixon (1972: 42) puts it:

> 'ERGATIVE ... involves the addition of:
> (i) -ŋgu to a disyllabic stem ending in a vowel;
> (ii) -gu to a trisyllabic or longer stem ending in a vowel;
> (iii) a homorganic stop plus -u to a stem ending in a nasal or -y;
> (iv) -ɽu, together with the deletion of the stem-final consonant, when the stem ends in -l, -r or -ɽ; ...
> SIMPLE GENITIVE involves the addition of -u for stems ending in a nasal, and the addition of -ŋu for all other stems ...'

THE PARADIGM ECONOMY PRINCIPLE

Table 3.8

Nominative	Base unchanged
Ergative	-C$_i$ u, -ṛu, -ŋgu, -gu
	(where C$_i$ is a stop homorganic with the last stem consonant)
Simple Genitive	-ŋu, -u

Table 3.9

Nominative	walguy 'brown snake'	bindirin 'lizard'	gubur 'bee'
Ergative	walguy-ḍu	biṉḍiriṉ-ḍu	gubu-ṛu
Simple Genitive	walguy-ŋu	biṉḍiriṉ-u	gubur-ŋu
Nominative	yaṛa 'man'	yamani 'rainbow'	
Ergative	yaṛa-ŋgu	yamani-gu	
Simple Genitive	yaṛa-ŋu	yamani-ŋu	

If one chooses to ignore this phonologically predictable allomorphy, then, the number of distinct inflexion patterns for Dyirbal nouns reduces to one.

3.1.2 Definitions

It is time now to consider the generalisation that appears to be emerging. For Hungarian, Zulu and Dyirbal data, as for our hypothetical Latin-like data, we have calculated an upper limit on the number of conceivably distinct inflexional patterns; we have then found that the actual number of distinct patterns is vastly smaller than this. In fact, if we decide to ignore phonologically predictable alternations, the number of distinct patterns turns out to be as small as it could possibly be — the bare minimum necessary to put all the available inflexional resources to work, as it were. In Zulu, for example, given that most of the Class–Number combinations have two exponents available as concordial prefixes and that the choice between them is not phonologically determined, there must be at least two patterns of distribution; and the actual total turns out to be two, as shown in Table 3.7. Similarly, in Hungarian, where phonological conditioning accounts for all the Plural allo-

47

morphy in Table 3.1 and for much of the allomorphy in the Singular, we are left with only two conjugations — just as many as is necessary to accommodate that element of allomorphy which is not phonological. The rest of this section will be devoted to formulating this generalisation in a precise and clearly testable fashion, and the rest of the chapter will be devoted to exploring its consequences and refining it.

It may seem natural at this stage to define the term 'paradigm' in such a way that phonologically conditioned allomorphy of the kind that we have observed is classed as intraparadigmatic. Doing this will enable us to say that, for example, the Hungarian verbs *olvasni* and *írni* in Table 3.2 belong to the same paradigm, despite the fact that one has -*sz* and the other -*ol* in the 2nd Singular Present Indicative Indefinite.[6] From there it will be a short step to formulating the emerging generalisation in terms of a strict upper limit on the number of paradigms into which the inflexional resources of a given wordclass may be organised. But there are two reasons for not defining 'paradigm' in this way. The first is consistency with other scholars' usage. Wurzel's notion 'Flexionsklasse' (inflexional class), which is closely allied to 'paradigm', is defined in such a way that, if two words have phonologically distinct exponents for some morphosyntactic propertycombinations, then they belong to distinct inflexional classes (1984: 66); *olvasni* and *írni* must therefore belong to distinct inflexion classes, since (as noted in Chapter 1) -*sz* and -*ol* must almost certainly be regarded as phonologically distinct even though their distribution is (within the normal conjugation) phonologically predictable. And Wurzel's decision here is not arbitrary; he regards it as important to be able to say, in some instances, that inflexional differences that are phonologically predictable nevertheless indicate distinct inflexion classes (1984: 143 fn. 29). The second, and more telling, reason is that, as we will shortly see, it will in any case be necessary to use a somewhat more abstract notion that the traditional 'paradigm' in order to arrive at a generalisation that will hold for a wider range of data. It will still be convenient, however, to approach this more abstract notion by way of the traditional one, and so define 'paradigm' first:

(301) A **paradigm** for a part of speech N in a language L is a pattern P of inflexional realisations for all combinations

of non-lexically-determined morphosyntactic properties associated with N such that some member of N exemplifies P (i.e. displays all and only the realisations in P).

Two comments on this definition are called for. First, it is vague in so far as we lack a precise criterion for determining in all instances whether two inflexional realisations are to be regarded as distinct. For example, should we regard the four Ergative suffixes of Dyirbal as distinct or not? To the extent that the distribution of allomorphs in doubtful cases is conditioned phonologically, this vagueness will be taken care of directly; other aspects, involving stem allomorphy, will be considered in Chapter 6. The second point concerns the term 'non-lexically-determined'. The effect of this term is to allow us to assign two lexical items to the same paradigm even though they (or, rather, their corresponding inflected forms) are not morphosyntactically identical. It requires us, for example, to exclude properties of Gender from those properties whose realisations may help to identify a particular nominal paradigm in a language such as Latin; consequently it allows us to say that *mensa* 'table' and *nauta* 'sailor' exemplify the same paradigm (or belong to the same declension-type) even though the former is Feminine and the latter Masculine. Defining 'paradigm' in this way certainly corresponds to traditional usage. More importantly, the phenomenon in question — the cross-cutting of classification based on declension- or conjugation-type by classification based on some inherent or lexically-determined morphosyntactic property such as Gender — is common enough so that to exclude the expression 'non-lexically-determined' in (301) would have embarrassing consequences. If we did exclude it, we would have to say not that *mensa* and *nauta* exemplified the same paradigm but that they exemplified two distinct paradigms which happened to be inflexionally identical; and we would have to say the same of (for example) *dêmos* (Masculine) 'people' and *nêsos* (Feminine) 'island' in Attic Greek, of *d'ad'a* (Masculine) 'uncle' and *t'ot'a* (Feminine) 'aunt' in Russian, and of *Tag* (Masculine) 'day' and *Boot* (Neuter) 'boat' in German, since the two nouns in each of these pairs differ in Gender even though the inflexions of both are the same.

We are now in a position to offer a provisional definition of the new notion 'macroparadigm' in terms of which our generalisations on paradigm economy will be formulated:

(302) Definition of **macroparadigm** (first version):

A macroparadigm consists of: (a) any two or more similar paradigms all of whose inflexional differences can be accounted for phonologically; or (b) any paradigm which cannot be thus combined with other paradigm(s).

Let us apply this notion to the Hungarian facts as discussed earlier. Concerning *ülni* and *érteni* in Table 3.2, one might well argue whether or not they exemplify different paradigms: should the 1 Sg endings *-ök* and *-ek* (for example) be classed as morphologically distinct, or should they be treated as merely different phonetic reflexes derived from a common phonological representation? The macroparadigm notion resolves us of the need to settle here this essentially phonological question. If we decide that *ülni* and *érteni* belong to the same paradigm, then they belong to the same macroparadigm; but, if we decide that they belong to different paradigms, the phonological predictability of their inflexional differences ensures that they belong to the same macroparadigm anyway. The same goes for *olvasni* and *írni*, since the crucial difference between *-sz* and *-ol* in the 2nd Singular can also be accounted for phonologically. The definition will not, however, allow us to combine the *ik*-conjugation verb *enni* with the normal conjugation verb *érteni* (for example), since the distribution of *-ik* and zero as exponents of 3rd Singular Indicative is not phonologically predictable.

There is an important difference between paradigms and macroparadigms when we consider them from the point of view of specifying realisations for combinations or bundles of morphosyntactic properties. For any one such property-bundle, a paradigm will by definition provide just one inflexional realisation. On the other hand, a macroparadigm may provide more than one: for example, *-(a)sz* and *-ol* for 2nd Singular in the Hungarian Indefinite Present Indicative. It will be convenient to invent a term for such sets of inflexions, defined as follows:

(303) A **macroinflexion** for some morphosyntactic property-bundle is the set of inflexional realisations for that

property-bundle consisting of all the (one or more) realisations appropriate to one macroparadigm.

This definition allows us to say (for example) that all the Dyirbal Ergative endings illustrated in Table 3.8 constitute a single Ergative macroinflexion, since the phonological predictability of the various exponents of Case ensures that all Dyirbal nouns belong to a single macroparadigm.[7]

We are at last in a position to state the generalisation that the Hungarian, Zulu and Dyirbal material seems to suggest:

(304) PARADIGM ECONOMY PRINCIPLE
When in a given language L more than one inflexional realisation is available for some bundle or bundles of non-lexically-determined morphosyntactic properties associated with some part of speech N, the number of macroparadigms for N is no greater than the number of distinct 'rival' macroinflexions available for that bundle which is most generously endowed with such rival realisations.[8]

This package of definitions will need revision in due course; what is presented here is a first, provisional version. But, before we look at further relevant evidence, it is worth reflecting how startlingly successful we appear to have been so far in answering a question posed in Chapter 2, namely: how far does language go to reduce the potential burden imposed on the memory by an array of inflexions like the hypothetical Latin-like ones of L in Table 2.3? What we were looking for was an actual upper limit to the number of affix distribution patterns for nouns in L, somewhere below the arithmetical upper limit of 27,648. But as well as an arithmetical upper limit, one can also calculate a lower limit for L. The Case most generously endowed with distinct affixes is Singular 2, which has four ($-e$, $-s$, $-m$, $-\emptyset$); so, assuming that their distribution is not phonologically predictable and that each is therefore a distinct macroinflexion, there must be at least four macroparadigms in L. Given these arithmetical limits, it would have been quite satisfying, perhaps, to find evidence for a constraint limiting the actual total to (say) twelve, or 28. But what the Paradigm Economy Principle predicts is that the actual total is no greater than the arithmetical lower limit. In our provisional formulation, then, the constraint that we have been seeking is as tight as it could possibly be. Not surprisingly, we will find reasons to relax the Principle somewhat, though not so as to undermine its spirit. Meanwhile, we will look at some consequences of the Principle, as presently stated, for phonological analysis and for diachrony.

3.1.3 Consequences

I remarked earlier that the definition of 'paradigm' at (301) was vague so long as there were no clear criteria for determining when two phonetically distinct inflexions were to be counted as morphologically distinct. To the extent that such allomorphy is phonologically conditioned, our definition of 'macroparadigm' solves the problem adequately for present purposes. But we can also imagine situations where the phonological analysis is dubious in another way — where two inflexions are phonetically identical but seem possibly to derive from distinct phonological representations through a process of neutralisation. In the absence of any general agreement about permissible 'abstractness' in phonology, this kind of phonological possibility could conceivably lend itself to manoeuvres designed to protect the Paradigm Economy Principle against disproof by rigging the phonological analysis of relevant inflexions appropriately. For example, let us imagine a hypothetical language L2, with three distinct Case macroparadigms for nouns (three declensions) as in Table 3.10 (where the affixes are to be understood as being in their 'surface' phonetic representations):

Table 3.10

	Decl 1	Decl 2	Decl 3
Case 1	-i	-a	-i
Case 2	-u	-u	-o
Case 3	-un	-un	-o

On the face of it, the Paradigm Economy Principle predicts that L2 will not be a possible human language, because, although there are three macroparadigms, there are no more than two rival realisations for each Case. But one could save the Principle from disproof by L2 if one posited that in Case 1, for instance, the surface -*i* in declension 3 was derived phonologically from another underlying segment (say /e/) and was therefore underlyingly distinct from the -*i* of declension 1; we would thus have three rival realisations after all for one of the Cases, and three distinct macroparadigms would therefore be permitted by the Paradigm Economy Principle. And insofar as that manoeuvre is theoretically possible, one might argue, the Principle is invulnerable to empirical disconfirmation and therefore vacuous. So, to preserve the empirical content of the Principle, it seems as if we are ineluctably drawn into the controversy on abstractness in phonology which I set out in Chapter 1 to avoid.

This kind of objection can, however, be answered satisfactorily. As long as there are uncertainties in phonological analysis, there are bound to be uncertainties about the empirical consequences of hypotheses in any other area of language to the extent that they presuppose phonological analyses. But the uncertainty need not render morphological hypotheses vacuous any more than uncertainty in semantics precludes the formulation and testing of empirical hypotheses about syntax. Let us consider again the L2 situation illustrated in Table 3.10 and the idea of deriving the -*i* in Case 1 of declension 3 from /-e/. If in L2 there were instances of [e] contrasting minimally with [i], so that any rule changing /e/ to [i] would have to be hedged about with phonologically ad hoc restrictions, we would need to feel very confident of the validity of the Paradigm Economy Principle, on the basis of evidence from a variety of languages, in order to be willing to countenance such a desperate ploy in defence of it. Even with such independent confirming evidence, we might choose to abandon the Principle in the light of Table 3.10 if it were apparent that the kind of ad hoc restrictions on the /e/ -to- [i] rule that would be needed would be unique in L2 and unparalleled in other languages. If, on the other hand, [i] never contrasted with [e] in final position in L2 and there was independent evidence for a vowel-raising rule, it would seem quite reasonable to invoke a phonological explanation for the absence of three distinct Case 1 suffixes in Table 3.10 and thus reconcile L2 with the Paradigm Economy Principle. What this hypothetical but (I hope) reasonably realistic example illustrates is that, even if there are no universally agreed limits on what is permissible in phonological representations and rules, it should not be hard in most actual instances to decide whether phonological manoeuvres to account for potential counter-examples to the Paradigm Economy Principle are justifiable or not. It also illustrates how a reasonably well established theory of what is and is not permissible in paradigmatic patterning on purely morphological grounds could in principle help to resolve phonological dilemmas. If, for example, we were firmly convinced of the validity of the Paradigm Economy Principle, on the basis of a wide range of independent morphological evidence, we might be persuaded by the data of Table 3.10 that [i] could legitimately be derived from some underlying segment such as /e/ even in the absence of any independent evidence in L2 to that effect and even at the cost of permitting types of phonological rule, or degrees of abstractness in underlying representations, that we would otherwise have preferred to outlaw. There are, no doubt, other kinds of phonological dilemma which a tight, independently justified theory of the paradigm could help to resolve, and the usefulness of such a theory for such purposes is, of course, one of the reasons for wanting to develop it.

The Paradigm Economy Principle also has consequences for morphological change. Let us imagine a third hypothetical language L3, with a set of Case affixes arranged in three declensions as in Table 3.11. These data are very similar to those of L2, set out in Table 3.10. The only difference is that for Case 1 of declension 1 the realisation is -*e*, not -*i*. Because of this, L3 has three distinct affixes for Case 1 and the existence of three paradigms is compatible with the Paradigm Economy Principle, without the need for any phonological jiggery-pokery. Let us now suppose that, by a phonological innovation, all *e* are raised to *i* (compare the development of [ɛ:] and [e:] to [i] in Hellenistic and Byzantine Greek, and the more recent shift of [e] to [i] in northern Greek dialects). This innovation will transform Table 3.11 into Table 3.10. If the Paradigm Economy Principle is correct, and if we reject the possibility of reconciling Table 3.10 with the Principle by invoking phonological neutralisation, then it follows that the pattern illustrated in Table 3.10 must change; either a new rival realisation must be 'invented' for one of the three Cases, so as to permit the maintenance of three distinct declensions, or else the number of declensions must be reduced, with perhaps the loss of one of the rival realisations for some of the other Cases. The prediction that the Paradigm Economy Principle makes is thus reasonably clear; and even though the data in any real language are unlikely to be as clear-cut as in our hypothetical example, the Principle certainly offers a new tool with which to try to make sense of, for example, certain inflexional developments affecting Indo-European languages.

Table 3.11

	Decl 1	Decl 2	Decl 3
Case 1	-e	-a	-i
Case 2	-u	-u	-o
Case 3	-un	-un	-o

Paradigms are certainly no more stable over time than the inflexions which they incorporate, and one could argue considerably less so. For an example of large-scale paradigmatic restructuring in different directions in related languages, one can cite the development of the various types of Indo-European 'i-stem' nouns in Sanskrit, Latin and Greek. In classical Sanskrit, most polysyllabic stems in long i follow a Case–Number paradigm very similar to, or perhaps best regarded as morphologically identical with, that of the a-stems, while stems in short i tend to resemble more closely the consonant-stems; in classical Latin, all i-stems are paradigmatically quite distinct from a-stems and some have adopted a 'mixed' inflexional pattern close to, yet not identical with, the regular consonant-stem one, to which some original consonant-stem nouns have also been attracted; while in Attic Greek i-stem nouns have developed peculiar affixes of their own (at least 'on the surface'), or else have acquired a new stem-final -d- after the i and thereby passed into the consonantal declension-type. One possible approach to these various developments is simply to account for them piecemeal, in terms of the borrowing of individual affixes by one declension from another, without attempting to find any deeper rationale. But, if the Paradigm Economy Principle is broadly correct, one sort of deeper rationale may be discoverable. I have argued elsewhere (Carstairs 1984a) that the Principle helps to make sense of an otherwise apparently rather haphazard series of inflexional changes affecting 'i-stem' and 'consonant-stem' nouns, as well as 'mixed' nouns, of the Latin third declension. And, to the extent that the Principle succeeds in this way, we have diachronic support for its validity. But there is certainly scope for much more work on its implications for linguistic change.

3.2 REVISIONS AND REFINEMENTS

3.2.1 Prima facie counterevidence to the Paradigm Economy Principle

One apparent corollary of the Paradigm Economy Principle has not so far been mentioned: if no more macroparadigms may exist for any part of speech than there are distinct realisations for that morphosyntactic property-bundle which is most generously provided with realisations, then surely it should be possible to determine unambiguously which paradigm (declension-type or conjugation-type) a word belongs to simply by referring to the form in which that word appears for the inflexionally most diverse property-bundle. More briefly, the bundle most generously provided with distinct inflexions ought to have a diagnostic role too; if one wants to indicate as succinctly as possible the inflexional pattern which a given word exhibits (for example, in a dictionary entry), it ought not to be necessary to cite more than this one diagnostic form. Yet anyone who has studied even a moderately highly inflected language knows that frequently more than one inflected form or 'principal part' has to be cited in dictionary entries and elsewhere in order to provide an adequate basis for predicting a word's whole inflexional behaviour. Is this not powerful evidence to the effect that the restriction imposed on inflexional organisation by the present version of the Paradigm Economy Principle is much too strong?

Implicit rejection of the Paradigm Economy Principle seems to be deducible also from the recent work on the structure of paradigms by Wurzel (1984) and Bybee (1985). Neither of these addresses precisely the question that led us to formulate the Paradigm Economy Principle, but both implicitly endorse the traditional view that to predict the inflexional behaviour of some lexical items in highly inflected languages requires more than one starting point, as it were. For Wurzel, this endorsement takes the form of claiming that more than one 'implicational paradigm structure condition' is necessary in order to predict the inflexional behaviour of some third declension Latin nouns. For Bybee, the emphasis is on the relative 'autonomy' of certain inflected forms; if an inflected word has two or more forms with a roughly equivalent high degree of autonomy, each of these may act as a centre of analogical influence within the paradigm and, in effect, constitute a distinct 'principal part'.

In response to this criticism, I would point out first that, from the fact that in some language more than one 'principal part' needs to be cited in order to identify the inflexional pattern of a word clearly, it does not necessarily follow that there must be more distinct macroparadigms than the present version of the Paradigm Economy Principle allows. Consider a hypothetical language with three nominal declension-types, each constituting a distinct macroparadigm, inflected for Case by means of prefixes as in Table 3.12. Here, it is clearly Case 3 which legitimates the maintenance of three distinct declension-types from the point of view of paradigm economy, since Cases 1 and 2 are each realised in only two ways. If, then, there is to be any single inflected form which will indicate unambiguously each noun's inflexional behaviour, it must be the Case 3 form. But consider an inflected form such as *antam* 'house (Case 3)'. We can determine from this without difficulty that the stem is -*tam* and that the word does not belong to declension-type C; but we cannot determine which of the other two declension-types it belongs to, since we cannot tell whether the prefix *an-* represents the /an-/ of Type A or the /aN-/ of Type B. This would not, of course, present any serious practical problem to the writer of a dictionary of our hypothetical language. Two obvious ways of presenting the necessary information on declension-type would be to cite forms of some other Case alongside those of Case 3 or else, while citing Case 3 forms only, to use a 'morphophonemic' symbol like our N to distinguish the Type B *an-* from the Type A one. What is important here is that, even if the first of these alternative courses is adopted, the hypothetical Case-system in Table 3.12 will still remain consistent with the Paradigm Economy Principle. For the linguist testing the correctness of the Principle, then, the moral is that even if the inflexional pattern of some language

Table 3.12

	Type A	Type B	Type C
Case 1	a-	i-	i-
Case 2	e-	a-	e-
Case 3	an-	aN-	en-

where N means a nasal homorganic with any following obstruent, otherwise *n*.[9]

seems to require the citation of more than one 'principal part' for expository convenience in identifying the inflexional pattern of nouns, verbs or whatever, the facts need not necessarily conflict with the Paradigm Economy Principle, even prima facie.

It must be admitted, however, that plenty of instances of the apparent need for multiple 'principal parts' exist which cannot be dealt with so neatly. For example, students of Latin and Attic Greek have traditionally had to learn two 'parts' for Latin nouns, four 'parts' for Latin verbs and six 'parts' for Greek verbs as in Table 3.13. Even without a thorough knowledge of these three languages, it is fairly easy to see that we cannot single out one property-bundle from among those quoted for each language as the one to play the diagnostic role seemingly required by the Paradigm Economy Principle. For example, among the Latin verbs in Table 3.13(b) we cannot select the Imperfective Indicative form because *amō*, *sonō* and *cadō*, alike there, diverge in the Perfective and the Supine; we cannot choose the Perfective because *cadō* and *spondeō*, alike in showing initial reduplication there, diverge in the Infinitive; and so on.

I will argue that facts of this kind require us to add a rider to the present formulation of the Paradigm Economy Principle and also to revise the definition of 'macroparadigm' at (302), so as to alter somewhat the empirical effect of the Principle. This revision, however, still leaves us with an extremely strong and restrictive hypothesis about paradigm organisation. More specifically, I will argue that all counter-evidence to the present formulation involves:

either
   (a) the realisation of lexically determined (as opposed to syntactically acquired) morphosyntactic or 'morphosemantic' properties;
or
   (b) a new notion 'slab', involving a distinction between more fundamental and less fundamental morphosyntactic categories;
or
   (c) stem allomorphy (hence a distinction between affixal and non-affixal inflexion).

Topic (c) will be dealt with in Chapter 6; topics (a) and (b) will

Table 3.13

a. Latin nouns

	Nom Sg	Gen Sg	
	dominus	dominī	'lord'
	bellum	bellī	'war'
	dux [duks]	ducis	'general'
	caput	capitis	'head'
	fructus	fructūs	'fruit'
	genu	genūs	'knee'

b. Latin verbs

1st Sg Impf Pres Ind Act	Impf Infin Act	1st Sg Pf Pres Ind Act	Supine	
amō	amāre	amāvī	amātum	'love'
sonō	sonāre	sonuī	sonitum	'sound'
terreō	terrēre	terruī	territum	'scare'
pōnō	pōnere	posuī	positum	'put'
cadō	cadere	cecidī	cāsum	'fall'
spondeō	spondēre	spopondī	sponsum	'pledge'

c. Greek verbs: 1st Person Singular Indicative

Active					Middle/Pass
Present	Future	Aorist		Perfect	Perfect
horô	ópsomai	eîdon		heóraka	heóramai or ômmai
bállō	balô	ébalon		bébleka	béblemai
lúō	lúsō	élūsa		léluka	lélumai

Passive Aorist		
óphthēn	'see'	
ebléthēn	'throw'	
elúthēn	'loose'	

occupy us in this chapter. In the light of these revisions, I will suggest in Chapter 7 how the Paradigm Economy Principle can be reconciled with, and even help to explain, the superficially quite lavish array of distinct inflexional patterns found among nouns in modern standard German.

3.2.2 The relevance of lexically determined morphosyntax and morphosemantics

The definition of 'paradigm' at (301) contains the term 'non-lexically-determined', for reasons already explained; we want to be able to say that (for example) the Latin nouns *mensa* (Feminine) 'table' and *nauta* (Masculine) 'sailor' belong to the same paradigm. But this is not to say that lexically determined categories should always be regarded as irrelevant to the determination of macroparadigms. Let us consider some more evidence from Russian, Dyirbal, Zulu and Latin.

Compare the following Russian nominal paradigms, and in particular the Accusative Case forms in Tables 3.14, 3.15 and 3.16. If we ignored the Accusatives, we could say that only three paradigms were exemplified here: one for *student* and *akt*, one for *professor* and *dom*, and one for *ženščina* and *kvartira*. But the difference in the Accusative Plural between *ženščina* and *kvartira* in Table 3.16 and the differences in both the Singular and Plural Accusatives within Tables 3.14 and 3.15 prevent us from identifying their paradigms in this way. In fact, on the basis of the definition of 'paradigm' at (301), we have to say that there are six distinct paradigms here; and, since none of the relevant alternations are phonologically conditioned, there are also six distinct macroparadigms. But, if this is so, the Paradigm Economy Principle is clearly at risk, since no morphosyntactic bundle here has anything like as many as six distinct realisations.

The solution to this problem lies, I suggest, in recognising the morphological importance of the semantic distinction between Animate and Inanimate nouns. In all Russian nouns denoting animate creatures, the Accusative Plural is the same as the Genitive Plural, and in the Singular too the Accusative is the same as the Genitive for certain Animate nouns, namely Masculines (not Feminines) belonging to those declension-types which do not supply a distinctive Accusative ending; thus, the Acc Sg is the same as the Gen Sg in the Masculine *student* and

Table 3.14

		a.	b.
Sg	Nom	student	akt
		'student'	'report; act (of play)'
	Acc	*studenta*	*akt*
	Gen	studenta	akta
	Dat	studentu	aktu
	Instr	studentom	aktom
	Loc	studente	akte
Pl	Nom	studenty	akty
	Acc	*studentov*	*akty*
	Gen	studentov	aktov
	Dat	studentam	aktam
	Instr	studentami	aktami
	Loc	studentax	aktax

Table 3.15

		a.	b.
Sg	Nom	professor	dom
		'professor'	'house'
	Acc	*professora*	*dom*
	Gen	professora	doma
	Dat	professoru	domu
	Instr	professorom	domom
	Loc	professore	dome
Pl	Nom	professora	doma
	Acc	*professorov*	*doma*
	Gen	professorov	domov
	Dat	professoram	domam
	Instr	professorami	domami
	Loc	professorax	domax

Table 3.16

		a.	b.
Sg	Nom	ženščina	kvartira
		'woman'	'flat, apartment'
	Acc	*ženščinu*	*kvartiru*
	Gen	ženščiny	kvartiry
	Dat	ženščine	kvartire
	Instr	ženščinoj	kvartiroj
	Loc	ženščine	kvartire
Pl	Nom	ženščiny	kvartiry
	Acc	*ženščin*	*kvartiry*
	Gen	ženščin	kvartir
	Dat	ženščinam	kvartiram
	Instr	ženščinami	kvartirami
	Loc	ženščinax	kvartirax

professor (illustrated in Tables 3.14(a) and 3.15(a)), but not in *mužčina* 'man', a Masculine noun which 'goes like' *ženščina*, nor in *mat'* 'mother', a Feminine noun whose Acc Sg is like the Nominative, not the Genitive (i.e. *mat'*, not *materi*).[10] Our first definition of 'macroparadigm' at (302) made use of the fact that some allomorphy is phonologically predictable. Here, by contrast, we have allomorphy which is semantically predictable. If we were to amend the definition of 'macroparadigm' so as to accommodate this kind of predictability too, the task of reconciling these Russian paradigms with the Paradigm Economy Principle would be solved: we would have three macroparadigms, not six, legitimised by the existence of three distinct macroinflexions *-ov~-y*, *-ov~-a* and *Ø~-y* for the Accusative Plural.

The Russian example just discussed illustrates the possible paradigmatic relevance of a semantic property. Dyirbal verb inflexion illustrates a lexically determined syntactic property (Transitivity) in a similar role. There is a prima facie instance of 'illegal' paradigm mixture in the partial verbal paradigms quoted below (Dixon 1972: 55, 68, 248) in Table 3.17. The forms relevant to us here are the Unmarked (Present/Past) Tense, the 'Do-it-quickly' stem and the Purposive form. There appear to be two distinct endings for each: *-n* and *-ɲu* for Unmarked Tense, *-nbal* and *-galiy* for 'Do-it-quickly', and *-li* and *-gu* for Purposive. Yet there are more than two distinct paradigms. *Balgal* and *baniy* are 'unmixed', the former selecting *-n*, *-nbal* and *-li* and the latter selecting *-ɲu*, *-galiy* and *-gu*; but *wayɲɟil* is 'mixed', since it goes like *balgal* in the Unmarked Tense and Purposive form (*wayɲɟin, wayɲɟili*) and like *baniy* in the 'Do-it-quickly' form (*wayɲɟigaliy*). Dixon makes it clear, however, that the membership of the *wayɲɟil* conjugation-type is not haphazard; it consists, in fact, of just those *l*-stem verbs (i.e. verbs with an Unmarked form in *-n*, like *balgan* 'hits/hit') which are Intransitive. So if we set up macroparadigms on the basis of syntactic as well as phonological predictability, we have grounds for uniting the *balgal* type and the *wayɲɟil* type into a single macroparadigm; for where their inflexional realisations for some non-lexically-determined property differ (namely in the 'Do-it-quickly' form), this difference can be correlated with a difference in some lexically determined syntactic category, namely Transitivity. Moreover, if we extend the 'macroparadigm' notion in this way, we no longer have here a counter-

Table 3.17

	'*l*-stems'		'*y*-stem'
Stem	balgal 'hit'	wayɲɟil 'go uphill'	baniy 'come'
Unmarked Tense	balgan	wayɲɟin	baniɲu
Future Tense	balgaɲ	wayɲɟiɲ	baniɲ
'Do-it-quickly'	balgalnbal	wayɲɟigaliy	banigaliy
Purposive Aspect	balgali	wayɲɟili	banigu

example to the Paradigm Economy Principle; for the number of macroparadigms here is not three but two, the same as the maximum number of distinct realisations for any one morphosyntactic bundle.

In Zulu, as we have already seen, all nouns belong to 'Classes' which play a considerable morphosyntactic role; verbs and predicate adjectives must agree in Class with their subject noun, and attributive adjectives and other modifiers must agree in Class with their head. It is customary to regard Classes as much like Indo-European Genders, only more numerous. But there is a difference. Each class in Zulu is, broadly speaking, associated with only one nominal prefix (or one pair of prefixes, Singular and Plural)[11] and only one set of concordial elements; whereas in a language such as Latin one Gender may be realised in a variety of ways, depending on the declension-type of the item (noun, adjective, participle or pronoun) which carries it. To put it another way: in Latin, Gender intersects with declension-type, whereas in Zulu, Class-membership determines declension-type. Indeed, for nouns, whose Class-membership is lexically fixed, Class-membership and declension-type are essentially the same thing. We can therefore think of each Class provisionally as a distinct paradigm and test whether the organisation of the Classes obeys paradigm economy.

Most Zulu nouns have distinct Singular and Plural forms (the exceptions being mainly what one would expect on semantic grounds, such as abstracts and mass nouns). The locus of this distinction, and hence the exponent of Number, is the prefix. It is thus appropriate to ask how many distinct prefixes exist for each of these two properties, and then test for compliance with the Paradigm Economy Principle by inquiring whether the number of relevant Classes (i.e. those in which Singular and Plural forms are distinguished) exceeds the number of prefixes for the more generously provided of the two properties Singular and Plural. The distinct prefixes are as follows:

(305) Singular: um(u)-, u-, i:-, isi-, in-, u:-
       Plural: aba-, o-, imi-, ama-, izi-, izin-

There are thus six prefixes for each of the two properties. The mathematical maximum number of distinct paradigms incorporating these prefixes is thus 36, while the maximum as predicted by the Paradigm Economy Principle is six. The actual number (barring a few marginal types)[12] is, however, seven:

Table 3.18

Class	1/2	1a/2a	3/4	5/6	7/8	9/10	11/10
Sg	um(u)-	u-	um(u)-	i:-	isi-	in-	u:-
Pl	aba-	o-	imi-	ama-	izi-	izin-	izin-

Two Classes (1/2 and 3/4) share a Singular prefix and two (9/10 and 11/10) share a Plural one, so that we have one paradigm too many from the point of view of the Paradigm Economy Principle. How, if at all, could a revised macro-paradigm concept help here? What we have to look for is a pair of Classes in Zulu which display a correlation between an inflexional contrast and a lexically determined semantic or syntactic contrast (like Animacy in Russian and Transitivity in Dyirbal). The obvious pairs of Classes to examine first are those which share a prefix for either Singular or Plural: 1/2 and 3/4 (which share *um(u)-* in the Singular) or 9/10 and 11/10 (which share *izin-* in the Plural). Both Class 9/10 and Class 11/10 are semantically rather heterogeneous, and certainly no consistent semantic contrast between them seems to stand out (Doke 1973: 53, 55). On the other hand, Class 1/2 is entirely homogeneous in that it contains exclusively nouns denoting human beings. What of Class 3/4? Doke remarks (1973: 44): 'This is sometimes called the "Tree" or "River" class, but in Zulu [by contrast with its cognate Classes in some other Bantu languages] it is mostly of a miscellaneous nature.' The crucial question for us, of course, is whether it contains any nouns denoting humans; for, if it does not, we will have found a straightforward and promising semantic contrast between it and Class 1/2.

The answer to this question is encouraging. Of the small group of Human nouns which belong to Class 3/4 and which therefore display the *um(u)-/imi-* pattern, examples are (Doke 1973: 47):

(306)   umsheshengwana   'sneaking informer'
        umbonamathunzi   'pessimist'

umhambuma   'tramp'[13]
umlindankosi   'king's bodyguard'

A significant generalisation about these words, I suggest, is that they nearly all have a pejorative connotation, the only common exception being *umhlobo* 'brother, relative', which sometimes has a Plural *imihlobo* rather than *abahlobo* when used in a figurative sense, not implying blood relationship.[14] We therefore have some prima facie ground for recognising a 'macro-Class' 1/2/3/4, with inflexion partly reflecting the morphosemantic properties Human and (let us say) Despised, thus:

(307) Class 1/2/3/4
      Singular: um(u)-
      Plural: Non-human: imi-
                Human: Despised: imi-
                          Non-despised: aba-

Any Human noun of the macro-Class which, like *umhlobo*, forms a Plural with *imi-* even though it does not carry a pejorative connotation will have to be treated as a lexically marked exception. We will therefore predict that it should be liable to acquire a 'regular' Plural in *aba-*; and, as we have seen, this prediction seems to be correct. (Doke's (1973: 46) words are: 'there is a tendency nowadays to use the [Class 1/2] plural *abahlobo*'.)

An obvious fact about (307) is that the Despised Human Plural prefix is exactly the same as the Non-human Plural prefix. In some sense, therefore, Zulu morphology treats Despised Humans as things. This fact tends to support the recognition of the macroparadigm, I suggest. There is a tendency in at least a few other languages for Human nouns with a pejorative connotation to belong to a Gender or declension-type which is in some way semantically inappropriate. An isolated example of this is the use in German of *Mensch* as a Neuter noun with the meaning 'hussy', in contrast to its neutral meaning 'human being' when in its normal Masculine Gender. A more systematic instance of the phenomenon, seemingly, is Gender-switch in the Ethiopian language Tigre, whereby diminutives of the opposite Gender to the noun from which they are derived (Masculine for Feminine and vice versa) acquire a pejorative sense (Palmer 1962: 47, 57-9, 61-2). Similarly, in those Polish declensions in which Plural Masculines display a morphological contrast between 'Viriles' (i.e. human males) and 'Non-viriles', a Non-virile inflexion may be deliberately substituted for a Virile one for pejorative effect, e.g. *Szwab* 'Swabian', *Szwabi* 'Swabians' versus *Szwaby* (with Non-virile -*y* instead of Virile -*i*) 'Krauts' (Gotteri 1981). I suspect that a careful search would reveal that the phenomenon is quite widespread. What this means is that the morphosemantic characteristics of the putative Zulu macro-Class 1/2/3/4 may really be simpler than is indicated in (307); at the point where morphosyntactic properties are realised, it may be appropriate to regard 'Despised Humans' as not really Humans at all, so the fact that their Plural prefix is *imi-* rather than either *aba-* or some third possibility (say, *izi-*) follows automatically from their macro-Class membership. We can say, essentially, that all Human nouns in the amalgamated macro-Class display a Plural prefix *aba-* except when, as in a few lexicalised instances, they are treated morphologically as Non-humans for pejorative effect.

I turn now to some Latin evidence, involving situations where compliance with the Paradigm Economy Principle is not at issue. Demonstrating the relevance of the amended macro-paradigm concept in such situations is important. If we can show the concept to be useful in morphological description independently of paradigm economy, we improve our chances of anchoring our approach to paradigms and our claims about their behaviour firmly within a more general framework of definitions and claims about inflexional morphology. Consider the Latin nominal paradigms in Table 3.19. There is room for argument about precisely how we should analyse the underlying phonological shapes of both stems and endings; but a traditional and relatively uncontroversial analysis would involve recognising four distinct Nom Sg endings, thus:

(308) Nom Sg of *dominus*:   -*us* (/domin + us/)
                  bellum: -*um* (/bell + um/)
                  dux: -*s* (/duk + s/)
                  caput: no affix (/kaput/)

Assuming that these four endings are indeed distinct, we will expect to find at least four distinct paradigms among the Latin nouns which exemplify them. Assuming further that the Nominative Singular is the most generously furnished property-bundle,

Table 3.19

		Sg	Pl		Sg	Pl
Nom	a.	dominus 'lord'	dominī	b.	bellum 'war'	bella
Voc		domine	dominī		bellum	bella
Acc		dominum	dominōs		bellum	bella
Gen		dominī	dominōrum		bellī	bellōrum
Dat		dominō	dominīs		bellō	bellīs
Abl		dominō	dominīs		bellō	bellīs
Nom	c.	dux [duks] 'general'	ducēs	d.	caput 'head'	capita
Voc		dux	ducēs		caput	capita
Acc		ducem	ducēs		caput	capita
Gen		ducis	ducum		capitis	capitum
Dat		ducī	ducibus		capitī	capitibus
Abl		duce	ducibus		capite	capitibus

the Paradigm Economy Principle will lead us to predict that there should be no more than four distinct paradigms among the class of Latin nouns with these four Nom Sg endings. On the basis of the data presented in Table 3.19, this seems correct.[15] What is the problem, then?

Clearly, there is no breach of paradigm economy here. Yet there is something about Table 3.19 which is potentially embarrassing. In the Nominative Singular, as we have seen, there are four distinct endings. If we look at the Nominative Plural, we will probably recognise three: -ī-, -ēs and -a, the last of these shared by two of the four nouns (*bellum* and *caput*). Yet when we look at the Genitive, Dative and Ablative Cases, the number of distinct inflexions drops to two. Moreover, the inflexions for each property-bundle are distributed in such a way that *dominus* and *bellum* share one while *dux* and *caput* share the other. The reason why this is potentially embarrassing is that, from the point of view of paradigm economy, it appears at first a mere accident. The existence of four distinct endings in the Nom Sg legitimises, as it were, the existence of four distinct endings for each of the other eleven Case–Number bundles. The fact that for six of the eleven bundles there are only two distinct endings and that the four nouns 'go together' in pairs as they do is unexplained. This need not perhaps be regarded as a serious embarrassment. After all, what we have been discussing, and what the Paradigm Economy Principle is meant to impose limits on, is paradigmatic distinctness, not paradigmatic resemblance; there are certainly more things to be said about paradigms, and further general constraints to be discovered, which have nothing to do with 'economy'.[16] Nevertheless, it would be very satisfying if the similarities we observe in the Genitive, Dative and Ablative forms could after all be shown to be a consequence of applying some notion we have developed already. I will hope to show, in fact, that they point to the application of the macroparadigm notion here.

One attribute of the four nouns in Table 3.19 has not so far been mentioned: their Genders. In fact, *dominus* and *dux* are both Masculine while *bellum* and *caput* are both Neuter. Is this an accident of the particular nouns we have chosen, or does it reflect some general association of particular Genders with particular paradigms in Latin? To some extent, both. Although the *dominus* type is predominantly Masculine, we can certainly find Feminine nouns which belong to it, particularly tree names such as *fāgus* 'beech' and *fraxinus* 'ash', and the *dux* type too includes Feminines, such as *lux* (Gen Sg *lūcis*) 'light'; but neither of these types includes any Neuters. On the other hand, neither the *bellum* nor the *caput* type includes any Masculines or Feminines. We thus have the ingredients we need to set up two macroparadigms in Table 3.19, linking *dominus* with *bellum* and *dux* with *caput* on the ground that their inflexional differences are associated with a consistent distinction between lexically determined properties: non-Neuter versus Neuter.

The linking of paradigms just achieved will come as no surprise to Latin scholars, who may even wonder what all the fuss is about. They are used to the fact that Neuters in Latin differ from non-Neuters in having a peculiar set of Nominative, Vocative and Accusative endings, and that every Neuter paradigm can be associated with some non-Neuter paradigm on the basis of identity in the endings for all (or nearly all) the other Cases; thus, *dominus* and *bellum* would be traditionally described as representing the non-Neuter and Neuter variants respectively of the 'second declension', and *dux* and *caput* as both belonging to the 'third declension'. But the fact that the macroparadigm concept yields such uncontroversial results here is a plus, not a minus. It means that what at first may have seemed a rather arbitrary device to protect the Paradigm Economy Principle from disconfirmation by certain evidence from Russian, Dyirbal and Zulu is after all no more than a notion well established (under whatever name) in the European description of Latin (and also Greek) since before the Renaissance. We have thus succeeded in finding a use for the notion 'macroparadigm' independent of paradigm economy.[17]

We have reached the point where it is appropriate to state precisely the amended definition of 'macroparadigm'. Our starting point will be the first definition at (302), which we can revise as follows:

(309) Definition of **macroparadigm** (second version):
A macroparadigm consists of:
(a) any two or more similar paradigms all of whose inflexional differences either can be accounted for phonologically, or else correlate consistently with differences in semantic or lexically determined syntactic properties;
or
(b) any paradigm which cannot be thus combined with other paradigm(s).

Perhaps the most important single phrase in this definition is 'lexically determined'; for this draws attention to a new difference between paradigms and macroparadigms, according to our revised definition. Paradigms are defined at (301) by reference to the inflexional realisations of morphosyntactic properties which are not lexically determined. This allows us to say, for example, that the Latin Masculine noun *dominus* 'lord' and the inflexionally identical Feminine noun *fraxinus* 'ash tree' belong to the same paradigm, despite their difference in Gender. On the other hand, our definition of 'macroparadigm' allows us to say that both *dominus* and *fraxinus* belong to the same macroparadigm as the Neuter noun *bellum*, despite the inflexional difference in the Nominative, Vocative and Accusative Cases; and we can say further that this inflexional difference serves a realisational function, inasmuch as Gender, though not realised elsewhere in the inflexion of second-declension nouns, does get realised in the Nom-Voc-Acc of *bellum*.

Adopting the revised definition of 'macroparadigm' has an immediate implication for the notion 'macroinflexion' and for the empirical consequences of the Paradigm Economy Principle. As already mentioned, in the Russian material in Tables

3.14-3.16 we now find not six macroparadigms but three, most of whose Accusative macroinflexions have two members, one for Animate nouns and the other for Inanimates. Similarly, the revised definition allows the syntactic property Transitive to come to the rescue of the Paradigm Economy Principle in the Dyirbal data in Table 3.17, and the semantic properties Human and Despised play a similar role in Zulu.

In section 3.2.1 I commented on the need in many languages for more than one 'principal part' to indicate a word's inflexional behaviour. It is natural to ask now to what extent the new definition of 'macroparadigm' mitigates the apparent damage to the Paradigm Economy Principle inflicted by material such as the Latin and Greek forms cited in Table 3.13. The answer is that it is relevant to the Latin noun forms, as already shown; the Latin and Greek verb forms remain to be accounted for in section 3.2.4. Meanwhile, we will look at another generalisation that the new definition of 'macroparadigm' facilitates.

3.2.3 Macroparadigm uniqueness

There is an element of vagueness in both our definitions of 'macroparadigm' hitherto, in that they both contain the expression 'any two or more similar paradigms'. How similar do two paradigms need to be in order to be candidates for assignment to a single macroparadigm? When we were considering only those inflexional differences that were predictable phonologically, no problem seemed to arise in practice: for example, the paradigms of the Hungarian verbs *olvasni* and *írni* are clearly similar in the sense that they are identical except in their 2nd Singular Indicative Indefinite forms (*olvas-ol* 'you read' versus *ír-sz* 'you write'). But now we have extended the definition of 'macroparadigm' so as to embrace other kinds of lexically determined property, the vagueness may seem more problematic. What if, for example, we found two distinct nominal paradigms containing only Masculines and one paradigm containing only Feminines but resembling each of the two Masculine paradigms equally? On the face of it, we could combine this Feminine paradigm equally validly with either of the two Masculine ones, so the choice would be arbitrary. I will in fact suggest that such instances of what we might call macroparadigmatic ambivalence never occur. To appreciate the significance of this claim, however, we need to realise what an extreme case of macroparadigmatic ambivalence would look like.

Let us examine a hypothetical set of paradigms exploiting most of the Singular inflexional resources of the Latin-like language L, given in Table 2.3.[18] These Singular inflexions are grouped in Table 3.20 into nine distinct paradigms, three for each of the three Genders, with each paradigm assigned a numeral in square brackets for convenience in identification. This pattern is clearly far removed from what we find in Latin, the inspiration for L's inflexions. But the important question here is whether it is consistent with the Paradigm Economy Principle on the basis of the revised definition of 'macroparadigm'. This depends on whether we can successfully group the nine distinct paradigms into macroparadigms in such a way that there are no more macroparadigms than there are 'macroinflexions' for the most lavishly provided slot. When we attempt such a macroparadigm grouping, however, the problem that we encounter is not that there is no solution but that there are too many. I will not attempt to list all possible solutions, but

Table 3.20

Masculine			
	[1]	[2]	[3]
Case 1	-s	-m	Ø
2	-e	-m	Ø
3	-m	-m	Ø
4	-i:	-is	-i:
5	-i:	-o:	-i:
6	-o:	-o:	-e
Feminine			
	[4]	[5]	[6]
Case 1	-s	-m	Ø
2	-e	-m	Ø
3	Ø	-m	-m
4	-i:	-i:	-is
5	-o:	-i:	-i:
6	-o:	-e	-o:
Neuter			
	[7]	[8]	[9]
Case 1	-s	-m	Ø
2	-e	-m	Ø
3	-m	Ø	-m
4	-is	-i:	-i:
5	-i:	-i:	-o:
6	-e	-o:	-o:

merely describe two or three, in order to demonstrate that this *embarras de richesse* indeed exists.

One fact about Table 3.20 which can easily be checked is that, in Cases 1 and 2, the three paradigms [1], [4] and [7] (which are M, F and N respectively) all share the same endings: -*s* for Case 1, -*e* for Case 2. Similarly, paradigms [2], [5] and [8] all share -*m* for these two Cases, and [3], [6] and [9] all share Ø. This suggests a possible way of grouping the nine paradigms into three macroparadigms: we can build on the inflexional identities in Cases 1 and 2, and attribute the inflexional diversity in the other four Cases to Gender differences, yielding the solution in Table 3.21. This solution complies with the revised Paradigm Economy Principle, in that the number of macroparadigms does not exceed that of the macroinflexions for the most generously supplied bundles — there being only three distinct macroinflexions for each of the six Cases.

Another solution, however, can be built on another set of shared endings. Again, it is easy to check that paradigms [1], [5] and [9] (M, F and N respectively) share the same endings for Cases 3 and 4, and that the same is true for the complementary threesomes [2], [6], [7] and [3], [4], [8]. This suggests the macroparadigm analysis in Table 3.22. Is there any ground for preferring either solution A or solution B over the other? Apparently none at all. But in any case these two are not the only solutions possible. By exactly similar reasoning we can build on further inflexional similarities (this time in Cases 5 and

Table 3.21

Macroparadigm solution A for Table 3.20:

	Masc	Fem	Neut
Macroparadigm I:	[1]	[4]	[7]
II:	[2]	[5]	[8]
III:	[3]	[6]	[9]

thus:

	I	II	III
Case 1	s	m	Ø
2	e	m	Ø

	I			II			III		
	M	F	N	M	F	N	M	F	N
3	m	Ø	m	m	m	Ø	Ø	m	m
4	i:	i:	is	is	i:	i:	i:	is	i:
5	i:	o:	i:	o:	i:	i:	i:	i:	o:
6	o:	o:	e	o:	e	o:	e	o:	o:

Table 3.22

Macroparadigm solution B for Table 3.20:

	Masc	Fem	Neut
Macroparadigm I:	[1]	[5]	[9]
II:	[2]	[6]	[7]
III:	[3]	[4]	[8]

thus:

	I			II			III		
	M	F	N	M	F	N	M	F	N
Case 1	s	m	Ø	m	Ø	s	Ø	s	m
2	e	m	Ø	m	Ø	e	Ø	e	m
3		m			m			Ø	
4		i:			is			i:	
5	i:	i:	o:	o:	i:	i:	i:	o:	i:
6	o:	e	o:	o:	o:	e	e	o:	o:

Table 3.23

Macroparadigm solution C for Table 3.20:

	Masc	Fem	Neut
Macroparadigm I:	[3]	[5]	[7]
II:	[2]	[4]	[9]
III:	[1]	[6]	[8]

thus:

	I			II			III		
	M	F	N	M	F	N	M	F	N
Case 1	Ø	m	s	m	s	Ø	s	Ø	m
2	Ø	m	e	m	e	Ø	e	Ø	m
3	Ø	m	m	m	Ø	m	m	m	Ø
4	i:	i:	is	is	i:	i:	i:	is	i:
5		i:			o:			i:	
6		e			o:			o:	

6) to arrive at yet a third solution, set out in Table 3.23. We have here a third solution which seems no better or worse than solutions A and B. Probably yet more equally plausible ways could be found of grouping the hypothetical paradigms of Table 3.20 into macroparadigms; but the important point is by now sufficiently well established, namely that there is no unique macroparadigm solution for these hypothetical data, and indeed none among the possible solutions which stands out as clearly preferable to the others.

This hypothetical example shows that extreme macroparadigmatic ambivalence is certainly conceivable. If it arose in practice, it would point to a serious deficiency in our present package of definitions concerning paradigm economy. I will suggest, however, that such ambivalence does not arise in practice. For the Russian, Dyirbal, Zulu and Latin material we have considered, it is easy to show that only one macroparadigm solution is plausible. And, since this is not a consequence of the Paradigm Economy Principle and its attendant definitions, it constitutes a significant new generalisation about paradigmatic organisation.

In the Russian examples in Tables 3.14-3.16, it is never in doubt which paradigms are, as it were, candidates for amalgamation. Seeking an Animate partner for the Inanimate noun *akt*, we can at once rule out *ženščina*, from which *akt* differs inflexionally in numerous Cases, and also *professor*, from which *akt* differs in the Nom Pl in a fashion unrelated to Animacy;[19] *student* remains as the obvious partner, differing from *akt* only in the inflexion of the Accusative forms. For Latin (cf. Table 3.19), similarly, no one would dream of combining the Neuter *bellum* with the Masculine *dux* (with which it shares no inflexions in common) rather than with the Masculine *dominus* (with which it shares inflexions in common for six out of twelve property-bundles). In Zulu ((305)-(307) and Table 3.18), finding a partner for the all-Human Class 1/2 on the basis of semantic predictability involves finding a Class with no Humans in it; and Class 3/4 happens to be not only the Class which is most similar inflexionally to Class 1/2 (sharing with it the Singular prefix *um(u)*-) but also the only Class containing no Humans at all (except for the small group of pejorative terms, morphologically non-Human).

The Dyirbal paradigms illustrated in Table 3.17 were analysed as constituting two macroparadigms: one '*l*-stem' one, containing *balgal* and *wayṇḍil*, with a macroinflexion for the 'Do-it-quickly' form whose members are distributed on the basis of Transitivity, and one '*y*-stem' one, containing only the paradigm of *baniy*. Once again, this is the only plausible macroparadigm analysis; to show this, we will examine the alternative carefully. The only conceivable alternative involves combining the *wayṇḍil* type with that of *baniy* rather than that of *balgal*. Bearing in mind that 80% of Dyirbal intransitive verbs are '*y*-stem' verbs like *baniy* (Dixon 1972: 54), we might consider assigning *wayṉḍil* and *baniy* to a single 'Intransitive' conjugation-type, sharing a single 'Do-it-quickly' marker *-galiy*.[20] But then what of the two distinct Unmarked Tense affixes *-n* and *-ɲu*, and the distinct Purposive affixes *-li* and *-gu*? Already, the fact that *wayṉḍil* has fewer inflexions in common with *baniy* than with *balgal* militates against this analysis. But there are further difficulties with it. The distribution of the Unmarked Tense and Purposive alternants clearly does not correlate with the Intransitive–Transitive distinction. Could we account for it phonologically? Superficially, in view of Dixon's terms '*l*-stem' and '*y*-stem' for the *balgal* and *baniy* conjugation-types, one could say: *-n* replaces *-ɲu* and *-li* (or *-i*) replaces *-gu* in just those Intransitive verbs whose stem is in *-l* rather than *-y*. This sounds superficially parallel to what we have said about the Hungarian 2nd Singular Indefinite Present Indicative: *-ol* replaces *-(a)sz* in just those verbs of the 'normal' conjugation whose stem ends in a sibilant or affricate. But there is a difference. In Hungarian, we observe a patent phonological difference in the shapes of the stems to which the relevant affixes are attached. In Dyirbal, on the other hand, there is no *-y* present 'on the surface' in either the Unmarked Tense or the Purposive forms of *baniy*, and an *-l* is present in the Purposive but not the Unmarked form of *wayṉḍil*. A phonological account of the distribution of the Unmarked Tense forms therefore relies on the possibility of justifying a consistent underlying phonological difference in the stem allomorphs to which the Unmarked Tense affixes are attached — a hard task, since the sole evidence for this supposed underlying difference resides precisely in the surface forms which it is meant to explain.

On this issue, to appeal to those other forms of '*y*-stem' and '*l*-stem' verbs in which the *y* or *l* is manifest 'on the surface' will settle nothing, because the same facts will be equally compatible with an alternative analysis according to which the 'stem-final' *-l-* and *-y-* do not belong to the roots of Dyirbal verbs at all, but are merely stem-forming affixes added to roots before some but not all Tense, Aspect or Mood markers. This alternative analysis departs from Dixon's; but it squares well with the realisation of not only the Unmarked but also the Future Tense, which shows no sign of a stem-final *-l* or *-y*. Moreover, treating the *-l* and *-y* as something added to verbal roots rather than as part of them absolves us from having to account for why the final segment of verbal 'stems' is subject to a phonological restriction which has no parallel elsewhere in Dyirbal. Under this alternative analysis, then, the *l/y* contrast defines an arbitrary morphological classification of Dyirbal verbs rather than a phonologically motivated one; consequently, we cannot look to the *l/y* contrast to yield a phonological motivation for either the *-n ~ -ɲu* alternation in the Unmarked Tense or the *-li ~ -gu* alternation in the Purposive within a supposed 'Intransitive' macroparadigm lumping *wayṇḏil* together with *baniy*. There therefore appears to be ample reason to regard our original macroparadigm solution, grouping *wayṇḏil* with *balgal*, as the only really plausible one.

It seems reasonable to hypothesise, then, that macroparadigmatic ambivalence does not occur, and that consequently the vagueness of the word 'similar' in the definitions of 'macroparadigm' will not lead to serious difficulties. We can state the ban on macroparadigmatic ambivalence as follows:

(310) MACROPARADIGM UNIQUENESS CLAIM
When paradigms are assigned to macroparadigms in accordance with the definition of 'macroparadigm', it will be found that each paradigm belongs to one macroparadigm and one only.

Of course, any generalisation based, as this one is, on evidence from only four languages must be regarded as tentative. But one aspect of the traditional terminology of morphological description, at least for Indo-European languages, certainly counts in favour of the Uniqueness Claim. We are used to statements such as: 'In Sanskrit, Neuter nouns differ from non-Neuters *of the i-stem declension* in interpolating an *-n-* before the ending in certain Cases,' or: 'In the Latin of the Imperial epoch, Neuters differ from non-Neuters *of the fourth declension* in preferring *-ū* over *-uī* as a Dative Singular ending.' What is significant about these statements is that it is taken for granted that the inflexionally peculiar Neuters belong to some one identifiable declension-type to which non-Neuters also belong. The Macroparadigm Uniqueness Claim does not forbid the existence of, say, a nominal paradigm limited to one Gender. What the Claim does forbid, however, is a situation where such a paradigm can, on the basis of the criteria for identifying macroparadigms, be paired equally readily with more than one other paradigm; or, in other words, it requires that if any pairing is possible it should be unique. And what the traditional terminology of the statements on Latin and Sanskrit indicates is that, in Indo-European languages at least, this requirement seems generally to be met. We do not find, for example, a Neuter-only paradigm in Latin which shares some of the inflexions of 'second-declension' Masculines and Feminines and some of the inflexions of 'fourth-declension' ones; rather, we find two distinct Neuter-only paradigms (those of *bellum* 'war', already quoted in Table 3.19(b), and of e.g. *genu* 'knee') which can each be assigned unambiguously to one and only one of the two declensions (the second and fourth respectively).

3.2.4 Slabs and paradigm mixture

I have not yet suggested any way of reconciling the Latin and Greek verbal examples in Table 3.13 with the Paradigm Economy Principle. Let us begin by asking a fairly obvious question: how do the principal parts of these verbs divide the labour, as it were, of predicting the shape of individual inflected forms within their paradigm? It is in the light of the answer to this question that I will propose a reconciliation.

Let us pose the question in more concrete terms, in relation to a particular example of a word with more than one principal part. I will choose the Latin verb *amō* 'I love' from Table 3.13. Four principal parts are listed there: the 1st Singular Imperfective Present Indicative Active, the Imperfective Infinitive Active, the 1st Singular Perfective Present Indicative Active and the Supine. Yet the total number of 'parts' or inflected forms of *amō* (if we treat the three participles as one form each, disregarding their adjectival declension) is no less than 103, arrived at as shown in Table 3.24.

How, then, do the four principal parts 'predict' the remaining 98 forms? Clearly, the number of logically possible ways in which the labour might be divided among them is massive. For example, one logically possible division of labour might be:

(311)   *amō* 'predicts' 1st Person forms in all Active Aspects, Moods and Tenses;
amāre 'predicts' all Infinitives and the Passive Past Subjunctive;
amātum 'predicts' all Participles;

Table 3.24

'Finite' forms (i.e. forms inflected for Person):

				Total
Imperfective:	Active:			
	Present	Past	Future	
Indic	6	6	6	
Subjunc	6	6	—	
Imper	2	—	2	34
	Passive:		as Active, less Future Imperative	32
Perfective (Active only):			as Imperfective Active, less Imperatives	30
'Nonfinite' forms:				
Participles:			Imperfective Pres Active	
			Imperfective Fut Active	
			Perfective Passive	3
Infinitives:			Imperfective Active	
			Imperfective Passive	
			Perfective (Active only)	3
Supine:				1
Grand total:				103

amāvī 'predicts' the rest (i.e. all 2nd and 3rd Person Active forms, all finite Present and Future Passive forms, and the Passive Past Indicative).

But anyone who knows Latin will know that the actual division of labour is quite different from this, and can in fact be much more simply described (at least so far as the 'finite' forms are concerned). For all Latin verbs, the division is in fact as follows:

(312) Except for the Participles:
1st Sg Impf Pres Indic Act and Impf Infin Act jointly predict all Imperfective forms (the Infinitive alone being sufficient for all verbs except a small group in -*iō*, such as *capiō* 'take', *fodiō* 'dig', *cupiō* 'desire'); 1st Sg Pf Pres Indic Act predicts all Perfective forms.
Among the three Participles:
Impf Infin Act predicts the Present Participle;
Supine predicts the remaining two.

What we observe in Latin, then, is a clear division of labour reflecting the division within the category Aspect between the properties Imperfective and Perfective. Logically, this could be a mere accident from the general linguistic point of view; in other words, a language in which the division of labour between the four principal parts was as in (311) rather than as in (312) is perfectly conceivable. But could such a language exist in fact?

In order to answer this question, we need to know what will count as evidence that the Latin-style division of labour reflects some general principle of morphological behaviour and is therefore more than a mere accident. Clearly, we need to find evidence for a division of labour in other languages which is similar in some identifiable respect. Fortunately, it is quite easy to find such evidence.

The most salient difference between (311) and (312) is as follows: in (312) (actual Latin) the main division of labour coincides with a simple contrast between two morphosyntactic properties, Imperfective and Perfective. Moreover, the main morphological realisation of these two properties (if one can be identified in any given word-form) is relatively close to the root. In (311) (a hypothetical pseudo-Latin), on the other hand, the division of labour reflects a rather complex set of contrasts between various combinations of properties, including properties which, in actual Latin at least, are realised relatively far from the root (e.g. 1st Person). What about other instances of inflexional behaviour involving more than one principal part? If we look at the division of labour in Attic Greek between the principal parts listed in Table 3.13(c), we find a state of affairs which, to say the least, resembles (312) much more closely than (311); for example, each of the six 1st Singular forms listed can be used to deduce all the remaining seven Person–Number forms which share the same Voice–Aspect–Tense combination, so that we do not need to refer to (say) the 1st Sg Aorist to determine the 3rd Pl of the Perfect — a logically quite conceivable state of affairs in a pseudo-Greek that one might construct on the lines of our pseudo-Latin at (311).

This resemblance between Latin and Greek might perhaps be put down not to any general morphological principle but rather to the fact that they are relatively closely related Indo-European languages; they might, in other words, have jointly preserved a characteristic which from the general linguistic point of view is merely an accident. But the resemblance certainly extends outside Indo-European. In Turkish, there are thirteen verbs whose 'Aorist' form is not predictable from the 'base' form by any rule (Lewis 1967: 116), and for these verbs two 'principal parts' are cited in the Concise Oxford Turkish Dictionary; but for our purposes the important point is that the second of these principal parts (the Aorist stem) is used to 'predict' all and only the Positive Aorist forms, thus preserving a correspondence with a simple morphosyntactic property contrast. Similarly, in those few Hungarian verbs which are irregular in certain Tenses, and whose behaviour is therefore not entirely predictable from a single principal part, the 'extra' principal parts are used to predict all and only the forms of a particular Tense or group of Tenses, and not some more complex subset of the verbal paradigm whose specification involves Person and Number too (cf. Bánhidi, Jókay and Szabó 1965: 418-21).

Two tentative conclusions seem to emerge. Firstly, certain morphosyntactic property contrasts, such as ones involving Aspect and Tense, seem to define partitions of verbal paradigms which are morphologically in some sense more fundamental than other property contrasts such as those of Person and Number. Secondly, when (despite the Paradigm Economy Principle) more than one principal part is needed to 'predict' the whole inflexional behaviour of a given verb, the division of labour between the principal parts corresponds to these more fundamental contrasts much more closely than one would expect in the absence of any general principle operating in that direction. The first conclusion is strongly supported by certain facts which are quite independent of paradigm economy: Hooper (1979; cf. Bybee 1985) reports that, out of a sample of 41 languages investigated, among those 14 which showed verb stem alternations with some clear semantic correlation, 13 had alternations corresponding to Tense or Aspect, one (Acoma) had alternations corresponding to Number but not Tense or Aspect, and none had alternations corresponding to Person.[21] The second conclusion must await support or disconfirmation from a much wider survey of prima facie breaches of paradigm economy than I have yet carried out. However, the Latin, Greek, Turkish and Hungarian facts already mentioned seem sufficient to justify some amendment of the paradigm economy package. This amendment will have the effect of reconciling the Paradigm Economy Principle with the role which the Latin and Greek 'principal parts' illustrated in Table 3.13 actually perform in relation to the rest of their paradigms, while ruling out the conceivable but nonexistent sort of role illustrated for Latin at (311). To some extent this reconciliation will involve stem allomorphy, which will be discussed in Chapter 6. But there is also a need to recognise as a factor contrasts in morphosyntactic properties such as that between Perfective and Imperfective in Latin. Let us introduce the term **slab** to refer to a subset of the macroinflexions within one paradigm consisting of all the macroinflexions which are associated with some specified morphosyntactic property. Thus, for example, in the *dominus/ bellum* macroparadigm illustrated in Table 3.19, the Singular slab consists of the macroinflexions -*us*/-*um*, -*e*/-*um*, -*um*, -$\bar{\imath}$, -$\bar{o}$, -$\bar{o}$, while the Genitive slab consists of the macroinflexions -$\bar{\imath}$, -$\bar{o}rum$. We are now in a position to introduce the rider (or 'codicil') to the Paradigm Economy Principle foreshadowed at the end of section 3.2.1:

(313) SLAB CODICIL to the Paradigm Economy Principle:
In a given language L some part of speech N may infringe the Paradigm Economy Principle if this infringement involves 'mixed' macroparadigms (i.e. macroparadigms containing no macroinflexion peculiar to them) which are divisible into slabs corresponding to certain fundamental morphosyntactic properties applicable to N in such a way that the slabs corresponding to any one such fundamental property obey the Paradigm Economy Principle (i.e. the inflexional resources available for that property are organised into as few slabs as possible).

I will comment on various aspects of this definition in the course of applying it to (b) and (c) of Table 3.13.

The formulation is vague to the extent that the notion 'fundamental morphosyntactic property' remains vague. But this is no serious embarrassment so long as there is evidence, such as that already presented here, to the effect that the distinction between 'more fundamental' and 'less fundamental' properties reflects something real in the way inflexion operates. We are entitled, in other words, to defer any attempt to make the Slab Codicil more precise in this respect, because it will automatically become more precise once more is known about the relationships at a relatively abstract level between different morphosyntactic categories, both universally and in the grammars of individual languages.[22] In any case, despite its present vagueness, the Slab Codicil is quite precise enough to discriminate clearly between those breaches of paradigm economy that it renders allowable and conceivable breaches that are still disallowed.

Consider the Latin verbal principal parts in Table 3.13(b) and the statement of their actual predictive functions at (312). If we look at the slabs corresponding to the fundamental morphosyntactic property Imperfective, we see that for nearly all verbs[23] only one principal part needs to be cited in order to predict which of the rival macroinflexions is chosen for any property-bundle containing the property Imperfective; and the same is true, *mutatis mutandis*, for Perfective slabs. But this amounts to saying that there are no more Imperfective or Perfective slabs than there are realisations available for the most generously provided property-bundle in each Aspect; in other words, even when paradigm economy is relaxed under the terms of the codicil, what one might call 'slab economy' is preserved. The Greek Aorist forms in Table 3.13(c) illustrate similar economy. The Tense contrast between Aorists and non-Aorists can be regarded as fundamental; consequently, among the Active forms of any verb, it is of interest to look at the behaviour of the slab consisting of all the Aorist forms (Indicative, Subjunctive, Optative, Imperative, Infinitive and Participle). What we find is that the entire inflexional composition is predictable on the basis of one diagnostic form; traditionally, as in Table 3.13(c), the 1st Singular Aorist Indicative is cited for this purpose. To see the sort of inflexional behaviour which is conceivable but forbidden by the Slab Codicil, it is enough to consider the Indicative suffixes of the Aorist Active, in Table 3.25.

Table 3.25

Sg	1	-on,	-sa
	2	-es,	-sas
	3	-e,	-se
Dual	2	-eton,	-saton
	3	-etēn,	-satēn
Pl	1	-omen,	-samen
	2	-ete,	-sate
	3	-on,	-san

Mathematically, the total of conceivable (partial) paradigms into which these affixes might be organised is $2^8 = 256$; yet the actual number of partial paradigms that we observe is just two, which we can illustrate in Table 3.26.

Table 3.26

Sg	1	eíd-on	'I saw'	élū-sa	'I loosed'
	2	eíd-es		élū-sas	
	3	eíd-e		élū-se	
Dual	2	eid-eton		elū-saton	
	3	eid-étēn		elū-sátēn	
Pl	1	eid-omen		elű-samen	
	2	eid-ete		elű-sate	
	3	eíd-on		elű-san	

In relation to Attic Greek Aorist inflexion, we can sum up the effect of the Slab Codicil to the Paradigm Economy Principle by saying that it permits the Aorist forms within a paradigm to be independent of the non-Aorist forms (in breach of strict paradigm economy), but does not permit the existence of more than the arithmetical minimum number of inflexional patterns for Aorists.

In Chapters 2 and 3 we have built up a package of definitions and claims relating to inflexional paradigms: definitions of 'paradigm', 'macroparadigm', 'macroinflexion' and 'slab', and formulations of the Paradigm Economy Principle, the Macroparadigm Uniqueness Claim and the Slab Codicil. This package seems sufficiently well motivated to constitute at least a suitable starting-point for further investigation. In this book, we will return to it in Chapter 6 (in connexion with stem allomorphy) and Chapter 7 (where it is applied to modern German noun inflexion).

NOTES

1. Hungarian examples are cited in Hungarian orthography. Acute accents indicate vowel length, *sz* represents [s], and *s* represents [ʃ]. The vowels in parenthesis are 'mobile', present or absent according to phonological characteristics of the stem. This characteristic will be relevant later. Anticipating the discussion, I will treat each affix concerned as one inflexion, not two.

2. In the 2nd Singular Subjunctive we have, at least at first sight, a counterexample to the Inflexional Parsimony Hypothesis, in that two inflexions are available for the same property-bundle in both conjugations. The Hypothesis will predict this situation to be unstable; either the two alternants Ø and *-ál* will be differentiated functionally or else one will tend to disappear. The situation in fact seems to be that the *-ál* form, originally proper to the *-ik* conjugation, is now used in both

conjugations to express a politer or less peremptory command than the Ø form (Peter Sherwood, personal communication). The prediction that the Hypothesis entails therefore seems to be correct.

3. The Class-labels are drawn from Rycroft & Ngcobo (1979). They, like Meinhof (1948) and many Bantu scholars, treat Plural Classes as distinct from Singular ones — thus, *umntwana* 'child' belongs to Class 1 but *abantwana* 'children' to Class 2. But I prefer to regard the distinction between *umntwana* and *abantwana* as purely one of Number, not Class (as does Doke (1973: 37)), and use the label '1/2' to refer to the Class of them both. In Meinhof's system, the same Class numbers are used in all Bantu languages for Classes whose prefixes are cognate; there are no Classes 12 and 13 in Zulu because the appropriate prefixes have been lost. In Zulu, the prefixes lose their initial vowels in some contexts, and some scholars therefore treat these vowels as outside the Class prefixes proper; but this does not matter for our purposes.

4. There is ample evidence in Zulu for a phonological (or at least morphophonological) process of vowel contraction, whereby $a + i$ becomes e and $a + u$ becomes o. This justifies us in identifying the concord *lo-* in *lomntwana* as a phonologically predictable alternant of the *la-* in, for example, *iqanda lakwebhokisi* 'the egg in the box' (cf. *kwebhokisi* 'in the box').

5. Class 15 seems to contain only mass nouns and abstract nouns without Plurals.

6. I myself formerly defined 'paradigm' in this way (Carstairs 1983; 1984b).

7. My analysis of the Dyirbal inflexional patterns in Table 3.9 as all belonging to the same macroparadigm does not of course rely on deriving all four realisations of the Ergative from a single underlying phonological representation. Dixon attempts to do this, however (1972: 288-9), apparently because (like Anderson (1974) and Hyman (1975)) he is unhappy about recognising phonologically predictable alternations which are not the outcome of phonological or morphophonological rules; but his account, as he admits, involves postulating an otherwise unmotivated difference in phonological behaviour between the Dative suffix *-gu* and a putative underlying Ergative /-gu/.

8. Because the number of macroparadigms for N cannot logically be *less* than the number of distinct macroinflexions for the most generously provided property-bundle, the stipulation 'no greater than' is empirically equivalent to 'the same as'.

9. The prefixes *an-* and *aN-* in this hypothetical language thus behave phonologically rather like the English negative prefixes *un-* and *in-/im-* respectively.

10. Comrie (1978) offers a thorough description and discussion of this phenomenon, not only in Russian but also in other Slavic languages.

11. As in section 3.1.1, I continue to use 'Class' to refer to patterns of Singular–Plural pairs rather than to Singular types or Plural types individually (see note 3).

12. The largest such marginal type is the group of ten or so nouns

(nearly all Human) which 'go like' Class 9/10 in the Singular and Class 5/6 in the Plural, e.g. *in-doda* 'man', Plural *ama-doda* (Doke 1973: 54; Rycroft & Ngcobo 1979: 62).

13. David Rycroft informs me that 'tramp' is a more appropriate gloss than Doke's 'pilgrim'.

14. The pejorative connotation of Class 3/4 Human nouns was pointed out to me by David Rycroft. The contrast in sense between *imihlobo* and *abahlobo* was confirmed by a native speaker, Fr. J. Ngubane.

15. There is a fairly small declension-type displaying a Nom Sg in *-us* but distinct from the type of *dominus*, namely that of 'fourth declension' nouns such as *fructus* 'fruit', *tribus* 'tribe'. The existence of this type seems to entail a breach of paradigm economy if we treat the Nom Sg as the 'diagnostic' slot. I will return to this later.

16. See, for example, the discussions of the paradigm by Wurzel (1984) and Bybee (1985).

17. The 'macroparadigm' concept also supplies a ready solution to the problem posed for paradigm economy by the Latin fourth declension, mentioned in note 15. Once inflexions have been combined into macroinflexions on the basis of Gender, it is no longer so clear that the Nominative Singular is inflexionally more diverse in Latin than all other slots; and, in fact, as Risch (1977: 234) in effect shows, at least as good a case can be made for treating as the 'diagnostic' slot for Latin nominal declension the Genitive Plural, in which the fourth and second declensions are inflexionally distinct (*-uum* versus *-ōrum*). Admittedly, for Roman infants acquiring a native command of Latin noun morphology, one might expect the choice of such a highly 'marked' property-bundle as diagnostic to present difficulties; but then there is evidence that such difficulties did in fact arise, in that the fourth declension, though inflexionally quite distinctive, seems nevertheless to be unstable and obsolescent from an early stage in the history of Latin (Ernout 1953: 63). But we have here in effect raised a question about the interaction between paradigm economy and the relative 'autonomy' (in Bybee's (1985) sense) of different inflected word-forms. I will not attempt to tackle this question here.

18. The entire Plural and the *-s* exponent of Singular-2 are omitted simply to make the illustration more manageable.

19. There may in fact be scope for combining the macroparadigm of *akt* and *student* with the very similar one of *professor* and *dom*. Comrie & Stone (1978: 89-91) quote evidence to the effect that the *-a* Nom Pl in Masculine nouns is especially characteristic of technical terms in technical contexts, e.g. *supa* 'soups' in caterers' usage instead of the usual *supy*, and *redaktora* 'editors' in journalists' usage instead of the usual *redaktory*. This suggests the development of a macroparadigm in which the Masculine Nominative Plural endings *-a* and *-y* are correlated at least partially with morphosemantic properties which one might label 'Technical' and 'Non-technical'. It is not surprising that two so similar macroparadigms should experience pressure towards coalescence through the 'functionalisaton' of the *-a/-y* contrast; in Wurzel's (1984) terminology, the effect is that the inflexional classes of

akt and *professor* cease to be 'complementary' and thereby become more 'stable' (128-30).

20. The label 'Intransitive' would not be altogether appropriate since some '*y*-stem' verbs are Transitive (Dixon 1972: 54); but all we need here is some arbitrary label, so that does not matter.

21. Similar conclusions emerge from Rudes's (1980) study of verbal stem suppletion.

22. Almost certainly, Bybee's (1985) notion of 'relevance', which I discuss more fully in Chapter 4, will play a part here; cf. also Rudes's observations (1980) on the property-contrasts which correlate with suppletion in verbs.

23. The qualification 'nearly' is necessary because of the behaviour of the small *capiō* group mentioned in (312). This group of verbs may, however be combinable into a single macroparadigm with the 'fourth conjugation' type *audiō* 'hear' on the basis of somewhat complex phonological conditioning: *capiō*-type verbs all have the stem shape CVC, where V is a short vowel and the second C is an obstruent (Ernout 1953: 147-50).

4

Homonymy Within Paradigms[1]

4.1 INTRODUCTION: APPROACHES TO INFLEXIONAL HOMONYMY

One way of regarding paradigm economy (the topic of Chapter 3) is as a paradigm-related constraint on what in Chapter 1 we called Deviation II — paradigmatic one-to-many relationships between morphosyntactic properties and their exponents. An independent constraint on Deviation II will be suggested in Chapter 5. In this chapter, by contrast, we will in effect be concerned with a paradigm-related constraint on Deviation IV — paradigmatic many-to-one relationships between morphosyntactic properties and their exponents, or homonymy within inflexional paradigms. The search for principles governing inflexional homonymy is not new and, superficially at least, we are now entering upon more well-trodden ground. Interest in inflexional homonymy in recent decades has focused on three main issues:

(a) the parallel between morphological and lexical homonymy on the one hand and phonological 'neutralisation' on the other;
(b) limits to the ambiguity engendered by inflexional homonymy and how this ambiguity is resolved;
(c) relationships between morphosyntactic properties on the 'plane of content' which either favour or inhibit homonymy in their inflexional realisations.

My preoccupation is somewhat different from all these, however, as I shall explain.

Since at least the 1930s linguists have noted certain similarities between 'neutralisation' in phonology and homonymy or 'syncretism' in inflexion. In 1957 the Institut de Linguistique in Paris published the replies of more than forty linguists to a questionnaire devised by André Martinet about the notion of neutralisation in morphology and the lexicon. This did not turn out to be a very profitable exercise (see TIL 1957). Insofar as one can generalise about the mass of views expressed,[2] it seems fair to say that the main preoccupation was with terminology rather than empirical claims; one finds much discussion of whether this or that morphological or lexical phenomenon resembles phonological neutralisation sufficiently closely to deserve the same label and of what, in general, the criteria for applying the term 'neutralisation' outside phonology should be, but one finds little in the way of generalisation about what morphological 'neutralisations' are possible and what are not. This is not because empirical generalisations of this kind were sought and not found, but rather because the linguists replying to the questionnaire did not see it as an opportunity to undertake the sort of investigation that we are engaged in here.

Apart from the criteria for applying the term 'neutralisation', what chiefly interested most respondents was how the ambiguities or potential ambiguities arising from neutralisation are resolved. This is not surprising, in view of the long tradition of linguistic and philosophical debate about the limits to ambiguity of all kinds, lexical and syntactic as well as morphological. The question of how ambiguities are resolved is explicitly to the fore in the study of neutralisation in Kasem by Callow (1968), who is strongly influenced by the ideas of Pike, and is also prominent in Pike's own (1965) work on morphological 'matrices' in German. More recently, Frans Plank (1979; 1980) has applied a range of data, particularly from late Latin and Romance languages, to the question whether one can attribute the nonexistence of certain inflexional homonymies or syntactically ambiguous constructions (or, diachronically, their removal through morphological or syntactic innovation) to the necessity to avoid certain intolerable ambiguities. Insofar as his work deals with inflexional homonymy, then, Plank is concerned with identifying conditions under which it is impermissible, or sufficient conditions for its avoidance.

Other linguists, by contrast, have concentrated on the other side of the coin, searching for conditions which favour inflexional homonymy or 'syncretism'. Hjelmslev (1935) asserted the need for a general theory of 'les lois générales qui dirigent le phénomène du syncrétisme, et qui permettraient de *prédire* [his emphasis] les syncrétismes possibles et les syncrétismes nécessaires d'un système donné'. Although in this remark 'syncrétisme' is implied to be a phenomenon of change, Hjelmslev sees clearly that uncovering the 'lois générales' will involve developing an 'explication *synchronique* [my emphasis]' for the phenomenon (1935: 60). His own general theory of syncretism was to have been one of the main topics of a promised sequel to *La catégorie des cas* (1935: iv) which regrettably never appeared.[3] At about the same time, Jakobson devoted section IX of his classic article 'Beitrag zur allgemeinen Kasuslehre' (1936) to a series of generalisations about syncretism within the Russian declension system: for example, 'Unterscheiden sich der N[ominativ] under der A[kkusativ], so ist entweder der Unterschied A[kkusativ]-G[enitiv] oder der entsprechende Unterschied D[ativ]-L[okativ] aufgehoben.' Although Jakobson's generalisations are language-particular, he clearly hoped that in the long run they would emerge as consequences of a general theory of 'Gesamtbedeutungen' in a Case system of the Russian type. It is therefore clear that, in spirit at least, Jakobson was working towards the same goal that Hjelmslev had set. It is also clear that the main focus of Jakobson's interest was the 'plane of content' rather than the link between 'content' and 'expression' — that is, he was interested in relationships between morphosyntactic properties themselves rather than between properties and their inflexional realisations. More recent explorations of a similar kind, looking at the German pronominal and Latin nominal Case systems, have been carried out independently by Bierwisch (1967) and Williams (1981: 266-9),[4] who attempt to account for the homonymies they observe by reference to binary morphosyntactic features.

For Jakobson and the others, the only fact that is of interest about the shapes of the relevant inflexions is which pairs or groups of them are homonymous; they are not concerned with the type of deviation that they exhibit (in the sense of Chapter 1). Our concern here, by contrast, is precisely with the search for constraints on those types of deviation. It follows that, even if the sort of goal that Jakobson had in view is ultimately reached and a general theory of 'Gesamtbedeutungen' incorporating certain constraints on syncretism is achieved, the question will still remain whether there are any further constraints connected with the relationship between properties and their exponents. And it is this latter question which will concern us.

More closely related to our question is one asked by Bazell (1960), Wurzel (1984), Plank (to appear) and especially Zwicky (1985). Bazell alleges a tendency towards homonymy in instances where a minimal morphosyntactic contrast coincides with a minimal phonological contrast between the relevant inflexions. This claim certainly involves the relationship between morphosyntactic properties and their exponents, although in order to make it precise one would need a reasonably clear idea of what constitutes a 'minimal' contrast. Wurzel's interest (1984: 205) is in 'the number and manner of formal distinctions in the paradigm', seen as one of the 'system-defining structural properties' of a particular language's inflexional system. Plank is more ambitious than Wurzel in suggesting that 'the number of exponents potentially available for nominal inflexion *in any language* [my emphasis] is limited to about 30', so that there must inevitably be some Case-homonymy in languages with large and elaborate Case-systems, cumulative exponence of Case and Number, and more than one nominal paradigm. Finally, Zwicky sketches a framework for describing inflexion in terms of which homonymies can arise as a result not only of 'realisation rules' applying to more than one morphosyntactic property-bundle in a paradigm but also of 'rules of referral' explicitly stating that, under appropriate conditions, property P is realised in the same way as property Q. Zwicky's rules of referral bear a close resemblance to what I will later call 'take-overs'; but since the claims that I put forward are independent of his descriptive framework, it seems better to maintain a separate terminology, at least for the present.

4.2 A GENERAL RESTRICTION ON SYSTEMATIC HOMONYMY

4.2.1 The structure of the argument

This chapter, then, will be devoted to the search for evidence for general constraints on property-to-exponent relationships involving Deviation IV. I will, in fact, propose a generalisation to the effect that every instance of systematic inflexional homonymy must display one or other of two sets of clearly specifiable characteristics. The word 'systematic' here is important. I will suggest that inflexional homonymies fall into two classes. The first class consists of sets of forms where the combined effect of morphological spell-out rules (or any analogous mechanism) and of phonological rules just happens to be an identical phonetic representation. The second class consists of sets of forms whose homonymy reflects some 'deeper' principle which must be explicitly incorporated in some way in any grammatical description which purports to be complete. Only homonymies of the second kind, I suggest, are subject to the generalisation I propose. This amounts to saying that I will specify necessary conditions for any homonymy to be considered systematic; it must comply with the proposed generalisation. But clearly, if such a proposal is to have any empirical content, an important prerequisite must be satisfied; it must be possible to determine readily in a reasonable number of instances whether a given homonymy is 'systematic' or 'accidental' independently of how it fits the generalisation. Unless we can determine this, the argument will be circular.

My argument will therefore take the following form. I will first argue that the distinction between systematic and accidental homonymies is well motivated, and that a reasonable number of clear cases can be identified on either side. I will then argue that there are at least some instances of systematic homonymy where the principle at work has to be regarded as morphosyntactic rather than purely syntactic, and where consequently the search for generalisations or constraints falls squarely within the scope of this chapter. At that point I will invite the reader to look at the list in the Appendix of more than forty inflexional homonymies, and point out a characteristic that many of them share. This will lead me to pose a question about the possible function of systematic homonymy, comparing and contrasting two versions each of two hypothetical Case–Number systems, one version illustrating homonymy and one not. The result of this discussion will be a link between homonymy and simplicity — specifically, a contrast between conceivable inflexional patterns which (according to a straightforward criterion of 'simplicity') are rendered simpler by the introduction of an element of Case homonymy, and conceivable inflexional patterns which such homonymy renders less simple. This argument is then applied to the homonymies in the Appendix in the following way: a great majority are found to belong to inflexional patterns of the kind in which homonymy contributes to simplicity, not complexity, according to the criteria applied to our earlier hypothetical examples. I therefore introduce a new definition of 'syncretism', in accordance with which we can now say that the great majority of systematic homonymies in the data presented are syncretisms. Turning to the remainder of the apparently systematic homonymies — those which are not syncretisms, according to the new definition — I will argue that they are nearly all examples of 'take-overs' (a term I define in due course) as well as having further features in common. We thus arrive at an empirical generalisation: all systematic homonymies are either syncretisms (as defined) or take-overs, with those further common features just referred to.

It will be seen that the appropriate test for my claims in this chapter lies in how well they cope with a mass of data, not with individual homonymies. If nearly all the homonymies that most linguists would be inclined to regard as systematic emerge as syncretisms or take-overs, and if nearly all the homonymies which are neither syncretisms nor take-overs look as if they could reasonably be attributed to factors other than some specifically morphological principle of organisation (for example, independently motivated processes of phonological neutralisation), then my empirical claim satisfies the test even if in a small minority of instances we are forced to classify as accidental a homonymy which we might otherwise be inclined to regard as systematic. The situation is somewhat similar to that which arises in syntactic research when a linguist 'allows the grammar to decide' whether certain rather doubtful sentences are grammatical or not. The fact that the syntactician treats some doubtful data in this way does not of itself vitiate his account of those data whose grammaticality is not in doubt.

I mentioned the need to test claims of the kind put forward here against a mass of data rather than against individual homonymies. But for such a test to be effective, we must obviously be confident that the mass of data which we use is not skewed or biased in some way which might affect the result. I will argue later that there is no reason to suppose that my actual data are skewed in this way, and that at the very least the onus of proof is on the objector who wants to claim that they are; but

I will readily admit that my claims about homonymy, just like all the empirical claims in this book, still stand in need of test against a larger range of data.

4.2.2 Systematic versus accidental homonymy

The morphological data from Latin in Table 4.1 illustrate behaviour common to all Latin nouns, pronouns, adjectives and participles, namely the lack of any overt morphological distinction between the Dative and Ablative Cases in the Plural.

Table 4.1

		Singular	Plural
a.	Dat	mensae 'table'	mensīs
	Abl	mensā	
b.	Dat	servō 'servant'	servīs
	Abl	servō	
c.	Dat	rēgī 'king'	rēgibus
	Abl	rēge	
d.	Dat	fīnī 'end'	fīnibus
	Abl	fīne	
e.	Dat	manuī 'hand'	manibus
	Abl	manū	
f.	Dat	faciēī	faciēbus
	Abl	faciē	
g.	Dat	mihi, mī 'me'	nōbīs 'us'
	Abl	mē	
h.	Dat	illī 'that (one), her, him'	illīs 'them'
	Abl	illō	

In traditional terms, this is described by saying that there is 'syncretism' of the Dative and Ablative Plural everywhere in Latin. This homonymy is stable over time; that is, at no period in the recorded history of Latin does any noun, adjective, participle or pronoun display distinct forms for these two Cases in the Plural. It is reasonable to conclude that we are dealing with something systematic and genuinely part of what the native Latin speaker 'knew', not a linguist's construct or a mere accidental homonymy between two Case-forms. (At the very least, the onus of proof is on the linguist who wants to contend otherwise.) Table 4.1 can be compared with the German verbal data in Table 4.2.

Table 4.2

		Singular	Plural
a.	1st	bin 'am'	sind 'are'
	3rd	ist 'is'	
b.	1st	habe 'have'	haben 'have'
	3rd	hat 'has'	
c.	1st	liebe 'love'	lieben
	3rd	liebt	
d.	1st	esse 'eat'	essen
	3rd	isst	
e.	1st	wasche 'wash'	waschen
	3rd	wäscht	

In both Tables 4.1 and 4.2, we find a pair of properties which, however they may be realised in the Singular (and, in the Latin examples especially, a considerable diversity of realisations is evident, at least 'on the surface'), are always realised homonymously in the Plural.

It is clear that thorough-going inflexional homonymies of this kind, which apply to all members of a given part of speech, can be productive. Evidence of this can be found by comparing Serbo-Croat with the closely related South Slavic language Slovenian. In Slovenian, as in Eastern and Western Slavic languages generally, Dative, Instrumental and so-called 'Locative' Cases are morphologically distinct in the Plural of nouns. In Serbo-Croat, although Dative and Locative forms are no longer distinct anywhere, so that there is no longer any justification for recognising these two Cases as morphosyntactically distinct (whether or not they may be distinct at some 'deeper' level), Instrumental and Dative–Locative are still distinct in the Singular of most nouns. In the Plural, however, the Dative–Locative is always homonymous with the Instrumental. Yet this homonymy is not explicable historically as due to purely phonological developments. Compare the earlier and later versions of the paradigm of *seljak* 'peasant' (Thomason 1976: 373-8), in Table 4.3.

On this, Thomason comments: 'Like the replacement of + *e* by + *u* in the singular, the replacement of loc.pl. + *ex* by + *ima* was the result of a complex *analogical* process [my emphasis].' The term 'analogical' here is implicitly contrasted with 'phonological'; the acquisition by Dative–Locative and Instrumental Plural of a common ending -*ima* (probably 'borrowed' from the

Table 4.3

		About 1250 AD	Today
Sg	Nom	seljak	seljak
	Voc	seljače	seljače
	Acc	seljaka	seljaka
	Gen	seljaka	seljaka
	Instr	seljakom	seljakom
	Dat	seljaku }	seljaku
	Loc	seljace }	
Pl	Nom	seljaci	seljaci
	Voc	seljaci	seljaci
	Acc	seljaki	seljake
	Gen	seljak	seljakā
	Instr	seljaki }	
	Dat	seljakom }	seljacima
	Loc	seljacex }	

Dual) cannot be explained purely in terms of phonological processes affecting the earlier endings *-om*, *-ex* and *-i*. But this amounts to saying that at some point a specifically morphological relationship came to be established in Serbo-Croat between the way the two Cases Instrumental and Dative–Locative were realised in the Plural; diachronically, the homonymy is not simply a by-product of phonological change. We therefore have historical confirmation for what the synchronic generality of the homonymy throughout Serbo-Croat declension suggests, namely that the homonymy is genuinely part of the linguistic system and not merely the accidental result of, say, phonological neutralisation.

We have evidence, then, that at least some inflexional homonymies are systematic, in the sense of being more than mere accidental by-products of phonological processes or morphological 'spell-out' rules. But are all such homonymies systematic? On the basis of comparison with other areas of grammar, namely syntax and the lexicon, the expected answer is no. In lexicalised metaphors such as 'the foot of the mountain', 'the mouth of the river', 'the shallowness of his thinking', the use of the words *foot, mouth, shallowness* will be felt by all or nearly all speakers to have some connexion with their non-metaphorical or concrete uses, and will be treated accordingly both in dictionaries and in any linguistic theory of the lexicon. On the other hand, no speaker feels any connexion other than a purely phonetic one between *beer* 'alcoholic drink made from barley' and *bier* 'conveyance for coffins', or between the noun *row* meaning 'line, series' and the verb *row* meaning 'propel with oars'. There is no systematic relationship here for dictionaries or descriptions of the English lexicon to capture; and there is no reason to quarrel with the traditional analysis under which *beer* and *bier* (and *row* noun and *row* verb) are treated as distinct lexical items which merely happen to overlap phonologically. But if accidental homonymy is possible between distinct lexical items, why not between the realisations of distinct morphosyntactic properties too?

It is easy enough to find instances of inflexional homonymy which it is plausible to interpret as morphosyntactically accidental. Consider the data in Table 4.4.

Table 4.4

a. English:	Present:	strike	} hit
	Past:	struck	
b. Turkish:	Accusative:	bahçe-yi 'garden (Acc)'	} ev-i 'house (Acc)' or 'his/her house'
	3 Sg Poss:	bahçe-si 'his/her garden'	
c. Dyirbal:	(Dixon 1972: 42):		
	Ergative:	yaɾa-ŋgu 'man (Erg)'	} yamani-gu 'rainbow (Erg *or* Dat)'
	Dative:	yaɾa-gu 'man (Dat)'	
d. German:	Nom Pl:	Gäste 'guests'	} Gärten 'gardens (Nom *or* Dat)'
	Dat Pl:	Gästen	

In all these instances, the homonymy in the right-hand column can be explained in terms of phonologically conditioned allomorphy, so that it can be regarded as morphosyntactically irrelevant. By this I mean that the inflected forms on the right have phonological characteristics which engender the homonymy as a by-product either of a general phonological process or of an alternation in which the choice between the alternants is determined by purely phonological characteristics of the environment (as happens with the Hungarian realisations *-(a)sz* and *-ol* for the property-combination 2nd Person Singular in the Present Indefinite Indicative of the 'normal' conjugation, referred to in Chapter 3). Which of these two kinds of phonological explanation is appropriate in any given example in

Table 4.4 does not matter for our present purposes; what does matter is that one or other of them can be invoked for each one. At the risk of labouring an obvious point, I will justify this claim for each example in turn.

The verb *hit* which appears in the right-hand column of Table 4.4(a) belongs to the small class of verbs which, like *rid, cut, put, set, spread,* display no morphological distinction between Present and Past Tense forms. Now, membership of this class is, synchronically at least, arbitrary in the sense that there is no way of predicting that (for example) *hit* is a member of it but the verb *fit* is not, having a Past Tense form *fitted* rather than *fit.* But, as is well known, the *hit* class verbs share an obvious phonological characteristic: they all end in a coronal plosive. It is therefore natural to look for some phonological or morphophonological explanation for the Present–Past homonymy; and, since the Past Tense of so many English verbs involves an affixed [t] or [d], a plausible explanation on these lines is not hard to find. One might say, for example, that the Past Tense forms of *hit*-class verbs are exceptions to the usual vowel-insertion process which, in a form such as *fitted,* breaks up what would otherwise be phonotactically inadmissible stop clusters, and undergo a kind of cluster-simplification instead. But the details of this explanation do not matter; what matters is that an explanation on these lines is plausible, and that to call the Present–Past homonymy here accidental from the morphosyntactic point of view is therefore legitimate in a way in which it would not be legitimate if, say, the homonymy extended to verbs ending in bilabial consonants or vowels.

In Turkish (Table 4.4(b)) the homonymy between the Accusative and 3 Sg Possessive suffixes observable with consonant-final stems is not found with vowel-final stems; and, whether we account for this by appeal to deletion, epenthesis or underlying allomorphy, the fact that the homonymy is restricted to a phonologically specifiable class of stems again suggests that from a morphosyntactic point of view it should be regarded as accidental. And the Dyirbal example in Table 4.4(c) is in relevant respects exactly parallel. The Dative suffix is *-gu* for all nouns; the Ergative suffix, on the other hand, has a range of exponents *-ŋgu, -gu, -bu, -du, -ɖu* and *-ɾu,* the choice between which is determined phonologically. Clearly, those nouns whose phonological characteristics are such that *-gu* is the appropriate realisation of Ergative (of which *yamani* 'rainbow' is one) will display no overt morphological contrast between the Ergative and Dative Cases; but this is of no morphosyntactic significance. Finally, in the German example in Table 4.4(d) we are entitled to say that the homonymy between Nominative and Dative in the Plural is phonologically explicable since (apart from those nouns with Plurals in -*s*) it is limited not to some lexically arbitrary or syntactically determined class of nouns but to precisely those nouns whose Nominative Plurals end in unstressed -*en*; and, for our purposes, it does not matter whether this is accounted for within the phonological component by a rule of 'degemination' affecting the sequence /n + n / (as Wurzel (1970) proposes) or more directly, by a 'spell-out' rule which assigns to the Dative Plural an overt realisation -*(e)n* only when the accompanying stem does not itself end in -*en*.

There are, then, a reasonable number of inflexional homonymies which can on more or less strong grounds be regarded as mere by-products of independent morphological or phonological rules or processes, and not as embedded systematically in the complex of rules which provide inflexional realisations for morphosyntactic properties or combinations of them. This does not mean, however, that we will always without hesitation be able to assign inflexional homonymies to either the systematic class (along with examples in Tables 4.1 and 4.2) or the accidental class (along with examples in Table 4.4). To illustrate the sort of doubts which may arise, I will turn again to examples from Latin.

Consider first example Table 4.1(b),

Table 4.1(b)

		Singular	Plural
b.	Dat	servō 'servant'	servīs
	Abl	servō	

Here we see that in the Singular as well as in the Plural the Dative and Ablative Case-forms of *servus* are homonymous. This is true of all Latin nouns and adjectives belonging to the large and productive 'second declension', but it is not true of the other declension-types except, to some extent, that shown in Table 4.1(d). Have we a systematic honomymy here or not? At least we can say that this homonymy is quite general within a subset of Latin nouns identified by clear independent criteria, namely their distinctive set of inflexional endings. What then of the homonymy illustrated in Table 4.5(a) below?

Table 4.5

	Singular: Nom	Gen		Singular: Nom	Gen
a.	canis	'dog'	b.	dux [duks] 'general'	ducis
	ignis	'fire'		custōs 'guardian'	custōdis
	collis	'hill'			
	civis	'citizen'		cīvitās 'citizenship'	cīvitātis
				mens 'mind'	mentis
			c.	consul 'consul'	consulis
				pater 'father'	patris
				caput 'head'	capitis

The homonymy here is just as stable during the classical Latin period as those mentioned before. But no Latin scholar would regard it as being on a par with the homonymy between the Dative and the Ablative Plural. This is not pure prejudice. The nouns of Table 4.5(a) do not constitute a well-defined distinct grouping, like the second declension. Rather, they are all, along with those of Table 4.5 (b) and (c), part of the superficially somewhat heterogeneous third declension, and share no distinctive morphological or other characteristics except the Nominative–Genitive homonymy. Moreover, I have presented evidence elsewhere (Carstairs 1984a) for saying that, in Golden Age Latin, the paradigm of Table 4.5(a) nouns is identical for purposes of paradigm economy with that of Table 4.5(b) nouns, which lack the homonymy in question; certainly, from the historical point of view, a large number of the nouns in type 4.5(b) formerly displayed this homonymy but lost it through the operation of a rule of syncope which was restricted to the Nominative. Finally, Nominative–Genitive homonymy does not occur in any other nominal or pronominal paradigm in Latin, whether Singular or Plural, nor in any adjectival paradigm except precisely that of for example *brevis* 'short', *gravis* 'heavy', which 'go like' the noun *ignis*. It seems clear that some line needs to be drawn between the Plural homonymy in Table 4.1 and that in Table 4.5(a), and that the latter can reasonably be called accidental; but which side of the line the Singular Dative–Ablative homonymy of *servus* in Table 4.1(b) should fall is not obvious.

A somewhat similar problem arises in Russian. I have already mentioned Jakobson's concern with homonymy in his 'Beitrag sur allgemeinen Kasuslehre'. Although he is concerned with generalisations about properties on the 'plane of content' rather than about the relationship between content and expression, it is just as important for him as it is for us (and perhaps even more important) to be able to distinguish systematic homonymies from accidental ones; and, in fact, he has no qualms about labelling certain Russian homonymies accidental. Thus (1936: 52): 'jede Endung des Instrumentals Sing. masc. fällt bei den russischen Adjektiva mit der Endung des Dativs Plur. zusammen (*zlym, božjim*); jede Endung des Nominativs Sing. masc. fällt bei den qualitativen Adjektiven mit der Endung ihres Genitivs Sing. fem. zusammen (*zloj–zloj, staryj–staroj, tichij–tichoj, sinij–sinej*; die graphischen Unterscheidungen sind künstlich), und nichtsdestoweniger ist die Getrenntheit der grammatischen Kategorien in jedem dieser Fälle ausser Zweifel. Das sind *bloss Paare homonymer Formen* [my emphasis] ...' In Jakobson's terms, clearly, 'mere pairs of homonymous forms' correspond to our accidental homonymies, and are to be distinguished sharply from the examples of systematic 'Kasussynkretismus' which he discusses in section IX of his article. Yet, according to Jakobson himself, the putatively accidental adjectival homonymies that he mentions are more, not less, pervasive than the instances of 'syncretism' that he treats in section IX, since the latter only occur in certain nouns and adjectives while the former occur in all adjectives without exception. Nor is any obvious phonological explanation available for these 'accidental' homonymies, on the lines suggested for the examples in Table 4.4. The truth is that Jakobson's instances of 'mere homonymy' are not distinguished from his 'Case syncretisms' by any criterion apart from the rather vague one of 'Getrenntheit der grammatischen Kategorien'; so 'Synkretismus' looks in some danger of becoming a mere label for those homonymies where some common element of meaning or function can be established within the framework of the 'allgemeine Kasuslehre'.

What these Latin and Russian examples show, then, is that inflexional homonymies exist whose status — whether accidental or systematic — is hard to determine on the basis of any clearly specifiable criterion. But this need not inhibit our search for generalisations about those whose status is clear; and any generalisations that we establish may themselves help to decide the status of the unclear instances. After all, unclear instances of homonymy in inflexion have parallels in the lexicon and in syntax. For example, it is not altogether obvious whether *ear* 'organ of hearing' and *ear* 'seed-bearing part of cereal plant' should be treated as distinct, homonymous items or whether the latter should be treated as a specialised, quasi-metaphorical use of the former (cf. 'the eye of the storm', 'the mouth of the river');[5] and linguists have disagreed as to whether it is syntax, semantics or pragmatics which should distinguish the 'specific' and 'nonspecific' readings of a sentence like *I am looking for a woman with green eyes* (in Spanish, *Busco a una mujer*... versus *Busco una mujer*...).

We can sum up our discussion of accidental and systematic inflexional homonymies, then, by saying that both types clearly exist, and the fact that we do not yet have explicit criteria for assigning certain problematic examples to one type or the other does not vitiate the distinction, any more than the existence of problematic examples in syntax, semantics and the lexicon vitiates the distinction between pairs of sentences which share a semantic or syntactic structure and pairs which do not, and the distinction between pairs of word-forms which belong to the same lexical item and pairs which belong to different lexical items. But, before we go on to search for constraints on systematic homonymy, we need to deal with a further possible objection that a determined sceptic might advance: is systematic inflexional homonymy a morphosyntactic phenomenon at all, or is it rather a syntactic one? This question is important, because if the answer is that all systematic inflexional homonymies involve the complete absence of a morphosyntactic property distinction rather than the homonymous realisation of distinct properties, then we ought not to be discussing homonymy at all in the context of a search for constraints on the relationship between morphosyntactic properties and their exponents; for this answer to our question will imply that Deviation IV (at least as a systematic phenomenon) does not exist. The next section will therefore be devoted to further clearing of the ground, showing that systematic inflexional homonymies can indeed be morphosyntactic rather than purely syntactic.

4.2.3 The morphosyntactic status of systematic homonymy

The two cardinal instances of systematic homonymy so far cited (Tables 4.1 and 4.2) share one important characteristic which distinguishes them both from the instances of allegedly accidental homonymy cited in Table 4.4 and from the more problematic Latin examples of Dative–Ablative homonymy in the Singular of the second-declension nouns and Nominative–Genitive homonymy in certain third-declension nouns (in Tables 4.1(b) and 4.5(a)). This shared characteristic is the generality of the homonymy within the parts of speech concerned: all Latin nouns, pronouns, adjectives and participles have homonymous Dative and Ablative Plural endings, and all German verbs (even the highly irregular *sein* 'be') have homonymous 1st and 3rd Plural forms in all Tenses and Moods. This characteristic is indeed the main reason for calling these homonymies systematic. Yet it also provokes the question whether in these instances it is really homonymy that we are dealing with. What is to stop us from saying that, in Latin words which inflect for Case, the Cases Dative and Ablative are just not applicable in the Plural, or, in other words, that the putative property-combinations 'Dative Plural' and 'Ablative Plural' are realised homonymously in all paradigms precisely because they do not exist as separate property-combinations at all? And a parallel question can be asked about the German example.

We have broached here, in effect, the possibility of a new way of looking at the systematic–accidental distinction. Those homonymies that we are least inclined to call systematic (e.g. those of Tables 4.4 and 4.5(a)) are also, it seems, those where we are most confident about the genuineness of the morphosyntactic distinction and therefore the existence of the homonymy. On the other hand, the homonymies that we are most strongly inclined to call systematic (such as that between Dative and Ablative Plural in Latin) seem also to be the instances where the genuineness of the morphosyntactic distinctions which underlie the alleged homonymies is most in doubt. Should we then simply treat 'systematic' as a not very appropriate label for homonymies which are apparent rather than genuine at the morphosyntactic level — that is, instances where the purported morphosyntactic distinction does not exist?

There are empirical grounds for answering no to this question. First, consider Latin sentences such as the following, where the Case of the participial forms is deliberately unidentified in the gloss:

(401) Mātrī et fīliae librum dedī
mother-Dat and daughter-Dat book I-gave
'I gave a book to the mother and daughter'

(402) Mātrī et fīliae in hortum ingressīs
mother-Dat and daughter-Dat into garden entered-??
librum dedī
book I-gave
'I gave a book to the mother and daughter when they had entered the garden'

(403) Ā mātre et fīliā in hortum ingressīs
by mother-Abl and daughter-Abl into garden entered-??
liber acceptus est
book received was
'The book was received by the mother and daughter when they had entered the garden'

(401) contains a straightforward conjoined noun phrase, unmodified, whose two conjuncts are both in the Dative Singular. In (402), however, the conjoined noun phrase is modified by a participial phrase containing one element (*ingressīs*) which would traditionally be described as agreeing with it in Number and Case. But the traditional account is hard to square with the approach to systematic homonymy that we are now considering, according to which 'systematic homonymy' does not involve homonymy at all at the morphosyntactic level. The conjoined noun phrase in (402) is syntactically Plural, as is usual in Latin, and *ingressīs* is, not surprisingly, Plural too. But, although each conjunct of the noun phrase is unequivocally Dative, we are not permitted under this approach to describe the participle *ingressīs* which agrees with it as Dative too, because *ex hypothesi* the Dative Case is incompatible with the Plural Number, and the Case to which *ingressīs* belongs is one peculiar to the Plural which combines the functions of Dative and Ablative. This peculiar Plural-only Case also crops up in

103

(403), where *ingressīs* modifies a conjoined noun phrase each of whose conjuncts is this time Ablative. We must therefore posit some sort of Case-change rule which will ensure that when either Dative or Ablative Singular nouns are conjoined the resulting noun phrase belongs to this peculiar Plural-only Case. But no such Case-change rule needs to be invoked for conjoined noun phrases whose conjuncts belong to Cases other than the Dative or Ablative. The only reason why we need such a rule is that our new approach to systematic homonymy commits us to claiming that *ingressīs* in (402) is indistinguishable from *ingressīs* in (403) not only 'after' its Case-ending has been spelt out but also 'before' — that is, not only in morphology but also in surface syntax. No such contortions are imposed on us if we stay with our earlier assumption, under which the *ingressīs* of (402) and that of (403) are allowed to be morphosyntactically distinct word-forms whose homonymy is purely a matter of inflexional realisation.

At first sight the choice between the two approaches may seem to depend purely on considerations of descriptive elegance, with no obvious empirical consequences. But this is not quite so. As I said earlier, the kind of feature-changing rule which the second approach necessitates is not independently required in Latin. But we can easily envisage a hypothetical 'pseudo-Latin' extremely similar to Latin in which it would be required — a pseudo-Latin, for example, in which a participle modifying a conjoined noun phrase with Nominative Singular conjuncts was inflected differently from a participle modifying a simple Nominative Plural noun, in that the modifier of the conjoined noun phrase was inflected like a modifier of a simple Plural noun phrase whose Case was not Nominative but Accusative. In this hypothetical Latin-like language, we would find contrasts as follows:

(404)   Fīliae   in hortum ingress*ae*   sunt
        daughters-Nom into garden entered-*Nom* are
        '(Her) daughters entered the garden'

(405)   Māter   [et] fīlia   in hortum
        mother-Nom and daughter-Nom into garden
        ingress*ās*   sunt
        entered-"*Acc*" are
        'The mother and daughter entered the garden'

A special rule would be needed in this language to ensure that the conjoined noun phrase of (405) differed syntactically from the simple Plural noun phrase of (404) in such a way as to trigger the difference in concord behaviour, and differed in a way which could be most naturally accounted for by changing the Case of the conjoined noun phrase from Nominative to Accusative. 'Feature-changing' rules of broadly this kind are by no means unknown; for example, in Icelandic such a rule is needed to ensure that, when a conjoined noun phrase some of whose conjuncts are Masculine and some Feminine has a predicate adjective agreeing with it, the Gender of the adjective will be Neuter (Einarsson 1945: 133).[6] But the fact that actual Latin does not exhibit the sort of behaviour illustrated in (404) and (405) militates against any invocation of feature-changing rules of this kind to cope with the Dative–Ablative Plural, since in actual Latin (as opposed to pseudo-Latin and Icelandic) such rules would have no independent motivation.

Despite the consistency of the pattern illustrated in the right-hand column of Table 4.1, then, there is good evidence for saying that the properties Dative and Ablative are indeed applicable in the Plural in Latin, just as much as in the Singular, and that the identity of form there is indeed due to a real systematic morphological homonymy. But it is still logically possible that there may be homonymies that are not real, in this sense — that is, instances where the morphosyntactic property distinction presupposed by the use of the term 'homonymy' does not exist. The arguments one can adduce for the existence of homonymy in word-forms such as *ignis* (Nominative–Genitive) and *servō* (Dative–Ablative) rely on the fact that these word-forms are used in sets of syntactic environments clearly subdivisible on the basis of overt morphological distinctions exhibited by other members of the same word-class. But the expression 'other members of the same word-class' is vague. How many other members are needed? Is just one enough? For an example of a practical difficulty caused by this vagueness we can look again at Latin. Morphologically and syntactically, a Genitive Case is extremely well motivated in Latin for nouns, adjectives and participles, and the Genitive Plural is in fact formally distinct from all other Case-forms even more generally than the Genitive Singular is (which, as we have seen, is homonymous with the Nominative in nouns like *ignis*, and is also homonymous with the Dative in nouns such as *mensa*).

Within the Genitive, there is no motivation for any more delicate distinction at the morphological level in these parts of speech. But with personal pronouns things are somewhat different. The Plural pronouns of the 1st and 2nd Persons (*nōs*) and (*vōs*) distinguish two Genitives: *nostrum* versus *nostrī* and *vestrum* versus *vestrī*. The syntactic functions of these two forms are more or less clearly distinct. Ernout (1953: 103) says: 'L'usage a distingué les deux formes: *nostrum, vestrum* s'emploient comme génitif partitif: *pars nostrum, vestrum*; *nostrī, vestrī* comme génitif objectif: *miserēre nostrī* 'aie pitié de nous'.' Should we then say that Partitive and Objective Genitives should count everywhere as two distinct Cases, which happen to be realised homonymously with all nouns, adjectives, participles and pronouns except the two we have mentioned? The problem is in fact very similar to the one posed by the modern English pronominal forms *I, he, she, they* versus *me, him, her, them*; do we conclude from them that an underlying contrast between Nominative and Accusative Cases should be recognised for nouns too? Another problem of this kind is posed by the contrast exhibited only in the verb *be* between a Past form ('John *was* in London yesterday') and an Irrealis form ('If John *were* in London today, ...'), which has been discussed by Huddleston (1975); on the strength of this one overt contrast, should we regard the morphosyntactic distinction as applicable to all English verbs?

To all these questions I suspect that (*pace* Huddleston) most linguists would answer no; the overt morphological distinctions are restricted to too few forms to justify positing a corresponding morphosyntactic distinction everywhere else.[7] But most linguists would probably also be hard put to it to decide precisely where the line should be drawn — that is, precisely how many overt morphological contrasts, and of what kinds, would justify generalising the morphosyntactic property distinction which these contrasts express. For our present purposes, the uncertainty does not matter. Just as with those homonymies which are not clearly either accidental or systematic, some of the problematic instances may ultimately be resolvable by reference to generalisations based upon the clear instances. For the time being, however, what matters is that clear instances do exist where a systematic homonymy must be recognised as a genuinely morphological phenomenon. We can now at last begin our search for constraints on Deviation IV in earnest.

4.2.4 The data of the Appendix: a first observation

43 homonymies are listed in the Appendix to this chapter. This list has no pretension to be a statistically respectable sample of inflexional homonymies drawn from all potential sources — that is, from all inflected languages. It is, rather, a fairly random collection drawn from languages which I happen to know something about, predominantly Indo-European ones. Initially, therefore, there is bound to be doubt about the legitimacy of basing any general conclusions on it. But I will assume for the time being that these data are indeed an adequate starting point for discussion; and I will argue in section 4.2.8 that the nature of the generalisations that seem to emerge from our discussion is such that they are unlikely to be spurious ones due to bias in the selection of the data. Superficially, this may seem a circular line of argument. But there is no logical guarantee that, having made our initial assumption about the adequacy of the Appendix, any general conclusion should emerge at all, let alone one which is intrinsically unlikely to be spurious. So the fact that general conclusions of that kind do emerge genuinely confirms the legitimacy of the initial assumption.

Column III in the Appendix is particularly important. In this column the morphosyntactic context for the homonymy is indicated; and in all instances of systematic morphosyntactic homonymy (as opposed to accidental homonymies and 'homonymies' which are syntactic or semantic rather than morphosyntactic in nature), some entry must occur under either (a) or (b) in Column III. The distinction between the two sides is that III (a) contains contexts consisting of morphosyntactic properties which are realised simultaneously with the homonymous properties (including, for example, Plural as the context for Dative–Ablative homonymy in Latin), while III (b) contains contexts which are wholly or partly non-simultaneous. To put it another way, in homonymies with an entry in III (a), Deviation III is always involved as well as Deviation IV.

Let us consider now the pattern of entries in III (a) and (b). One conceivable pattern, and the pattern we would probably expect to find on the assumption that systematic homonymy is subject to no general constraints specifically to do with the property-exponent relationship, is that of a roughly even distribution of entries, with about the same totals in III (a) and III (b). Yet this is not what we observe in Appendix A. For the great majority of entries (34 out of 43), the conditioning context includes properties which are simultaneous, and hence specified in III (a). The majority of the examples therefore illustrate the cooccurrence of Deviation IV with Deviation III. Is there any logical necessity for this? The answer is no. It is easy to construct examples which display homonymy without a morphosyntactic context which is realised simultaneously.

Consider the Turkish nominal paradigm in Table 4.6.

Table 4.6

	Singular	Plural
Nom	ev 'house'	ev-ler
Acc	ev-i	ev-ler-i
Gen	ev-in	ev-ler-in
Dat	ev-e	ev-ler-e
Loc	ev-de	ev-ler-de
Abl	ev-den	ev-ler-den

This illustrates inflexional behaviour without sensitivity (cf. (112)), without simultaneity and without homonymy. Now consider a nominal paradigm, Table 4.7, for a hypothetical language closely resembling Turkish.

Table 4.7

	Singular	Plural
Nom	ev	ev-ler
Acc	ev-i	ev-ler-i
Gen	ev-in	ev-ler-in
Dat	ev-e	ev-ler-e
Loc	ev-de	ev-ler-de
Abl	ev-den	

In this hypothetical paradigm, there is sensitivity, in that Ablative is realised as -*den* in the context Singular but -*de* in the context Plural; furthermore, this sensitivity results in homonymy in the Plural, in that both Locative and Ablative are realised alike. We can also easily envisage a hypothetical paradigm in which the Case-ending for the Locative and Ablative in the Plural differs from that of both Cases in the Singular — being, say -*be*; in such a paradigm, clearly, the Locative as well as the Ablative is realised sensitively.

The hypothetical paradigm in Table 4.7 and the variant just mentioned both illustrate the logical possibility of homonymy with a morphosyntactic context which is not realised simultaneously (except insofar as the 'unexpected' Plural Case-forms are regarded as sharing the realisation of Plural). But, on the basis of the evidence presented in the Appendix, this sort of homonymy is uncommon in comparison with homonymies in which the same morphological material realises both the properties whose distinction is 'neutralised' and the property or properties which furnish the context for that neutralisation. There are three possible reasons for this: it may be due to bias in the sample of languages cited (admittedly heavily weighted towards Indo-European); it may be a mere accident, not rooted in any general linguistic constraint on the realisation of morphosyntactic properties; or it may indeed have a general linguistic explanation. Of these three, the last is at least worth considering. I will suggest in the next section what this explanation might be — why, in other words, non-accidental homonymy should be largely restricted to cumulated or simultaneous inflexional realisations.

4.2.5 A possible function for systematic homonymy

Let us assume, as argued in section 4.2.2, that there is a genuine linguistic phenomenon of systematic inflexional homonymy distinct from mere accidental homonymy of inflexional realisations. One way of approaching a general linguistic explanation for it is to consider what characteristics it must have in order to contribute to morphological simplicity (in a naïve, pre-theoretical sense of the term), or in order to help native speakers to learn and remember some aspect of the grammar of their native language more easily. Starting from an *a priori* notion like this of the function of systematic homonymy, we will arrive at certain conclusions about the circumstances which will favour it and the manner in which it should be represented in grammatical descriptions. These conclusions can then be tested against linguistic evidence such as that presented in the Appendix. I will argue that the conclusions which flow from the most plausible *a priori* view of the function of systematic homonymy do in fact square very well with the linguistic evidence so far presented. In particular, they include a prediction that homonymy should be commonest among forms which realise more than one morphosyntactic property simultaneously. This suggests the desirability of a new technical term or terms for systematic homonymies of kinds which promote morphological simplicity; we will turn to that question in section 4.2.6.

Let us consider first a hypothetical paradigm involving more than one morphosyntactic category but displaying neither morphological homonymy nor any kind of simultaneous realisation (including cumulation). Let us suppose that it is a nominal paradigm, and that the categories concerned are Number and Case. We are not concerned with the phonological shape of the inflexions except insofar as they realise more than one property simultaneously or homonymously; we can therefore represent the inflexions (which we can assume to be suffixes) by arbitrary letters, given the conventions that (a) a sequence of two letters indicates two separable morphs and (b) distinct letters indicate phonologically distinct morphs. The hypothetical paradigm is given in Table 4.8.

Table 4.8

	Singular	Plural
Nom	a	p a
Acc	b	p b
Gen	c	p c
Dat	d	p d

Such a pattern (what Pike (1963; 1965) calls a 'simple matrix') is quite plausible for natural languages, since it is very similar to what we observe in Turkish (see Table 4.6) or Hungarian nouns. I want to concentrate here on one aspect of it: memorability. There are five inflexional realisations for the morphosyntactic properties and their combinations to be learnt and remembered, as shown in Table 4.9.

Table 4.9

p	Plural
a	Nominative
b	Accusative
c	Genitive
d	Dative

Compare this now with an inflexional paradigm which still lacks cumulation but in which there is homonymy, Table 4.10:

Table 4.10

	Singular	Plural
Nom	a	p a
Acc	b	p b
Gen	c	p c
Dat	d	p c

In this paradigm there are still only five inflexional realisations to be memorised, but there is an added complication in the way two of them (*c* and *d*) are distributed. This complication can be expressed on the following lines:

(406) In Plural contexts, Dative is realised by the morph which is generally associated with Genitive; or, Dat → Gen / Pl + _____.

How this fact might be represented in a grammatical description is not important for the moment; what is important is that it is an 'extra' fact which would seem likely, *a priori*, to make the task of remembering the paradigm in Table 4.10 more burdensome than that of remembering that in Table 4.8.

In Table 4.10 we posited homonymy without any increase over Table 4.8 in the number of suffixes involved. But one can well envisage a paradigm with homonymy in which there is such an increase, Table 4.11.

Table 4.11

	Singular	Plural
Nom	a	p a
Acc	b	p b
Gen	c	p e
Dat	d	p e

This paradigm seems, on the face of it, to present an even greater memory burden than that in Table 4.10, since the speaker must remember six, not five, suffixes (see Table 4.12) as well as a rule for the occurrence of the 'extra' one (see (407)).

Table 4.12

p	Plural
a	Nominative
b	Accusative
c	Genitive
d	Dative
e	Genitive, Dative

(407)   In Plural contexts, Gen and Dat are both realised by the same morph (or: Dat = Gen / Pl + _____), namely *e*.

Where there is no cumulation, then, it seems *a priori* that paradigms with homonymy should always impose a greater burden on speakers' memories than paradigms without any homonymy. What if we turn to paradigms involving cumulation? Let us suppose that in our hypothetical language Case and Number are cumulated. Its nominal paradigm could then be represented as in Table 4.13 (in what Pike calls an 'optimal' or 'ideal' matrix).

Table 4.13

	Singular	Plural
Nom	a	e
Acc	b	f
Gen	c	g
Dat	d	h

Here, in contrast to Table 4.8, there are not five but eight suffixes to remember, Table 4.14.

Table 4.14

a	Nom	Sg	e	Nom	Pl
b	Acc	Sg	f	Acc	Pl
c	Gen	Sg	g	Gen	Pl
d	Dat	Sg	h	Dat	Pl

Let us compare this now with a paradigm in which, as in Tables 4.10 and 4.11, there is homonymy between the Genitive and the Dative in the Plural, Table 4.15.

Table 4.15

	Singular	Plural
Nom	a	e
Acc	b	f
Gen	c	g
Dat	d	g

In paradigms without cumulation, as we have seen, homonymy seems *a priori* to increase the memory burden. With cumulation, on the other hand, we find the opposite. In contrast to the eight realisations listed in Table 4.14, we find for paradigm Table 4.15 a need to memorise only seven realisations, as in Table 4.16 (or, at most, seven realisations plus one 'rule' on the lines of (408)).

Table 4.16

a	Nom Sg	e	Nom Pl
b	Acc Sg	f	Acc Pl
c	Gen Sg	g	$\left\{ \begin{array}{l} \text{Gen} \\ \text{Dat} \end{array} \right\}$ Pl
d	Dat Sg		

(408) Genitive and Dative have the same realisation in the Plural, or: Gen = Dat / ___ .
　　　　　　　　　　　　　　　　　　　　　　　Pl

The upshot of our discussion is that homonymy has contrasting consequences for the memorability of inflexional paradigms, *a priori*, according to whether or not they also exhibit cumulation. When we examined the hypothetical paradigms in Tables 4.8, 4.10, 4.11, 4.13 and 4.15, what emerged (as Table 4.17 shows) is that, without cumulation, homonymy makes paradigms *a priori* more difficult; with cumulation, however, it makes them easier, if we assume that a rule such as (408) is easier to remember than a distinct inflexion such as *h* for Dat Pl in Table 4.14. Moreover, without cumulation, one can envisage two sorts of homonymy, the first involving no 'new' inflexions (as in Table 4.10) and the second involving at least one such 'new' inflexion (as in Table 4.11); and the second of these introduces more difficulty than the first.

Table 4.17

			Facts to be remembered:	Example:
a.	Without cumulation:			
	i.	no homonymy	5 affixes	4.8
	ii.	homonymy between two Cases without new distinct affix	5 affixes plus rule (406)	4.10
	iii.	homonymy between two Cases with new distinct affix	6 affixes plus rule (407)	4.11
b.	With cumulation:			
	i.	no homonymy	8 affixes	4.13
	ii.	homonymy between two Cases	7 affixes plus rule (408)	4.15

4.2.6 Syncretism, take-over and the Systematic Homonymy Claim

We began the previous section by assuming that the function of systematic homonymy might be to contribute to memorability and learnability. Among the three conceivable kinds of homonymy discussed, only one was found to do so: that of Table 4.17 (b.ii). Moreover, of the other two kinds, one (that of Table 4.17 (a.ii)) was found to introduce less complication than the second (that of Table 4.17 (a.iii)). It is time now to confront these conclusions, based entirely on assumptions and *a priori* reasoning, with some empirical evidence. Having done so, we can decide whether there is any ground for removing the recurrent phrase '*a priori*' from our reasoning in section 4.2.5 and whether the distinction drawn between the three types of homonymy does indeed seem likely to reflect some linguistic reality.

The empirical predictions which flow from our conclusions are, in general terms, fairly plain:

(409) The commonest and most stable instances of systematic inflexional homonymy will be of the 4.17 (b.ii) type (that is, the morphosyntactic properties which constitute the context for the homonymy will be realised simultaneously with the properties neutralised).

(410) Other instances of systematic inflexional homonymy will generally turn out to be of type 4.17 (a.ii) rather than type 4.17 (a.iii).

We will deal with (409) first.

In terms of the Appendix, (409) predicts that entries in Column III (a) (for simultaneous contexts) will be commoner than entries in Column III (b) (for non-simultaneous contexts). This prediction is confirmed. First we need to exclude those examples which are accidental or where the genuineness of the purported morphosyntactic contrast is in doubt; and, while recognising the difficulty of the decision in some instances, we can reasonably exclude ten of the 43, as indicated in Column VI, for reasons given in the Comments on the Appendix. Of the remainder, the 26 examples without any entry in Column III (b) (i.e. those whose morphosyntactic context is entirely simultaneous) heavily outnumber the seven examples with an entry in Column III (b). The examples in each of the three categories are:

(411) (i) Certainly or probably to be analysed as morphologically unsystematic: 7, 12, 13, 19, 26, 29, 31, 38, 42, 43

(ii) With purely simultaneous morphosyntactic context: 1, 2, 3, 4, 5, 6, 10, 11, 14, 15, 16, 17, 18, 20, 21, 22, 23, 24, 25, 27, 28, 30, 32, 33, 34, 41

(iii) With at least partly non-simultaneous morphosyntactic context (i.e. entry in Column III (b)): 8, 9, 35, 36, 37, 39, 40

Let us therefore find a use for the traditional term 'syncretism' by defining it in such a way that it can replace the rather unmemorable term 'of the 4.17 (b.ii) type' which appears in our prediction at (409). We will need a definition on the following lines:

(412) A systematic inflexional homonymy is a **syncretism** if

(a) the homonymous forms are simultaneous exponents of more than one morphosyntactic property, and

(b) the conditions under which the homonymy occurs (or: the context for the homonymy) can be stated entirely in terms of properties thus realised.

We can now restate our prediction at (409) as follows:

(413) The commonest and most stable instances of systematic inflexional homonymy will be syncretisms.

Using the notation introduced in (408), a syncretism is a homonymy expressible in the following fashion:

(414) $A = B\ /\ \underline{\quad}$
$$C$$

where A, B and C are morphosyntactic properties or combinations of them and '=' means 'has the same realisation as'.

I do not attach great importance to this notation, however, except as a device for illustrating graphically the contrast between syncretisms and other actual or conceivable types of homonymy. For example, in the version of pseudo-Turkish discussed earlier in which both Locative and Ablative were realised in the Plural by a suffix -*be* distinct from the realisation of either Case in the Singular, that homonymy would be expressed as follows:

(415) $Loc = Abl\ /\ Plural + \underline{\quad}$

The context for the homonymy here is clearly not of the kind characteristic of syncretisms, as I have just defined them, because it involves properties with sequentially ordered, not simultaneous, realisations.

There is, of course, no point in defining terms for their own sake; a definition is useful or sensible only to the extent that it facilitates the formulation of strong, interesting generalisations. Now, our definition of syncretism at (412) certainly facilitates the formulation of the empirical claim at (413). But this claim is itself not particularly strong; it asserts only a statistical tendency, placing syncretisms towards one end of a scale of types of homonymy ranging from commonest to least common.

The claim it makes about the sort of homonymy illustrated by pseudo-Turkish in Table 4.7 is correspondingly weak; it says only that this will be relatively rare or perhaps 'highly marked'. Can we, then, claim anything more precise than (413), and thereby establish the usefulness of the term 'syncretism' more positively? The answer, I believe, is yes. To show this, I will need to turn to the second of our two predictions, that at (410).

Prediction (410), like prediction (413), is supported by evidence from the Appendix. All seven systematic homonymies for which there is an entry in Column III (b) (that is, the seven which are definitely not syncretisms, under our present definition) can plausibly be classified as falling under 4.17 (a.ii). They all, too, have an entry in Column IV of the Appendix, headed 'Take-over (if any)'; for I propose to define at (416) a new term which will facilitate the reformulation of prediction (410) as (417):

(416)   A systematic inflexional homonymy is a **take-over** if it involves the realisation of two or more morphosyntactic properties (A and B) in some context by an inflexion which elsewhere realises only one of these properties (B). In such circumstances we can say that B takes over A, or that there is a take-over of A by B.[8]

(417)   Instances of systematic inflexional homonymy which are not syncretisms will generally turn out to be take-overs.

A systematic homonymy that is neither a syncretism nor a take-over will be one such as we find in the Locative and Ablative Plural in the pseudo-Turkish paradigm given in Table 4.18 (contrast actual Turkish in Table 4.6):

Table 4.18

	Singular	Plural
Nom	ev 'house'	ev-ler
Acc	ev-i	ev-ler-i
Gen	ev-in	ev-ler-in
Dat	ev-e	ev-ler-e
Loc	ev-de	ev-ler-be
Abl	ev-den	

The Locative–Ablative homonymy here is not a syncretism, because the morphosyntactic context (Plural) is realised separately from the neutralised properties by the suffix *-ler*; and it is not a take-over, because the hypothetical Locative–Ablative Plural suffix *-be* does not elsewhere (i.e. in the Singular) realise either Locative or Ablative. Most linguists will probably agree that there is nothing especially outlandish about this hypothetical paradigm. Nevertheless, paradigms containing syncretisms of the '*ev-ler-be*' kind are completely absent from the data in the Appendix. On the basis of this, it may seem reasonable to strengthen (417) at once by omitting the qualification 'generally'. But I propose to defer a more formal statement of any constraint on inflexional homonymies until we have investigated a question which arises naturally from the existence of take-overs. In the course of our *a priori* discussion in section 4.2.5, we found that all homonymies without cumulation increase complexity, even if those of the kind that we are now calling 'take-overs' increase it less than those of the kind illustrated in Table 4.18. Why, then, should take-overs exist at all? Our suggestion of a functional explanation for syncretisms (in terms of memorability) is considerably weakened, one might argue, if we cannot offer any parallel explanation for other types of systematic inflexional homonymy. I will attempt to answer this objection in two stages. First I will suggest that, in certain instances, the prima facie counterfunctionality of take-overs in general is overridden by language-particular considerations of 'system-congruity', in Wurzel's (1984) sense. Then I will point to conditions which even these take-overs must satisfy and which can be incorporated into the general constraint on Deviation IV towards which we are working.

Let us consider in some detail the homonymy involving the properties Definite and Indefinite in the Hungarian Past Tense (example 37 in the Appendix). Part of the paradigm for the Hungarian verb *ír* 'write' is given in Table 4.19.

The aspect of this paradigm that interests us is the homonymy between the two 1st Singular Past forms. The form *írtam* 'looks' Definite rather than Indefinite, because all Definite 1 Sg forms end in *-m* (like the Present Definite form *írom* also shown in Table 4.19), whereas all other Indefinite 1 Sg forms end in *-k* (like the Present Indefinite *írok*); the expected 1 Sg Past Indefinite form would thus be '*írtak*'.[10] What we have is therefore a take-over, and moreover one which is not a syncretism, because part

Table 4.19

			Indicative: Indefinite	Definite[9]
Present:	Sg	1	ir-ok	ir-om
		2	ir-sz [i:rs]	ir-od
		3	ir	ir-ja
	Pl	1	ir-unk	ir-juk
		2	ir-tok	ir-játok
		3	ir-nak	ir-jak
Past:	Sg	1	ir-t-am	ir-t-am
		2	ir-t-ál	ir-t-ad
		3	ir-t	ir-t-a
	Pl	1	ir-t-unk	ir-t-uk
		2	ir-t-atok	ir-t-átok
		3	ir-t-ak	ir-t-ák

of the morphosyntactic context (namely Past Tense) is clearly realised separately from the neutralised properties by means of the suffix -*t*- which crops up in all Past Tense forms. Now, a function for this take-over suggests itself when we notice that the form *irtak* does in fact occur in the Past Indefinite, namely as the 3rd Plural form; so the Definite–Indefinite homonymy in the 1st Singular has a clearly identifiable consequence within the Indefinite Past, namely the avoidance of a homonymy between 1st Singular and 3rd Plural forms. This might be a pure accident, of no systematic significance. However, such avoidance of homonymy within a set of forms sharing the same Tense–Mood–Definiteness properties is a general characteristic of Hungarian; it is therefore a prime candidate for the status of a 'system-defining structural property', locating Hungarian on the parameter of 'the number and manner of formal distinctions in the paradigm' (Wurzel 1984: 81-9, 205-6). Thus the *irtam* take-over, though apparently counterfunctional in general terms, helps to ensure conformity with a language-particular structural property.

There seems to be a similar dislike in Finnish of homonymy between Case-forms sharing the same Number. In Table 4.20 below we find no Case-homonymy at all, but two instances of Number-homonymy in the Comitative and Instructive Cases (examples 39 and 40 in the Appendix). The Comitative suffix for both Singular and Plural, as illustrated in Table 4.20, is -*ine*, which 'looks' Plural inasmuch as -*i*- (or an allomorphic variant

Table 4.20

	Sg	Pl	Sg	Pl
Nominative	pöytä	pöydät	tehdas	tehtaat
	'table'		'factory'	
Genitive	pöydän	pöytien	tehtaan	tehtaiden
Partitive	pöytää	pöytiä	tehdasta	tehtaita
Essive	pöytänä	pöytinä	tehtaana	tehtaina
Translative	pöydäksi	pöydiksi	tehtaaksi	tehtaiksi
Inessive	pöydässä	pöydissä	tehtaassa	tehtaissa
Elative	pöydästä	pöydistä	tehtaasta	tehtaista
Illative	pöytään	pöytiin	tehtaaseen	tehtaisiin
Adessive	pöydällä	pöydillä	tehtaalla	tehtailla
Ablative	pöydältä	pöydiltä	tehtaalta	tehtailta
Allative	pöydälle	pöydille	tehtaalle	tehtaille
Abessive	pöydättä	pöydittä	tehaatta	tehtaitta
Comitative	pöytine[11]	pöytine	tehtaine	tehtaine
Instructive	pöydin	pöydin	tehtain	tehtain

-j-) occurs in all Finnish Plural Cases except the Nominative and is in many of them the sole characteristic distinguishing them from the corresponding Singular Cases. The Instructive ending *-in* 'looks' Plural for the same reason. We can therefore regard these two homonymies as takeovers by the Plural. Furthermore, if we regard absence of Case homonymy as a system-defining structural property of Finnish, the Instructive take-over acquires a diachronic motivation. There was once a Singular-only Instructive form, now obsolete, which happened to be homonymous with the Genitive Singular, in violation of the structural property just mentioned; the takeover by the Plural form has thus served to enhance system congruity in Wurzel's terms (Hakulinen 1957: 68; Aaltio 1964: 256).[12]

How persuasive one finds these suggested motivations for certain homonymies will depend on one's attitude to Wurzel's notion of system-dependent 'naturalness' as a whole. I have in any case suggested such a motivation for only two of the seven relevant homonymies in the Appendix. But our main concern is not with conditions which favour Deviation IV, but rather with constraints on its occurrence. We have not yet exploited a further common factor which unites six of the seven take-overs of (411 iii). This common factor involves a notion of **dominance** that was introduced into the discussion of inflexional homonymy by Hjelmslev (1935: 107-8): 'L'interdépendance entre les catégories [grammaticales] est un fait de *domination*. Dans un système grammatical, certaines catégories sont dominantes et certaines autres catégories sont dominées ... La domination consiste en ceci que *la catégorie dominée engage de syncrétismes sous la pression de la catégorie dominante* [his emphasis]'. As an example, he cites in Latin the syncretisms between Cases sharing the same Number and the absence of syncretisms between Singular and Plural in any Case as evidence for the dominance of Number over Case in Latin. Hjelmslev does not develop his notion of dominance very far; but there is a striking resemblance between it and a collection of observations about morphosyntactic categories assembled by Bybee (1985). What interests Bybee, studying a sample of 50 languages designed to minimise genetic and areal bias, is the frequency with which a variety of verbal categories including Aspect, Tense, Mood, Number and Person are given derivational or inflexional expression in these languages, and the way this correlates with the position of inflexional exponents of these categories in relation to each other and to the verb root.[13] The upshot is that the frequency with which an inflexional category appears in the sample correlates closely with the relative position in which its exponents stand in verb-forms; for example, Person (due to subject concord) is expressed inflexionally in fewer languages than Mood is, and its exponents are generally placed further from the root than those of Mood. Bybee sums up (1985: 35): 'These results suggest a "diagrammatic" relation between the meanings and their expression, such that the "closer" (more relevant) the meaning of the inflectional morpheme is to the meaning of the verb, the closer its expression unit will occur to the verb stem'.[14] From now on I will use the term 'relevance hierarchy' as a convenient label for the hierarchy of categories jointly established by criteria of sample frequency and realisational position, without necessarily accepting all aspects of Bybee's semantic definition of relevance (1985: 13-19), and without accepting her assumption that all inflexions are historically derived from 'full words' (1985: 38). Bybee suggests that a similar hierarchy of relevance applies to nominal categories, noting Greenberg's observation (1963: 112) that, if Number and Case are both realised inflexionally on the same side of the noun root, Number almost always comes between Case and the root.

We have here, then, a pair of categories about which both

Bybee and Hjelmslev have something to say: for Bybee Number is more 'relevant' than Case, while for Hjelmslev Number 'dominates' Case, at least in Latin. Can we therefore identify Bybee's 'relevance' with Hjelmslev's 'dominance'? The answer is no, for a reason that brings us directly back to the take-overs that we are interested in. Bybee's relations of 'relevance' are explicitly language-independent. For Hjelmslev, on the other hand, the dominance of one category over another is language-particular: 'On verra qu'il y a des langues ou les faits de domination sont toutes autres qu'en Latin, où par example les cas dominent les nombres et non inversement' (1935: 108). A language of this kind will be Finnish, where (as we have seen) the Comitative and Instructive Cases 'dominate' the category of Number. These Finnish take-overs thus illustrate a conflict between dominance and 'relevance'. But in this respect they are not unique: if Person–Number[15] is at the bottom of the 'relevance' hierarchy for verbs just as Case is for nouns, then six of the seven take-overs in (411 iii) illustrate just the same conflict, as shown in Table 4.21.

Table 4.21

Appendix example	Category or categories within which homonymy occurs	Morphosyntactic context
8	Tense, Mood	Aspect, *Person–Number*
9	Tense, Mood	Aspect, *Person–Number*
35	*Case*	Number
36	Definiteness	Mood, *Person–Number*
37	Definiteness	Tense, *Person–Number*
39	Number	*Case*
40	Number	*Case*

In Table 4.21 we have italicised the category which is lowest on the 'relevance' hierarchy in each row. In all the examples except 35, this category is part of the morphosyntactic context, not the category within which the homonymy occurs. By contrast, if we look at any of the other systematic homonymies in the Appendix (i.e. the syncretisms listed at (411 ii)), we find that 'relevance' and dominance coincide: either the homonymous properties belong to a category which is clearly less 'relevant' than any in the morphosyntactic context (e.g. the Latin Case syncretisms in examples 1-3, 5 and 6 and the Italian Person–Number syncretism of 30), or else the relative relevance of the categories concerned is unclear (e.g. Person and Number in German and Lithuanian verbs at examples 27 and 28, or Case and Gender in various languages at examples 4, 10, 14 and 20). Putting together all the observations we have so far made about the systematic homonymies of the Appendix, we can now formulate a general claim about homonymy in inflexion as follows:

(418) SYSTEMATIC HOMONYMY CLAIM
All systematic homonymies within inflexional paradigms are either (a) syncretisms (as defined at (412)) or (b) take-overs in which relevance conflicts with dominance (i.e. the morphosyntactic context contains properties belonging to categories which are lower in the relevance hierarchy than the category to which the neutralised properties belong).

Reverting to the classification of the Appendix examples at (411), we find that, of the systematic ones, those of (411 ii) come under part (a) of the Systematic Homonymy Claim and those of (411 iii) come under part (b) — except, apparently, the Arabic Genitive–Accusative homonymy of example 35, to which we will return in section 4.3.2.

Clearly we want the Systematic Homonymy Claim to predict the nonexistence of homonymies of the '*ev-ler-be*' type illustrated in Table 4.18. It succeeds in doing so, because '*ev-ler-be*' exhibits neither syncretism nor take-over. But in this respect the Claim makes no advance over the prediction at (417) that systematic non-syncretisms will be take-overs. Where the Claim does go beyond (417) is in predicting also the nonexistence of homonymies of the '*ev-ler-de*' type illustrated in Table 4.7. In this hypothetical pseudo-Turkish Locative–Ablative Plural homonymy, a property belonging to the more 'relevant' category of Number provides the context for the take-over of one property (Ablative) by another (Locative) belonging to the less 'relevant' category of Case. This is a kind of systematic homonymy that the Claim at (418) does not permit;[16] and, at least on the strength of the evidence presented so far, it is right not to permit it. Table 4.7 thus illustrates the respect in which our recourse to the notions of 'dominance' and 'relevance' has enabled us to tighten the constraint on Deviation IV beyond what would otherwise have been possible. Obviously the Claim remains vague to the extent that the notion of relevance is itself vague. The detailed formulation and testing of the sort of typological generalisations that interest Bybee pose numerous problems, some of which I have already alluded to; decisions have to be made about the cross-linguistic identification of grammatical categories, about the morphological segmentation of inflected word-forms, and about the boundary between inflexion and derivation. There is a further fundamental problem about how such generalisations are to be related to a 'theory of grammar' in the Chomskyan sense. But the vagueness in the claim (which will in any case diminish as progress is made on the relevant typological issues) is quite precisely circumscribed, and the predictions that flow from the claim about the occurrence or nonoccurrence of conceivable types of systematic homonymy are strong.

4.2.7 Consequences of the Systematic Homonymy Claim for language change

There is a tug-of-war between memorability (to which syncretism contributes) and the avoidance of ambiguity (with which syncretism conflicts). This tug-of-war can be expected to have consequences for language change. *A priori*, we would expect that languages with persistent inflexional homonymies, unless they do away with these homonymies analogically, should develop non-morphological means of expressing those morphosyntactic properties most affected, and in particular should do so more readily than languages without inflexional homonymies. Insofar as this rather vague expectation is testable, the evidence seems to bear it out. A number of linguists have attributed the 'analytic' tendencies of certain Indo-European languages and the phenomenon of linguistic 'drift' in general largely to the ambiguities engendered by the phonological attrition of inflexional endings (see e.g. Vennemann (1975) and the references he cites); other linguists have vigorously rejected this explanation (e.g. Lakoff 1972; M.B. Harris 1978). But the Systematic Homonymy Claim has as one corollary a rather more novel and more precise expectation about morphological change, relevant to the long-standing controversy about drift and particularly to the question whether the relationship between the phonological attrition just mentioned and the loss of inflexional endings is one of cause and effect, or whether they should both be seen rather as somehow aspects of a single process, influencing one another mutually.

Let us assume first that the Systematic Homonymy Claim is incorrect, so that syncretisms (as defined at (412)) are not as such any more likely to be systematic than homonymies which are not syncretisms. The origin of homonymies within inflexional paradigms cannot then be attributed even in part to any specifically morphological principle involving simultaneous exponence, and, if we compare the relative weight of phonological and specifically morphological factors in the Indo-European analytic 'drift', the balance is likely to come down squarely on the side of the phonological factors. But then, if we look at the distribution of phonological innovations of the kind that are said to have contributed to the loss of inflexion in Europe, we find (at least at first sight) a rather mysterious correlation: these innovations seem to be especially characteristic of 'fusional' rather than agglutinating languages. That is, it is in languages where cumulation of morphosyntactic properties is, or has been, typical, such as the Germanic, Romance and Slavic languages, that phenomena such as the neutralisation of vowels in final or unstressed syllables and the loss of final consonants have putatively caused pernicious large-scale homonymy and consequent loss of inflexions, rather than in languages where cumulation is less typical, such as Hungarian and Turkish. We are faced with choosing between two equally unattractive conclusions; either the 'agglutinating' languages just happen to be phonologically more conservative than many of the 'fusional' ones, or else such phonological innovations as have occurred in the agglutinating languages just happen not to have resulted in inflexional homonymy of the kind found in the fusional ones.

Let us suppose, on the other hand, that the Systematic Homonymy Claim is broadly correct. If so, then in 'fusional' languages there is a specifically morphological factor independent of any phonological ones contributing to the incidence of homonymy, namely the fact that only in fusional languages can systematic homonymies of the kind I have called 'syncretisms' occur. Assuming that widespread inflexional homonymy, however caused, will hasten the drift towards analyticity, the Systematic Homonymy Claim will thus imply that, other things being equal, fusional languages will become analytic faster than agglutinating ones do. The Systematic Homonymy Claim thus points to an explanation for the correlation which in the last paragraph I called 'mysterious'. If some sound change introduces a homonymy in an agglutinating paradigm, that homonymy has to be regarded as accidental, and is consequently relatively vulnerable to removal by 'analogical' processes; on the other hand, a homonymy introduced in a fusional paradigm can be treated as systematic, and will therefore be less vulnerable to removal by morphological means (as opposed to syntactic ones, involving the replacement of 'synthetic' by 'analytic' or periphrastic modes of expression).

The Systematic Homonymy Claim thus implies a prediction about the relative speed of the drift to analyticity which an admittedly quite cursory look at the European evidence seems to confirm. It tends, too, to confirm the view of Martin Harris and others that, even if phonological change may contribute to inflexional attrition, it is not its sole cause. One is tempted to speculate further about the relationship between morphological cumulation and phonological change. If 'agglutinating' languages are indeed phonologically more conservative than 'fusional' ones — or, at any rate, display fewer phonological innovations with 'neutralising' effects likely to engender morphological homonymy — can we say that a general principle of morphological organisation embodied provisionally in the Systematic Homonymy Claim may have an inhibitory effect on sound changes of certain types in languages with certain morphological characteristics? We are used to thinking of phonological innovation (or the lack of it) as proceeding quite independently of morphology and syntax, even though it may have quite radical morphological and syntactic consequences; but if my speculation is correct, then an influence may operate in the opposite direction too, inasmuch as certain phonological innovations tending to create morphological homonymies may be inhibited in 'agglutinating' languages (as opposed to 'fusional' ones) in virtue of a general propensity to avoid morphological homonymies which are unsystematic, at least in circumstances where an ambiguity is likely to arise. This speculation squares well with the suggestion by various scholars that certain phonological characteristics are typical of 'agglutinating' languages (Lehmann 1973: 61-2; Neustupný 1978: 113-46). On the other hand, it runs counter to Lightfoot's contention (1979: 123-4, 149) that, in linguistic change, 'grammars practice therapy rather than prophylaxis', since what I am positing for agglutinating languages is essentially a prophylactic avoidance of certain kinds of sound change. On balance, the speculation certainly seems to me worth investigating; but to do so now would take us too far afield.

4.2.8 The reliability of the Appendix

I promised to revert later to the question whether the generalisations emerging from our discussion risked turning out to be spurious because of bias in the selection of the data in the Appendix on which they are based. As I have said, the Appendix contains a relatively high representation from Indo-European. But the bias would seriously endanger our conclusions (in particular, the Systematic Homonymy Claim) only if it could be shown that there were, or might be, 'family-specific' reasons why simultaneous exponence of contextual and neutralised properties should favour homonymy, or, conversely, why sequential exponence should inhibit it.

To demonstrate such reasons, it would not be sufficient merely to show that many Indo-European homonymies (such as the Neuter Nominative–Accusative one) are old and well established; for this very persistence could equally be attributed to the fact that these homonymies are syncretisms (in my sense) and therefore conform to the Systematic Homonymy Claim. Rather, one would need to show that Indo-European languages have an inherited penchant for homonymy quite independent of factors such as simultaneity in inflexional realisation. But the only way to show this would be to show that systematic homonymies crop up in Indo-European 'agglutinated' structures (by contrast with, say, Turkish and Hungarian ones) just as freely as in 'fused' structures. Yet this does not seem to happen; and the absence of such 'agglutinated' homonymies cannot simply be put down to an Indo-European distaste for agglutination altogether, since 'agglutinating' as well as 'fused' morphological structures are common in attested Indo-European languages of all times and places (cf. Latin *amā-t-ur* (LOVE + 3 Sg + Passive) 'he is loved' alongside *amā-minī* (LOVE + $\{ \begin{smallmatrix} 2\ \text{Pl} \\ \text{Passive} \end{smallmatrix} \}$) 'you (Pl) are loved').

We can be reasonably confident, then, that the Indo-European bias in the Appendix is not seriously distorting. Quite apart from this, it is logically possible that even without any family-specific tendency towards homonymy as such, systematic homonymy should be relatively more frequent in Indo-European than in other language families. This will be not merely possible but probable if it is the case that the factors which (I have argued) facilitate systematic homonymy generally, such as simultaneous exponence, are relatively more frequent in Indo-European too — something which has indeed been suggested by some linguists; thus, Hjelmslev (1935: 83) claimed that the Case-systems of Indo-European languages were quite unusual in their lack of 'regularity' (i.e., in effect, their high incidence of sensitivity, homonymy and simultaneous exponence). So, although it is certainly desirable to adduce evidence from more language families in testing a generalisation of the nature of, and as ambitious as, the Systematic Homonymy Claim, the Claim seems at least sufficiently adequately supported to furnish a starting-point for further investigation.

4.3 SOME INDIVIDUAL HOMONYMIES

Attached to the Appendix are comments on many of the individual homonymies listed there. In the rest of this chapter, however, I will offer a more extended commentary on certain of the homonymies which present features of special interest. In section 4.3.1 we will look at two homonymies which have been resolved diachronically — that is, where earlier homonymous realisations have been replaced by distinct ones. In section 4.3.2 we will look at an Arabic homonymy which raises questions about how the Systematic Homonymy Claim should be related to the formal mechanisms for associating morphosyntactic properties with their exponents. Finally, in section 4.3.3 we look at an instance where the Claim impinges on a superficially quite unrelated issue: the definition of 'macroparadigm'. The Claim has implications also for the subject-matter of Chapter 5; but discussion of that must wait until section 5.1.3.

4.3.1 Homonymy losses in Italian and Georgian

Other things being equal, a systematic homonymy is likely to be diachronically stable. If we found a widespread propensity to resolve all inflexional homonymies by morphological innovation as soon as they arose, we would almost certainly hesitate to regard any such homonymies as morphologically systematic; in other words, we would almost certainly reject the notion of systematic inflexional homonymy entirely. If, on the other hand, the Systematic Homonymy Claim is basically correct, the destruction of a homonymy by inflexional innovation must generally be a sign either that (a) the homonymy was unsystematic in the first place or (b) the morphosyntactic properties involved, or their realisations, have changed in such a manner as to render the homonymy unsystematic if it is maintained. Examples 29 and 41 in the Appendix can plausibly be interpreted as illustrating circumstances (a) and (b) respectively.

The medieval Italian Imperfect Indicative Tense of *parlare* 'speak' is given in Table 4.22.

Table 4.22

Sg	1	parl-av-a
	2	parl-av-a
	3	parl-av-a
Pl	1	parl-av-amo
	2	parl-av-ate
	3	parl-av-ano

The hyphens are inserted to draw attention to the element -*av*-. This appears throughout the Imperfect and nowhere else in the paradigm, so it is clearly the exponent of Imperfect here, while Person and Number are realised by the suffix which follows.[17] On the other hand, the homonymy of the three Singular Persons is peculiar to the Imperfect, so it is the property Imperfect which constitutes the morphosyntactic context for it. But, if so, the homonymy cannot be considered systematic, because it conforms to neither part (a) nor part (b) of the Systematic Homonymy Claim; it violates part (a) because Imperfect is not realised simultaneously with the Singular Persons, and it violates part (b) because there is no conflict between dominance and relevance here, Person–Number being lower in the relevance hierarchy than Tense. The homonymy must therefore be considered accidental — and, moreover, an accidental homonymy that cannot be attributed to phonological factors in the way that (for example) the homonymy between -*i* 'his/her/its' and -*i* 'Accusative' in Turkish *evi* 'his house *or* house (Acc)' can be (see Table 4.4(b)).

This conclusion turns out to be a welcome one, however, when we observe what happens in modern Italian. In the Present Tense of all Italian verbs, the three singular Persons have distinct realisations as exemplified in Table 4.23(a); and in modern Italian the Present Tense endings for the 1st and 2nd Persons Singular have been adopted in the Imperfect too (see Table 4.23(b)):

Table 4.23

		a.	Present	b.	Imperfect
Sg	1		parl-o		parl-av-o
	2		parl-i		parl-av-i
	3		parl-a		parl-av-a
Pl	1		parl-iamo		parl-av-amo
	2		parl-ate		parl-av-ate
	3		parl-ano		parl-av-ano

The situation, then, is that purely phonological changes between Latin and Italian, namely the loss of final consonants, created a new homonymy in the Imperfect in medieval Italian of a kind which, according to the Systematic Homonymy Claim, must be classified as accidental: Latin -*ābam*, -*ābas*, -*ābat* > -*ava*, -*ava*, -*ava*. Moreover, this new homonymy lacked any synchronic phonological underpinning, in that the homonymous -*a* suffixes were not phonologically conditioned allomorphs of suffixes elsewhere distinct, as in the examples in Table 4.4. But the fact that in due course the homonymy was removed tends to confirm that to classify the homonymy as accidental is indeed correct.

The Systematic Homonymy Claim does not, of course, entail any requirement that accidental homonymies should immediately be removed as soon as they arise. Such a requirement would clearly be wrong, since in another Romance language (Spanish), for similar historical reasons, a similar homonymy arose between 1 Sg and 3 Sg in the Imperfect, which is likewise 'accidental' in my framework but which has not been removed by any later morphological innovation (see Table 4.24).

Table 4.24

Sg	1	habl-ab-a	'I spoke'
	2	habl-ab-as	etc.
	3	habl-ab-a	
Pl	1	habl-ab-amos	
	2	habl-ab-ais	
	3	habl-ab-an	

What the Italian example demonstrates, though, is that to rush to chalk up as counter-evidence to the Systematic Homonymy Claim all 'accidental' homonymies which are phonologically unaccountable in purely synchronic terms is over-hasty; it is at least worth investigating whether later historical changes, if known, do not actually convert the apparent counterevidence into confirming evidence.

In contrast with the Italian example the ancient Georgian homonymy presented as example 41 is a straightforward syncretism with no particularly remarkable features: the Dative, Ergative and Ablative Cases are homonymous in the context of the simultaneously-realised Plural. But consider the partial nominal paradigms of the noun *kal* 'daughter' given in Table 4.25, illustrating a contrast between ancient and modern Georgian (Vogt 1971):

Table 4.25

	Singular (ancient and modern)	Plural (ancient)	Plural (modern)
Nom	kal-i	kal-ni	kal-eb-i
Dat	kal-s	kal-ta	kal-eb-s
Erg	kal-ma	kal-ta	kal-eb-ma
Gen	kal-is	kal-ta	kal-eb-is

Clearly, a morphological innovation has taken place (for whatever reason) whereby a Plural paradigm in which Number and Case were realised simultaneously, at least in some Case-forms, has been replaced by one where they are realised sequentially, with a separate identifiable Plural marker -*eb*-.

Logically, when this Plural marker was introduced, the pattern of homonymy observable in the ancient Georgian Plural could have been retained; modern Georgian might, in other words, have ended up with a form such as '*kal-eb-ta*' realising homonymously Dat, Erg and Gen Pl. What we actually observe in modern Georgian, however, is an inflexional pattern displaying no homonymy and no sensitivity either: a straightforward identity of Case-endings between Singular and Plural. It would be unrealistic, without a thorough study of Georgian historical morphology, to point to any one factor as causing the obliteration of the homonymy. But we can at least say that, if the Systematic Homonymy Claim is correct, the observed development is quite natural, whereas the development of a new homonymous form such as our hypothetical '*kal-eb-ta*' would not be expected. The reason is that '*kal-eb-ta*' would have been no longer a syncretism nor even a take-over, but would have had to be analysed as accidental, and would thus have represented an increase in complexity over the form *kal-ta* which it replaced. What actually happened, on the other hand, represents a decrease in complexity inasmuch as it introduces the maximally simple one-to-one pattern of exponence.

In the study of linguistic change, it is the development of homonymies which has attracted most comment, not their removal. But with the help of a distinction (such as that offered here) between morphologically systematic and unsystematic homonymies, we can begin to redress the balance. The fact that we can now say something sensible about diachronic aspects not only of homonymy in general (as in section 4.2.7) but also of particular homonymies is an encouraging by-product of the Systematic Homonymy Claim.

4.3.2 An Arabic Case-homonymy and its implications

In this book I am primarily concerned with establishing the correctness of certain generalisations about the property–exponent relationship, not with the formal mechanisms for representing these relationships in linguistic descriptions. Nevertheless, certain implications about these mechanisms seem to flow directly from the Systematic Homonymy Claim. If we are right in saying that syncretisms (as defined at (412)) are systematic, then we will expect to find them explicitly represented somewhere in an adequate description of the languages concerned. Thus, for example, we will expect to find in a grammar of Latin an explicit statement that Dative and Ablative

Plural are always realised homonymously. But, since deciding that a homonymy is a syncretism depends on knowing that the properties concerned are realised simultaneously, the grammar must also provide information about the sequence in which the properties are realised. Finally, the grammar must also state what the realisation is. It is tempting, therefore, to think in terms of three types of inflexional rule — sequencing rules, homonymy rules and spell-out rules — applying in that order, and most recent attempts at a formal treatment of inflexion make at least some distinctions on these lines.[18] One reason why I hesitate to adopt explicitly a descriptive framework of this kind, however, is the fact that ordering paradoxes arise. Common sense suggests that, if some homonymy depends on sequencing and some spell-out depends on homonymy, then sequencing can never depend on the output of spell-out rules — that is, on the phonological shape of the inflexions concerned. Unfortunately, just this sort of dependence does sometimes occur, albeit rarely. For example, in the Zulu Immediate Past Continuous Tense the Tense-marker *be-* or *b-* '*precedes* the Participial Subject Concord *except* where the latter has *no consonant*' (Rycroft & Ngcobo 1979: 100), thus:

(419) a. in-tombi i- *b-* i- funda izolo
           Sg-girl Sg-Past-Sg-read yesterday
           'the girl was reading yesterday'
       b. izin-tombi *be-* zi-funda izolo
           Pl-girl Past-Pl-read yesterday
           'the girls were reading yesterday'

In (419 a) the nonconsonantal concord-marker *i-*, exhibiting extended exponence, both precedes and follows the marker of Tense, but in (419 b) the consonantal marker *zi-* only follows it.

The relevance of this to the Arabic Case-homonymy at example 35 lies in the fact that there, too, we seem to find an untypical interaction between 'rules' of the three kinds — an interaction which may perhaps account for what is otherwise the only direct counterexample in the Appendix to the Systematic Homonymy Claim. In some classical Arabic nominal paradigms, namely those with 'sound' (i.e. purely suffixal) Plural inflexion, the Genitive and Accusative Cases are realised homonymously in the Plural, as shown in Table 4.26.

Table 4.26

		Singular	Plural	Singular	Plural
Indef	Nom	muʕallim-un	muʕallim-ūna	ḥayawān-un	ḥayawān-ātun
		'teacher'		'animal'	
	Gen	muʕallim-in	muʕallim-īna	ḥayawān-in	ḥayawān-ātin
	Acc	muʕallim-an	muʕallim-īna	ḥayawān-an	ḥayawān-ātin
Def	Nom	muʕallim-u		ḥayawān-u	ḥayawān-ātu
	Gen	muʕallim-i	(as above)	ḥayawān-i	ḥayawān-āti
	Acc	muʕallim-a		ḥayawān-a	ḥayawān-āti

In this respect, these Plurals differ from the 'broken' Plural pattern of *rajulun* 'man', which exploits vowel change, as shown in Table 4.27.

Table 4.27

		Singular	Plural
Indef	Nom	rajul-un	rijāl-un
	Gen	rajul-in	rijāl-in
	Acc	rajul-an	rijāl-an
Def	Nom	rajul-u	rijāl-u
	Gen	rajul-i	rijāl-i
	Acc	rajul-a	rijāl-a

In shape, the Acc–Gen forms *ḥayawānātin* and *ḥayawānāti* 'look' Genitive rather than Accusative, because *-i(n)* is, in the Singular of all three nouns as well as in the Plural too of *rajulun*, a marker of Genitive solely. The homonymy is therefore, seemingly, a take-over. Moreover it is not a syncretism, since the morphosyntactic context Plural has a clearly distinct exponent in the paradigm of *ḥayawānun*, namely the suffix *-āt-*. Yet, since Number is higher in Bybee's relevance hierarchy than Case, relevance and dominance coincide here. The take-over is therefore not of the kind which is classified as systematic under part (b) of the Systematic Homonymy Claim. It must therefore be accidental, apparently. And superficially, at least, the same reasoning applies to the behaviour of *muʕallimun*. The shape of the homonymous forms *muʕallimīna* again suggests a take-over of Acc by Gen; and here again there seems to be a distinct exponent of Plural, namely *-na*, so here, too, we seem to have a take-over which is not a syncretism and in which relevance and dominance do not conflict.

HOMONYMY WITHIN PARADIGMS

There is, however, a difference between *ḥayawānātun* and *muᶜallimun* in the order in which the markers of Number and Case occur. As Tables 4.26 and 4.27 indicate, there are in fact three ways in which the stem, the Plural inflexion and the Case inflexion may be ordered in classical Arabic:

(420) a. 'Broken' Plurals (e.g. *rajulun*): $\begin{bmatrix} \text{Stem} \\ \text{Pl} \end{bmatrix}$ + Case
 b. 'Sound' Plurals in -*ūna* (e.g. *muᶜallimun*): Stem + Case + Plural
 c. 'Sound' Plurals in -*ātun* (e.g. *ḥayawānun*): Stem + Plural + Case

Now, describers of Arabic seem traditionally to regard the main morphological distinction in declension as that between 'broken' Plurals and the rest; the distinction between different types of 'sound' Plural is less fundamental. Taking our cue from this, we can easily enough describe the various linear orders illustrated in (420) in terms of two stages of sequencing:

(421) Sequencing rules for Arabic Plurals:
 a. Stage 1 (distinguishing 'broken' and 'sound' Plurals):

$$\begin{bmatrix} \text{Stem} \\ \text{Pl} \\ \text{Case} \end{bmatrix} \rightarrow \begin{cases} \begin{bmatrix} \text{Stem} \\ \text{Pl} \end{bmatrix} + \text{Case} & / \text{ broken-Plural nouns} \\ \text{Stem} + \begin{bmatrix} \text{Pl} \\ \text{Case} \end{bmatrix} & / \text{ sound-Plural nouns} \end{cases}$$

 b. Stage 2 (distinguishing two types of 'sound' Plural):

$$\begin{bmatrix} \text{Pl} \\ \text{Case} \end{bmatrix} \rightarrow \begin{cases} \text{Case} + \text{Plural} & / \text{ -}\bar{u}na \text{ class} \\ \text{Plural} + \text{Case} & / \text{ -}\bar{a}tun \text{ class} \end{cases}$$

The next step is to relate to these sequencing rules the homonymy rule (or rules) needed to account for the Acc–Gen homonymies.

Our common-sense expectation, given the dependence of syncretism on sequencing, is that any take-over which relies for its legitimacy on being also a syncretism (thus coming under part (a) of the Systematic Homonymy Claim) must take effect only after all sequencing rules have applied. This means that any syncretistic Case take-over would have to apply after Stage

135

2 of sequencing at (421). But clearly no syncretism (in our technical sense) is possible at that stage; all morphosyntactic properties have by then been fully 'unpacked' and linearised in sequence, so there is no longer any possibility of specifying a simultaneous morphosyntactic context. But, if we take seriously the separation of sequencing into two stages in (421), another ordering possibility presents itself; we can envisage the take-over as taking effect between Stage 1 and Stage 2, thus:

(422) Sequencing: Stage 1 (= (421 a))
       Genitive takes over Accusative in the context Plural
       Sequencing: Stage 2 (= (421 b))

With this rule-ordering, the take-over has a chance to apply at a point where at least some nouns (namely all those with 'sound' Plurals) still have Plural and Case packed together in one bundle, so that its application to them yields a syncretism, in conformity with the Systematic Homonymy Claim; however, the take-over automatically fails to apply to those nouns (namely those with 'broken' Plurals) in which Plural and Case have already been separated, because its application there would yield a result which violated the Systematic Homonymy Claim. The fact that the homonymy occurs precisely where it does — in both types of 'sound' Plural but in no 'broken' Plurals — is thus accounted for. In Table 4.28 I illustrate how the rules apply in the 'derivation' of the inflexional realisations for the Accusative Plural of all three of our exemplary nouns:

Table 4.28

	Broken Pl	Sound Pl in -*ūna*	Sound Pl in -*ātun*
Morphosyntactic representation	[RAJUL, Plural, Acc]	[MUʕALLIM, Plural, Acc]	[ḤAYAWĀN, Plural, Acc]
Sequencing: Stage 1	[RAJUL, Pl] + Acc	M. + [Pl, Acc]	Ḥ. + [Pl, Acc]
Gen–Acc take-over	Cannot apply	M. + [Pl, Gen]	Ḥ. + [Pl, Gen]
Sequencing: Stage 2	Does not apply	M. + Gen + Pl	Ḥ. + Pl + Gen
Spell-out	rijālan	muʕallimīna	ḥayawānātin

There is admittedly a danger in allowing homonymy rules to be interspersed among sequencing rules too freely. By invoking this privilege, we might even 'reconcile' the Systematic Homonymy Claim with hypothetical homonymies of the pseudo-Turkish kinds illustrated in Tables 4.7 and 4.18, thereby rendering the Claim empty. Clearly, then, there must be limits on the kind of manoeuvre we have adopted for the Arabic example. But, if we are prepared to accept that untypical rule interactions may sometimes occur, example 35 seems an eminently suitable instance in which to recognise one. At the very least, we have blunted the impact of the only direct counterexample to the Systematic Homonymy Claim that the Appendix presents.

4.3.3 Nominative–Accusative Neuter homonymies in Indo-European

In Chapter 3 we discussed at some length the relevance to paradigm economy of lexically determined categories such as Gender in nouns and Transitivity in verbs. Our conclusion was that identical inflexional patterns should not be considered distinct paradigms solely on the basis of difference in properties of this kind (so that the Latin *mensa* Fem 'table' and *nauta* Masc 'sailor' could be said to belong to the same paradigm in spite of their Gender difference), but that distinct inflexional patterns could be assigned to the same 'macroparadigm' if all their inflexional differences corresponded consistently to a difference in some lexically determined property (so that Latin *dominus* 'lord' Masc and *bellum* 'war' Neut could be assigned to the same macroparadigm despite their inflexional differences in the Nominative and Accusative). One could paraphrase this conclusion by saying that, for the purposes of paradigm economy, a lexically determined property A counts as having an inflexional realisation in some word-form if and only if there is some other property B within the same category which triggers a different realisation from A for at least one bundle of non-lexically-determined properties in the paradigm. On this basis, Neuter is realised inflexionally in most Latin, Greek and Russian noun paradigms in the Nominative and Accusative and nowhere else (examples 4, 10, 14, 20), since in most paradigms it is only in the Nominative and Accusative that Neuter nouns differ inflexionally from non-Neuters.

This conclusion, reached without reference to any considerations about homonymy within paradigms, turns out to be very convenient for our present purposes too. It allows us to say that the -*a* of Latin *bella* 'wars' realises not only the properties Plural and Nominative or Accusative but also Neuter, simultaneously; so, since Neuter is the morphosyntactic context for the Nom–Acc homonymy, it allows us to say that this homonymy is a syncretism. Suppose, on the other hand, that we had concluded that lexically determined morphosyntactic properties ought never to count as being inflexionally realised at all for the purpose of grouping inflexional patterns into paradigms. If we apply this conclusion to the Neuter Nom–Acc homonymy, we find that it destroys the characteristic which entitles us to call the homonymy a syncretism, because the contextual property Neuter is no longer realised simultaneously with the neutralised properties; and in the Plural at least we cannot call this homonymy a take-over either, since the ending -*a* does not 'look' either specifically Nominative or specifically Accusative. In order to go on calling this homonymy 'systematic', then (as we would clearly wish to do, in view of its remarkable persistence and regularity throughout Indo-European), we would have to either invent some special definition of 'syncretism' applicable only to lexically determined morphosyntactic contexts or weaken the Systematic Homonymy Claim or both.

The upshot is, then, that the Paradigm Economy Hypothesis and the Systematic Homonymy Claim are not altogether independent, as one might expect, but provide a certain measure of support for one another in that one and the same way of handling lexically determined properties contributes to the most economical and 'natural' formulation of both.

NOTES

1. This chapter constitutes a much expanded version of Carstairs (1984c). Where it differs from both this and Chapters 8 and 9 of Carstairs (1981b) (as on the definition of 'take-over' and the formulation of the Systematic Homonymy Claim), it supersedes them both.

2. The rapporteur for the exercise, Geneviève Corréard, comments on 'l'extrême diversité des réponses', and Bazell's remark (page 25) is apt: 'If the opposition between linguists is to be neutralised, the "archiopinion" will turn out to be zero.'

3. The section on syncretism in Hjelmslev (1961) (pages 87-93) does not go beyond definitions and a few remarks about logical entailment and set theory.

4. Williams's effort is severely and, in my view, rightly criticised by Joseph and Wallace (1984).

5. Historically, as it happens, the two uses of *ear* are definitely distinct, cognate with German *Ohr* and *Ähre* respectively. But this is, of course, irrelevant for determining how the native speaker perceives them in modern English. See Bloomfield (1935: 436) for discussion.

6. Icelandic thus contrasts with better-known languages such as Italian which, in male chauvinist fashion, require Masculine concord in such circumstances.

7. It is not clear to me whether the Case system that Chomsky (1980) posits for English noun phrases is morphosyntactic (in my sense) or purely syntactic. If the former, then we have here an instance where the syntactic evidence in favour of an alleged general morphosyntactic distinction is allowed to compensate for the lack of morphological evidence for it.

8. Notice that, according to the definitions presented here (by contrast with Carstairs (1981b)), a homonymy may be both a syncretism and a take-over at the same time. Examples are 21 and 22 in the Appendix, and also example 35, according to the analysis suggested in section 4.3.2. In most syncretisms, however, the shape of the exponent does not point to either of the homonymous properties as the one that 'takes over'. Zwicky's (1985) framework provides for only one kind of explicit systematic homonymy, namely 'referral', similar to our take-over; it seems likely, however, that decisions about the direction of referral in that framework will often be unavoidably arbitrary.

9. The Definite forms are used with a 'definite' 3rd Person direct object (i.e. one accompanied by a demonstrative or possessive adjective or the definite article).

10. Vago (1980: 53) arrives independently at what is in effect a view of the 1st Sg Past Indef ending as derived by take-over from the 1st Sg Past Def. He posits a 'morphological rule' as follows:

m-Suppletion
$$\begin{bmatrix} 1\ \text{Sg} \\ +\ \text{PAST} \end{bmatrix} \rightarrow [\ +\ \text{DEF}\ ]$$

11. On nouns (as opposed to attributive adjectives), the Comitative suffix will never in fact appear 'naked', as here, but always followed by a Personal Possessive suffix, e.g. *pöytine-en* 'with her table(s)'.

12. The English translation of Hakulinen's work (1961: 74) oddly contradicts both Aaltio and Hakulinen himself (in the German version) on the subject of the Singular use of the Plural Instructive form; but this seems to be a translator's or proof-reading error.

13. Bybee's willingness to identify categories across languages and her identification of 'categories' that are realised derivationally with ones realised inflexionally (the only ones which can count as morphosyntactic, in our framework) provoke a variety of questions about both facts and definitions. But the generalisations she establishes seem suf-

ficiently striking to allay doubts about the correctness of the overall picture.

14. The diagrammatic relation suggested by Bybee recalls the Mirror Principle enunciated by Baker (see section 5.2.3 below), but the linguistic evidence that motivates them seems, superficially at least, quite different.

15. Person and Number are combined here because they are so often realised cumulatively (Bybee 1985: 35).

16. Or, rather, the Claim requires that, if homonymies of the '*ev-ler-de*' kind do occur, they must be analysed as non-systematic or accidental. Example 29 in the Appendix is a relevant instance; and diachronic evidence supports the 'accidental' analysis there (see section 4.3.1).

17. One might prefer to segment the forms as *parla-v-a* etc., in which case it will be -*v*- that is the exponent of Imperfect; but this does not affect our present argument.

18. Warburton (1973), arguing for a sort of compromise between WP and IA approaches to modern Greek verb morphology, draws a distinction between 'segment transformations', which 'unpack' certain complexes of morphosyntactic properties into strings, and the realisation rules which subsequently assign phonological shape to the properties. Selkirk (1982: 71-4) achieves a rather similar sequencing of morphosyntactic categories by means of 'word structure rules' for inflexional affixes. In Zwicky's (1985) framework, systematic homonymies arise partly through explicit rules of referral and partly through rules of exponence applying to more than one property. By contrast, Anderson (1982) and his colleagues (Thomas-Flinders (ed.) 1981) are not primarily concerned with inflexional homonymy and, though they allow for manipulation of morphosyntactic representations before the spell-out stage, they in effect treat sequencing and spell-out as parts of the same operation.

APPENDIX TO CHAPTER 4: A SELECTION OF INFLEXIONAL HOMONYMIES

	I Language	II Homonymous properties and word-class restrictions	III Morphosyntactic context: (a) simultaneous	III (b) not simultaneous	IV Take-over (if any)	V Dominance-relevance conflict?	VI Accidental or non-morphological?
1	Latin	Dat, Abl of all Case-inflected words	Plural			No	No
2	Latin	Dat, Abl of all second-declension forms	Singular			No	Unlikely
3	Latin	Gen, Dat of all first-declension forms	Singular			No	Unlikely
4	Latin	Nom, Acc of all Case-inflected words	Neuter			Unlikely	No
5	Latin	Nom, Acc of all Case-inflected forms of third, fourth and fifth declensions	Plural		By Nom (in old *i*-stem forms)	No	No
6	Latin	Dat, Abl of third-declension adjectives	Singular		By Dat	No	No
7	Latin	Nom, Gen of third-declension nouns and adjectives with Nom Sg in -*is*	Singular			No	Probably
8	Latin	Fut Indic, Subjunc in verbs		Perfective; Pl, 2 Sg, 3 Sg	By Subjunc in 3 Pl; by Indic elsewhere	Yes	Perhaps
9	Latin	Fut Indic, Pres Subjunc of third- and fourth-conjugation verbs		Imperfective; 1 Sg	By Pres Subjunctive	Yes	No
10	Greek (Ancient)	Nom, Acc of all Case-inflected words	Neuter			Unlikely	No
11	Greek (Ancient)	2nd and 3rd Persons of verbs in some Tenses	Dual; Indic, Subjunc		By 2nd Person	No	No

Appendix to Chapter 4: continued

	I	II	III (a)	III (b)	IV	V	VI
12	Greek (Ancient)	Indicative and Subjunctive of verbs in -ō ('thematic')	1 Sg; Pres; Active			Yes	Yes
13	Greek (Ancient)	Fut Indic, Aorist Subjunc of verbs with identical stems for Future and ('sigmatic') Aorist	1 Sg; Active			Yes	Yes
14	Sanskrit	Nom, Acc of all Case-inflected words	Neuter			Unlikely	No
15	Sanskrit	Instr, Dat, Abl of all Case-inflected words except clitic personal pronouns	Dual			No	No
16	Sanskrit	Gen, Loc as for example 15	Dual			No	No
17	Sanskrit	Dat, Abl as for example 15	Plural			No	No
18	Sanskrit	Gen, Abl of all nouns, adjectives and participles except in the -as declension	Singular			No	Perhaps
19	Vedic	2nd and 3rd Persons of Verbs with 'athematic' Aorist stems	Sg; Indic	Aorist		No	Yes
20	Russian	Nom, Acc of all Case-inflected words	Neuter			Unlikely	No
21a	Russian	Nom, Acc as for example 20	Plural; Inanimate		By Nom	No	No
21b	Russian	Nom, Acc as for example 20	Singular; Inanimate; Masc		By Nom	No	No
22a	Russian	Acc, Gen as for example 20	Plural; Animate		By Gen	No	No
22b	Russian	Acc, Gen of all Case-inflected words except in the -a declension	Singular; Animate; Masc		By Gen	No	No
23	Russian	Dat, Loc of -a-declension nouns	Singular			No	No
24	Russian	Gen, Dat, Instr, Loc of adjectives	Sg; Fem			No	No

25	Russian	Gen, Dat, Loc of Feminine 'soft-stem' nouns	Singular		No	No
26	Russian	1, 2, 3 Persons of verbs	Past		No	Probably
27	Lithuanian	Sg, Pl of Verbs	3rd Person		Unclear	No
28	German	1, 3 Persons of verbs	Plural		Unclear	No
29	Italian (medieval)	1, 2, 3 Persons of verbs	Singular	Imperfect	No	Yes
30	Italian (modern)	1, 2, 3 Persons of verbs	Singular; Pres; Subjunc	By 3 Sg	No	No
31	French	Sg, Pl of nouns except for most in -a/ and a few others			No	Yes
32	English	Possessive, Nonpossessive except for some nouns with irregular Plurals (e.g. *man*)	Plural		No	Unlikely
33	Hebrew	3 Fem, 2 Masc of verbs	Sg; Imperfective		No	No
34	Classical Arabic	Definite, Indefinite of nouns with 'sound' Plurals in *-ūna*	Plural		Unclear	No
35	Classical Arabic	Gen, Acc of all nouns with 'sound' Plurals	Plural	By Gen	No (but see section 4.3.2)	No
36	Hungarian	Definite, Indefinite of verbs	1, 2 Pl	By Indef	Yes	No
37	Hungarian	Definite, Indefinite of verbs	1 Sg	By Def	Yes	No
38	Hungarian	Indicative, Subjunctive of verbs except those with stems in *-t*	1 Pl; Definite	By Subjunc	Yes	Yes
39	Finnish	Sg, Pl of nouns	Comitative Case	By Pl	Yes	No
40	Finnish	Sg, Pl of nouns	Instructive	By Pl	Yes	No
41	Georgian	Dative, Ergative, Genitive of nouns	Plural		No	No
42	Dyirbal	Instrumental, Ergative of nouns, adjectives, 'markers'			No	Yes
43	Dyirbal	Dative, Allative of nouns, adjectives			No	Probably

Comments on the Appendix

1. A stable homonymy from earliest to latest Latin.
2, 3. Early Latin innovations.
4, 10, 14, 20. An inherited Indo-European trait. See section 4.3.3.
5. Spread to old *i*-stem nouns by the 1st century AD, with loss of the distinct Acc Pl ending -*īs*. See Carstairs 1984a.
6. Developed by about 1st century AD. Clearly systematic, since it distinguishes participles used adjectivally (which display the homonymy) from participles used verbally (which do not); some adjectival exceptions, however, such as *vetus* 'old' and comparatives in -*ior*.
7. See discussion of Table 4.5 in section 4.2.2.
8. Gradual merger, still incomplete in Plautus's time (c. 200 BC). Take-over of Indicative by Subjunctive in 3 Pl, of Subjunctive by Indicative elsewhere.
9. Take-over of Future Indicative by Present Subjunctive. See section 5.1.3.
10. See on 4.
11. The homonymy does not occur in those Indicative forms which carry a prefixed *e*- (the 'augment') peculiar to the Indicative — i.e. in those forms where Indicative is not realised wholly simultaneously with Number, Person and Voice. Nor does it ever occur in the Optative, which always has a clearly identifiable exponent -*oi*-, -*ai*- or -*ei*-. Hence the homonymy is restricted to forms where it can be classed as a syncretism.
12. Present Indicative and Subjunctive endings typically differ in having short and long vowels (or diphthongs) respectively. But the 1 Sg -*ō* has no short-vowel alternant. The homonymy therefore results naturally from spell-out and is best seen as accidental.
13. The Person–Number endings of the Future Indicative are like those of the Present Indicative in most -*ō* verbs, and those of the Aorist Subjunctive are like those of the Present Subjunctive. Hence, see comment on 12.
14. See on 4.
15, 16. The clitic forms of the 1st and 2nd Person pronouns have a Dat–Acc–Gen homonymy instead, and there are no clitic forms for Instr or Abl. This confirms that these homonymies are indeed morphological rather than purely syntactic (cf. section 4.2.3).
17. Distinct in 1st and 2nd Person pronouns, which have a clitic Dative form homonymous with those for Accusative and Genitive instead; hence a genuinely morphological homonymy (cf. comment on 15, 16).
18. The importation of the Gen–Abl distinction from the pronominal declension into the -*as* declension may indicate that the homonymy should be analysed as accidental in other nouns.
19. The homonymy is clearly due to fairly recent phonological developments and is removed later by substitution of other types of Aorist stem (Kiparsky 1972: 203-5). Accidental, therefore.
20. See on 4.

21, 22, 23. One might argue that Singular or Plural (as appropriate) belongs in column VI rather than column V, since there are some Russian nouns in which Number is unambiguously realised by the position of the primary stress. If so, these homonymies cannot be classified as syncretisms, and, since dominance does not conflict with relevance here, they are incompatible with the Systematic Homonymy Claim. But it is argued in section 6.3 that non-affixal inflexion (such as stress alternation) must be ignored for the purposes of paradigm economy; and, if we decide to ignore it for the purpose of classifying homonymies also, these homonymies become syncretisms and hence compatible with the claim. The implications of this decision need to be investigated further, however.

26. One might argue that the category Person is simply not relevant to verbs in the Past Tense, just as Gender is not relevant in the Present. If so, this is not a morphological homonymy.

29. See section 4.3.1.

30. There is no tendency to remove this homonymy, in contrast with example 29 — not surprisingly, since it can readily be classified as a systematic syncretism.

31. Phonologically accountable, probably accidental. Alternatively, perhaps, an indication that there is no genuine morphosyntactic Number contrast in most modern French nouns (as opposed to determiners); if so, not a morphological homonymy.

32. The status of the Possessive marker -'s as a clitic rather than an affix (cf. Janda 1980) may seem to rule this out as a morphological homonymy. But if the Possessive Plural -s' of regular nouns is an inflexion (as argued by Carstairs 1985), then this can be regarded as a syncretism.

33. An old, stable homonymy, found in the 'prefix conjugation' of all Semitic languages. The existence of further homonymies in some but not all Semitic prefix conjugation systems raises questions about the extent to which the Systematic Homonymy Claim can help to account for the relevant historical developments.

35. See section 4.3.2, where it is argued that this is a syncretism, and therefore systematic, despite the presence of Plural in column VI rather than column V.

36. The homonymy in the 1st Person is relatively new (late 19th century). Vago (1980: 57) talks of the Definite suffix being 'replaced by' the Indefinite one, thus supporting a take-over analysis.

37. See discussion of Table 4.19 in section 4.2.6.

38. The nature of the restriction in column II suggests that this homonymy is accidental. If not, then the relevant exponent shapes suggest a take-over of the Indicative by the Subjunctive.

39, 40. See discussion of Table 4.20 in section 4.2.6.

41. See section 4.3.1.

42. The Instrumental and Ergative are probably best regarded as a single Case morphosyntactically, even if the syntactic functions are clearly distinguishable, as Dixon (1972) argues.

43. It seems best to treat Dative and Allative on the same lines as Nominative and Accusative in English; as the latter contrast is restricted

to personal pronouns, so the former is restricted to 'markers'. Since 42 and 43 are the only clear prima facie examples of morphological homonymy in Dyirbal, it may be possible to say that Dyirbal eschews this kind of homonymy altogether — not surprisingly, if the Systematic Homonymy Claim is correct, since Dyirbal has few if any instances of simultaneous exponence (Deviation III).

5
Syntagmatic Constraints on Allomorphy

This chapter is concerned with the search for constraints on Deviation II. This is the deviation that involves 'sensitivity' on the part of one morphosyntactic property either to other properties realised in the same word-form (where the allomorphy is 'grammatically conditioned') or else to the stem of the word itself (where the allomorphy is 'lexically conditioned'). The first part of the chapter proposes a generalisation concerning the direction in which such conditioning can operate; the second part discusses the relationship between this generalisation and certain other recent proposals relevant to Deviation II.

5.1 INWARD AND OUTWARD SENSITIVITY

5.1.1 Identifying pure sensitivity

Mel'čuk (1976: 73) remarks that, although the term 'suppletion' is generally restricted to the relationship between phonologically dissimilar realisations of the same lexical item (as in *go/went*, Russian *idu/šol* 'I am going/(I) was going'), phonologically dissimilar realisations of the same morphosyntactic property seem to stand in just the same relationship. This point is also explicitly emphasised by the proponents of 'Natural Generative Phonology'. But why is suppletion traditionally exemplified by alternations between roots only? There must be some difference between the behaviour of roots and that of inflexions which has obscured the parallelism that Mel'čuk noted. The main difference, in fact, seems to be one of frequency and ordinariness. In most languages, root suppletion is unusual, limited to rather few, even if frequently occurring, lexical items. Some linguists have therefore seen it as a rather marginal phenomenon which they need pay little attention to when constructing a model for lexical and morphological description. But, whether or not this attitude is justified where root suppletion is concerned, it is clearly quite inappropriate as regards non-phonologically-conditioned inflexional 'suppletion', simply because inflexional alternations of this kind are much too common in even moderately inflected languages to be considered marginal. A terminological distinction has therefore grown up; we tend to speak of suppletion between phonologically dissimilar roots associated with the same lexical item, but grammatically or lexically conditioned allomorphy between phonologically dissimilar realisations of the same morphosyntactic property.

Examples of grammatically or lexically conditioned allomorphy were given in (112). One of these examples was the realisation of Plural in English nouns. Although English is generally regarded as being poor in inflexional morphology, it is easy to find further English examples, as shown in Table 5.1.

Table 5.1

	Inflexional property	Suppletive realisations
a.	Past Tense	-ed
		Ø (e.g. *put*)
		vowel change (e.g. *drove*)
b.	Past Participle[1]	-ed
		Ø (e.g. *put*)
		-en (e.g. *driven*)
		vowel change (e.g. *sung*)

One might argue that Ø and -*ed* here are not in fact phonologically unrelated; the fact that the former is limited to roots ending in -*d* or -*t* may point to a phonological representation such as [[put] d]. But the important point for our present purpose is that there are at least two realisations of Past Tense, namely -*ed* and vowel change, and three of Past Participle, namely the same two plus -*en*, which are clearly not phonologically related and whose distribution is determined lexically or grammatically, not phonologically. And as soon as we turn from English to a highly inflected language such as Latin, we find much more elaborate arrays of rival realisations for the same morphosyntactic property, for example in Table 5.2.

Table 5.2

Inflexional property	Part of speech	Suppletive realisations
2 Sg	Verb	-s (-ās, -ēs, -is, -īs) istī -re (-āre, -ēre, -ere, -īre) -ris (-āris, -ēris, -eris, -īris) -e
Dat Sg	Noun	-ae, -ō, -ī, -uī, -ū, -ēī
Infinitive	Verb	-re, -rī, -ī, -isse
Perfective	Verb	-v- ([w]), -u-, -s-, ablaut, reduplication

Almost equally elaborate allomorphy can be found in Hungarian.[2]

Table 5.3

Inflexional property	Part of speech	Suppletive realisations
2 Sg Indef	Verb	-ol, -(a)sz-, -j, -ál
2 Sg	Noun	-od, -ad

This very proliferation poses a problem. In our search for constraints on Deviation II, we need a starting point. Where shall we concentrate our attention first?

One point which will strike anyone who knows anything of either Latin or Hungarian is that many of the examples in Tables 2.2 and 2.3 are not examples of Deviation II by itself; they also involve Deviation III (many-to-one syntagmatic realisation), identified at (113) with Matthews' 'cumulative' or 'overlapping' exponence. Thus, in Table 5.2, the Dative endings listed all realise Singular as well; and in Table 5.3 the first two verbal endings given are restricted to the Present Indicative and so may be said to help realise that combination of properties also. It is not surprising that many instances of Deviation II should also be instances of Deviation III; after all, many-to-one syntagmatic realisation of morphosyntactic properties presupposes the impossibility of segmenting the morphological material into one 'morph' per property, which in turn presupposes a kind of mutual sensitivity between the properties so realised. If, however, we wish to concentrate on Deviation II specifically, without the risk of our data being contaminated by any constraints on overlapping or cumulative exponence, we ought to concentrate on instances of Deviation II by itself — what I will call instances of **pure sensitivity**.

One possible objection to the plan of campaign just outlined is that there can never be any such thing as pure sensitivity — that we can never find Deviation II unaccompanied by any of the other deviations. Let us suppose that, in some inflexional paradigm, a certain morphosyntactic property (or property-combination) P is sensitive to its grammatical environment in such a way that it is realised as *a* normally but as *b* when some other property (or combination) Q is present, thus:

(501) Property: P (without Q)   P (with Q)
       Realised as: *a*   *b*

An example of this state of affairs can be found in Latin; in Active verb-forms the 2nd Singular is realised as -*s* (perhaps with a preceding thematic vowel) in all contexts except the Perfective Present Indicative, where the realisation is -*istī*. If we oversimplify slightly by ignoring the property Present, we can represent this as is shown in Table 5.4.

Table 5.4

Property:	2 Sg (without Pf Indic)	2 Sg (with Pf Indic)
Realised as:	-*s*	-*istī*
e.g.	amās 'you love'	amāvistī 'you (have) loved'
	amābis 'you will love'	
	amāvissēs 'you had loved (Subjunc)'	
	etc.	

In such a situation, one might say, *b* realises Q just as much as it does P; in Latin, -*istī* realises Perfective Indicative just as much as it does 2nd Singular. But then we have here an instance of many-to-one syntagmatic realisation, in that a single signifiant *b* realises (or helps to realise) two signifiés, P and Q. The example thus involves Deviation III as well as Deviation II. Yet (the objection continues) all logically possible examples of Deviation II are of this kind, since they all involve an analogue of *b*; and it is arbitrary to deny to this analogue of *b* some share in realising the conditioning property (analogous to Q) as well as the property with which it is allegedly primarily associated (the analogue of P).

In answering this objection, I will not deny that the analogue of *b* in any conceivable example of Deviation II has some share in realising the analogue of Q. But I will argue that we can nevertheless identify circumstances in which it makes sense to talk of pure sensitivity. These will be circumstances in which the conditioning property Q has a **principal exponent** apart from *b*, by which I mean that Q is unambiguously realised independently of the sensitive inflexion (*b*) by some inflexion (call it *x*) which also realises Q in some or all contexts where P is not present. We can illustrate this on the lines of (501) as follows:

(502)   Property: P (without Q)   Q (without P)   QP
        Realised as: a, c, ...,   x, y, ...   xb
                       possibly b

In terms of our Latin example, this can be interpreted as follows:

Table 5.5

Property:	2 Sg (without Pf Indic)	Pf Indic (without 2 Sg)	2 Sg Pf Indic
Realised as:	-s	-v- (in paradigm of amā- 'love')	-v-istī
e.g.	amās amābis amāvissēs etc.	amāvī 'I (have) loved' amāvit '(s)he (has) loved' etc.	amāvistī 'you (have) loved'

Although Deviation III is present in (502) inasmuch as *b* realises Q as well as P, what we see there is not complete overlap of the properties P and Q in a single unsegmentable inflexion but rather the extended realisation of Q by two inflexions, *x* and *b*. Of these, the first serves by itself to realise Q in other environments and, moreover, has no part in realising the sensitive property P. This distinguishability of the two inflexions *x* and *b* is crucial in allowing us to say that the sensitivity of P to Q in (502) is pure. Our definition of pure sensitivity thus requires us to exclude from consideration for present purposes all instances of Deviation III where there is complete overlap of the properties concerned, as in the realisation of Case and Number in Latin declension. Any constraints we discover on pure sensitivity may, of course, turn out to apply to sensitivity of other kinds too; but, by restricting ourselves in the way I suggest, we can be sure that such constraints will be independent of any which intrinsically involve overlap or cumulation.

A further example will illustrate the distinction between pure sensitivity and other types. The French word-forms *parlerons* [parlə'rɔ̃] '(we) will speak' and *parlerions* [parlə'rjɔ̃] '(we) would speak' represent the 1st Person Plural of the Future and the Conditional respectively. Comparison with the other Persons of these two Tenses suggests a segmentation into a stem *parler-* [parlər] which is shared by both Tenses, and a Personal ending which is not. Clearly the stem affix *-er-* does not unambiguously realise either Future or Conditional by itself. But the Personal endings do not do so either, since each is shared with some other Tense: *-ons* with the Present *parlons* [par'lɔ̃] '(we) speak' and *-ions* with the Imperfect *parlions* [par'ljɔ̃] '(we) were speaking'. Rather, it is the combination of the stem-forming affix and the Personal ending which jointly distinguishes the Future from the Conditional in the 1st Person Plural. So, in this example, the way in which the property-combination 1st Person Plural is realised is certainly sensitive to some other accompanying property, namely one belonging to the category Tense; but we cannot say that either of the two Tenses, Future and Conditional, is unambiguously realised independently of Person, so we cannot call this an instance of pure sensitivity.[3]

5.1.2 Pure inward sensitivity

Having defined pure sensitivity, we can now begin to consider whether it has any use in stating constraints on inflexional behaviour. As a first step, we need to appreciate how wide is the range of conceivable inflexional behaviour which conforms to our definition. To help illustrate this, I present in Table 5.6 a set of hypothetical verbal endings for Tense, Person and Number, realised in that order: each Person and Tense has two allomorphs, one of which (in italics) is limited to a single morphosyntactic context.

Most linguists, when presented with this paradigm, would, I think, find something implausible about it. Yet a close examin-

Table 5.6

		Present	Past	Future
Sg	1	-*e*-n	-o-*k*	-ai-n
	2	-a-l	-o-l	-ai-*p*
	3	-a-r	-o-r	-*u*-r
Pl	1	-a-n-t	-o-n-t	-ai-n-t
	2	-a-l-t	-*i*-l-t	-ai-l-t
	3	-a-*s*-t	-o-r-t	-ai-r-t

ation reveals a structure which, although it departs from one-to-one exponent-to-property patterning, does so only in the direction of pure sensitivity and, moreover, in a fashion which can be stated quite succinctly, as in Table 5.7.

Table 5.7

a.	Sequence of realisation of categories: Tense + Person (+ Number)	
b.	Realisations of Tense:	
	Present	*e* in 1st Sg
		a elsewhere
	Past	*i* in 2nd Pl
		o elsewhere
	Future	*u* in 3rd Sg
		ai elsewhere
c.	Realisations of Person:	
	1st	*k* in Past Sg
		n elsewhere
	2nd	*p* in Fut Sg
		l elsewhere
	3rd	*s* in Pres Pl
		r elsewhere
d.	Realisation of Number:[4]	
	Plural	*t*

This statement does, however, provoke a fairly obvious question: what would the hypothetical set of endings look like if no sensitivity were present and if only the 'elsewhere' realisations listed for each property in Table 5.7 were to occur? The result would be as in Table 5.8. This in turn suggests a possible explanation for the implausibility of Table 5.6: perhaps it is the sheer quantity of sensitivity displayed in Table 5.6, as opposed to the maximally perspicuous pattern of Table 5.8, which is enough to exclude it as an actual Tense–Person–Number

Table 5.8

		Present	Past	Future
Sg	1	a-n	o-n	ai-n
	2	a-l	o-l	ai-l
	3	a-r	o-r	ai-r
Pl	1	a-n-t	o-n-t	ai-n-t
	2	a-l-t	o-l-t	ai-l-t
	3	a-r-t	o-r-t	ai-r-t

paradigm in an actual language. If so, it is obviously superfluous to look for any deeper or more subtle explanation in terms of general constraints or sensitivity.

This possible explanation can, however, be shown to be false. All we need do to demonstrate this is find a set of Person–Tense–Number forms in an actual language which displays as much sensitivity as Table 5.6 or more, from the point of view of the sheer volume of allomorphy. Once again Latin furnishes as set of forms meeting this requirement. Consider the verb-forms in Table 5.9 (all of which are Active Indicative):

Table 5.9

		Imperfective Present	Perfective Present	Imperfective Future
Sg	1	regō 'I rule'	rexī [reksi:]	regam
	2	regis	rexistī	regēs
	3	regit	rexit	reget
Pl	1	regimus	reximus	regēmus
	2	regitis	rexistis	regētis
	3	regunt	rexerunt	regent

If we try to draw up for Table 5.9 a description of how the relevant morphosyntactic properties are realised, on the lines of Table 5.7, the result is unavoidably quite complex, no matter what our view of Latin phonology and of the underlying phonological representations of the various 'morphs'. One version might be as follows:

(503) a.   Sequence of realisation of categories:

$$\text{Aspect } (+ \text{ Tense}) + \begin{Bmatrix} \text{Person} \\ \text{Number} \end{Bmatrix}$$

(i.e. Person and Number are cumulated)

b. Realisation of Aspect:
   Perfective   -*v*-, -*u*-, -*s*-, reduplication, vowel lengthening
c. Realisation of Tense:
   Future   *a* in 1st Sg
           e elsewhere
d. Realisation of Person–Number:

		/V__	/C__
1st Sg	-*i* in Pf Pres; elsewhere:—	*m*	*ō*
2nd Sg	-*istī* in Pf Pres; elsewhere:—	*s*	*is*
3rd Sg		*t*	*it*
1st Pl		*mus*	*imus*
2nd Pl	-*istis* in Pf Pres; elsewhere:—	*tis*	*itis*
3rd Pl	-*erunt* in Pf Pres; elsewhere:—	*nt*	*unt*

I grant that one could shunt the complexity represented in the final column out of one's morphological into one's phonological description, by dint of positing several morphologically sensitive 'minor' phonological rules. But one is still left with an irreducible minimum of sensitivity in one's account of how the six properties (or combinations of properties) Perfective, Future, 1st Sg, 2nd Sg, 2nd Pl and 3rd Pl are realised — just as much as in the hypothetical example Table 5.6, described in Table 5.7. Moreover, one could argue that the complexity at (503) involves not merely pure sensitivity but also cumulation of the properties Person and Number, and is therefore exacerbated. So the reason why the hypothetical paradigm in Table 5.6 seems so implausible cannot be that the sheer quantity of sensitivity involved is greater than any actual human language will tolerate. Is this apparent implausibility then solely due to prejudice? To answer this question, we clearly need to look at more illustrations of actual inflexional behaviour, and I will introduce material from Turkish, Hungarian and Zulu.

Turkish does not have arbitrary declension- and conjugation-classes of the kind that we are familiar with in Latin, and Hungarian does so only to a relatively small extent. Yet both Turkish and Hungarian display plenty of examples within the verbal inflexional system of sensitivity on the part of Person and

Number to properties of Tense (or Aspect) and Mood. This can be seen in Tables 5.10 and 5.11, in which certain unequivocal instances of Person–Number allomorphy are highlighted by italics:

Table 5.10

		Turkish *gel-* 'come' Aorist Simple	*di*-Past Simple
Singular	1	gel-ir-im	gel-di-m
	2	gel-ir-sin	gel-di-n
	3	gel-ir	gel-di
Plural	1	gel-ir-*iz*	gel-di-*k*
	2	gel-ir-siniz	gel-di-niz
	3	gel-ir-ler	gel-di-ler

Table 5.11

		Hungarian *vár-* 'wait' Present Indefinite	Past Indefinite	Conditional Indefinite
Singular	1	vár-ok	vár-t-am	vár-n-ék
	2	vár-sz	vár-t-ál	vár-n-ál
	3	vár	vár-t	vár-n-a
Plural	1	vár-unk	vár-t-unk	vár-n-ánk
	2	vár-tok	vár-t-atok	vár-n-átok
	3	vár-*nak*	vár-t-*ak*	vár-n-*ának*

It is not important for our purposes precisely what Tense, Aspect or Mood properties are involved in the distinction between the various columns in Tables 5.10 and 5.11. What matters is that (except in the Hungarian Present) these properties are unambiguously realised immediately to the right of the root by an element (-*ir*- or -*di*- in Turkish, -*n*- or -*t*- in Hungarian) which is constant for all Persons and Numbers and therefore plays no part in realising any individual Person–Number combination.[5] These elements therefore count as principal exponents of Tense–Aspect–Mood, according to our definition; and the associated Person–Number endings, insofar as their variation in shape cannot be accounted for phonologically, display pure sensitivity. One does not need to delve deeply into Turkish or Hungarian phonology to determine that the sensitivity in question is indeed phonologically unaccountable, at least in part. For example, the contrast in the 1st Person

Plural between the -*iz* of Turkish *geliriz* and the -*k* of *geldik* cannot be plausibly accounted for either by positing a common phonological representation from which the different surface forms are derived by phonological rules, or by positing distinct underlying representations whose distribution is phonologically determined; rather, these are distinct realisations of 1st Person Plural whose distribution is determined by other morphosyntactic properties realised elsewhere in the word. The same may be said about the contrast between the Hungarian *várnának* 'they would wait' and *vártak* 'they waited'. One might argue whether the realisation of Conditional is underlyingly -*n*- (as suggested in Table 5.11), -*na*- or -*ná*- (i.e. /na:/); but the choice between these phonological analyses will not by itself account for the difference between the 3rd Plural endings -*(a)nak* in the Conditional and -*ak* in the Past. Rather, one must allow that there are distinct realisations for 3rd Person Plural which are sensitive to properties of Aspect, Mood or Tense, realised principally elsewhere.[6]

A further example of pure sensitivity can be found in Zulu, this time in nominal morphology.[7] In Table 5.12 I give a sample of Zulu nouns with the Class-prefix separated from the root by a hyphen, and in Table 5.13 I illustrate the possessive construction (with possessive prefixes italicised).

There is good evidence elsewhere in Zulu for a phonological contraction process changing /a + i/ to [e] and /a + u/ to [o] — a process which has parallels in the Romance languages and in Sanskrit. This suggests that we might derive the forms *womntwana, wezintombi* etc. in Table 5.13 from an underlying representation incorporating the 'basic' forms of the possessor nouns given in Table 5.14.

Table 5.12

Class		Singular	Plural	
	1/2	um-ntwana	aba-ntwana	'child'
	1a/2a	u-thisha	o-thisha	'teacher'
	3/4	um-nyango	imi-nyango	'door'
	5/6	i-qanda	ama-qanda	'egg'
	7/8	isi-hlalo	izi-hlalo	'seat'
	9/10	in-tombi	izin-tombi	'girl'
	11/10	u-thi	izin-ti	'stick'
	14	ubu-so	ubu-so	'face'
	15	uku-fa		'death'

Table 5.13

Class and Number of head noun:		
a. 3/4 Sg	umnyango *wo*mntwana	'the child's door'
5/6 Sg	iqanda *lo*mntwana	'the child's egg'
7/8 Sg	isihlalo *so*mntwana	'the child's seat'
11/10 Pl	izinti *zo*mntwana	'the child's sticks'
14 Sg/Pl	ubuso *bo*mntwana	'the child's face'
b. 3/4 Sg	umnyango *we*zintombi	'the girls' door'
5/6 Sg	iqanda *le*zintombi	'the girls' egg'
7/8 Sg	isihlalo *se*zintombi	'the girls' seat'
11/10 Pl	izinti *ze*zintombi	'the girls' sticks'
14 Sg/Pl	ubuso *be*zintombi	'the girls' faces'

Table 5.14

Class and Number of head noun:				
3/4 Sg	a.	wa + umntawana	b.	wa + izintombi
5/6 Sg		la + umntawana		la + izintombi
7/8 Sg		sa + umntawana		sa + izintombi
11/10 Pl		za + umntawana		za + izintombi
14 Sg/Pl		ba + umntawana		ba + izintombi

This analysis is supported by what we observe in constructions where the analogue of the possessor (*umntwana* or *izintombi* in Table 5.13) happens to begin with a consonant (e.g. when it is a locative expression), thus:

(504) a. phakathi (kwebhokisi) iqanda *la*phakathi (kwebhokisi)
       'inside (the box)'   'the egg inside (the box)'
    b. kwaZulu   izintombi *za*kwaZulu
       '(in) Zululand'   'the girls in Zululand'
    c. lapha 'here'   umnyango *wa*lapha
                               'the door here'

It is, in fact, usual to treat the first element in *laphakathi* (see (504a)) as a 'possessive concord' morphologically identical to the first element in *lomnyango* or *lezintombi* (see Table 5.13), and to analyse the underlying forms of the possessive concords for all the noun Classes as in Table 5.15.

Table 5.15

Class	Singular	Plural
1/2	wa-	ba-
1a/2a	wa-	ba-
3/4	wa-	ya-
5/6	la-	a-
7/8	sa-	za-
9/10	ya-	za-
11/10	lwa-	za-
14	ba-	ba-
15	kwa-	

So far, the relationships between morphosyntactic properties and their realisations here seem quite straightforward. Just as we would regard the -*a* of *piccola* 'little' in the Italian phrase *la piccola finestra* 'the little window' as realising the Gender property Feminine acquired in agreement with the head noun *finestra* 'window', so we can regard the *la*- of *laphakathi* in (504a) and underlyingly present in *lezintombi* in Table 5.13 (b) as realising the Class property 5/6. And just as we can draw up a Gender–Number paradigm for the Italian adjective *piccolo* as in Table 5.16, so we can draw up a Class–Number paradigm for a Zulu noun such as *intombi* 'girl' exhibiting all the possible possessive concords as in Table 5.17. No sensitivity is observable in the way the concordial properties are realised, so far; we have had to posit only a single set of prefixes, listed in Table 5.15. But consider now the concordial Class–Number paradigm for a Singular Class 1a noun such as *uthisha* 'teacher', shown in Table 5.18. The forms we would expect to see here, on the basis of Tables 5.15 and 5.17, are: Class 1/2 Sg *wothisha, Pl *bothisha, 7/8 Sg *sothisha and so on. The forms that we in fact find depart from what we would expect in two ways: firstly, the normal Class-prefix appropriate to Class 1a/2a Sg, namely *u*-, is replaced by *ka*-; secondly, the set of concords listed in Table 5.15 is replaced by a distinct set, as in Table 5.19.

Table 5.16

	Singular	Plural
Masculine	piccolo	piccoli
Feminine	piccola	piccole

Table 5.17

a. Possessor noun Singular (*intombi*)

Class of head noun:	Number of head noun: Singular	Plural
1/2, 1a/2a	wentombi	bentombi
3/4	wentombi	yentombi
5/6	lentombi	entombi
7/8	sentombi	zentombi
9/10	yentombi	zentombi
11/10	lwentombi	zentombi
14	bentombi	bentombi
15	kwentombi	

b. Possessor noun Plural (*izintombi*)

Class of head noun:	Number of head noun: Singular	Plural
1/2, 1a/2a	wezintombi	bezintombi
3/4	wezintombi	yezintombi
5/6	lezintombi	ezintombi
7/8	sezintombi	zezintombi
9/10	yezintombi	zezintombi
11/10	lwezintombi	zezintombi
14	bezintombi	bezintombi
15	kwezintombi	

Table 5.18

Class of head noun:	Number of head noun: Singular	Plural
1/2, 1a/2a	kathisha	bakathisha
3/4	kathisha	kathisha
5/6	likathisha	kathisha
7/8	sikathisha	zikathisha
9/10	kathisha	zikathisha
11/10	lukathisha	zikathisha
14	bukathisha	bukathisha
15	kukathisha	

There are clearly strong resemblances between the two sets of concords in Tables 5.15 and 5.19. Nevertheless, the choice between them is certainly not phonologically determined; there is no phonological reason, for example, why the Class 9/10 Plural concord should be *za-* in *izintombi zakwaZulu* 'the girls of Zululand' (see (504b)) but *zi-* in *izintombi zikathisha*

Table 5.19

		Singular	Plural
Class	1/2	∅	ba-
	1a/2a	∅	ba-
	3/4	∅	∅
	5/6	li-	∅
	7/8	si-	zi-
	9/10	∅	zi-
	11/10	lu-	zi-
	14	bu-	bu-
	15	ku-	

'the teacher's girls'. Clearly, there is sensitivity at work here. The realisation of the concordial Class properties is sensitive to whether or not the noun to which they are attached is Class 1a/2a Sg.

The time has come to consider whether there are any common features of the Latin, Turkish, Hungarian and Zulu phenomena which may point towards a generalisation. There is in fact a feature shared by nearly all the instances of sensitivity we have looked at, relating to the direction of the sensitivity which is displayed. In each instance, since the sensitivity is pure, the morphosyntactic property which triggers the allomorphy (property Q, in terms of our earlier discussion) has a principal exponent which is clearly distinguishable from the exponent of the property which displays sensitivity (property P). We can therefore ask about the order of these exponents relative to the root: is the exponent of P closer to the root than the exponent of Q, or vice versa? If there were no constraints affecting pure sensitivity, we would probably expect no consistency in the relative order of P and Q, so that our question would have no clear general answer. But examination of the data presented so far points to a high degree of consistency: Q is nearly always closer to the root than P. Thus, in Latin the 2nd Sg ending *-isti* triggered by the property Perfective is further from the root (or more peripheral) than the realisation of Perfective (cf. Table 5.9, (503)); in Turkish and Hungarian the relevant Person–Number markers are more peripheral than the Tense–Aspect–Mood markers that determine the choice between them (cf. Tables 5.10 and 5.11); and in Zulu the special set of possessive markers which occur with Singular nouns of Class 1a are more peripheral than the Class 1a marker itself, *ka-* (cf. Table 5.18).

Tentatively, then, let us assume that some constraint does operate here, and formulate it provisionally as follows:

(505) PERIPHERALITY CONSTRAINT (first formulation):
The realisation of a property may be sensitive inwards, i.e. to a property realised more centrally in the word-form (closer in linear sequence to the root), but not outwards, i.e. to a property realised more peripherally (further from the foot).

What light does this constraint shed on the implausible hypothetical paradigm in Table 5.6? In that paradigm, Tense is realised more centrally than Person. Yet the realisation of individual Tenses is sensitive to properties realised more peripherally (for short, 'more peripheral properties'), namely 1st Person, 2nd Person and 3rd Person. This contravenes directly the Peripherality Constraint as stated at (505). If the Constraint is broadly correct, therefore, we have an explanation for the implausibility of Table 5.6. Later in this chapter we will find reasons to revise our formulation of the Constraint, but the revision will not alter the Constraint's implication that Table 5.6 displays a pattern of inflexional sensitivity that could not occur in an actual language.

5.1.3 Peripherality and homonymy

Can we say, then, that 'inward' sensitivity — sensitivity of more peripheral properties to more central ones — is the only kind that exists, and that 'outward' sensitivity never occurs under any circumstances? The answer is no. But, before discussing a class of genuine counterexamples to the Peripherality Constraint in its present version, I will discuss a counterexample which is only apparent, involving systematic homonymy. Among the Latin data presented in Table 5.9 is the 1st Sg Imperfective Future form *regam*. This is analysed in (503) as containing a Future marker -*a*- and 1st Sg suffix -*m*. However, the Future marker that occurs in all other Persons is -*e*-;[8] consequently, the realisation of Future is sensitive to Person. Furthermore, -*m* realises 1st Sg unambiguously in a range of verb-forms, such as *rexeram* 'I had ruled', *rexissem* 'I had ruled (Subjunctive)', and so on; it is therefore a principal exponent of 1st Sg, and the sensitivity involved is pure. Yet, since the exponent of 1st Sg is more peripheral than that of Future, this example seems to contravene the proposed Peripherality Constraint.

The problem takes on a different complexion, however, if we include in the Latin data under consideration certain Imperfective Subjunctive and Passive forms:

Table 5.20

		Active Fut Indic	Pres Subjunc	Passive Fut Indic	Pres Subjunc
Sg	1	regam	regam	regar	regar
	2	regēs	regās	regēris	regāris
	3	reget	regat	regētur	regātur
Pl	1	regēmus	regāmus	regēmur	regāmur
	2	regētis	regātis	regēmini	regāmini
	3	regent	regant	regentur	regantur

We find here a consistent homonymy between the 1st Sg forms. As Table 5.20 shows, it applies in both the Active and the Passive. Moreover, it is a feature of Latin attested at all periods until periphrastic Future formations like *regere habeō* take over, whereas 'analogical' 1st Sg Future forms such as *regem* and *reger*, distinct from the Present Subjunctive forms, are exceedingly rare. The homonymy seems clearly systematic, therefore; and, in terms of Chapter 4, it is a take-over, consistent with the Systematic Homonymy Claim inasmuch as the morphosyntactic context (1st Singular) belongs to a pair of categories (Person—Number) which are lower in the relevance hierarchy than the categories of the neutralised properties (Tense, Mood). Somewhere in an adequate description of Latin grammar, therefore, must be represented the following fact:

(506)   In the third and fourth conjugations, Present Subjunctive takes over Future Indicative in the morphosyntactic context 1st Singular Imperfective.

The details of the representation do not matter, for present purposes. The essential point is that (506) is a statement about how the realisations of different property combinations are ordered in certain Latin word-forms, and not a statement about what these realisations actually are. (506) is therefore in one sense more abstract, or further removed from the actual surface shapes, than statements specifying the actual phonological representations of 'Present Subjunctive' or '1st Singular' in different contexts. This point is crucial, because it is only in connexion with statements of this second kind that questions of sensitivity can arise, and thus only to statements of this second kind that the Peripherality Constraint applies. In other words, in any word-form, the arrangement of morphosyntactic properties whose realisation must comply with the Peripherality Constraint is not what one might call the 'underlying' arrangement, but rather the arrangement which emerges from the enforcement of any language-particular specifications on syncretism or take-over.

How does this bear on the realisation of the property-combination 1st Sg Impf Fut Indic in association with the Latin third-conjugation verb-root *reg-*? The grammar of Latin will specify that the two relevant word-forms (Active and Passive) are subject to the take-over stated at (506), rendering them homonymous with the corresponding Present Subjunctive forms. This has the effect of ensuring that 1st Sg Impf Future Indicative forms are never spelt out, or related to their realisations, directly, but always indirectly, by way of the rules or statements which realise the 1st Sg Impf *Present Subjunctive*. So it is only the latter combination of properties which (in association with third and fourth conjugation verbs) ever has to run the gauntlet of the Peripherality Constraint; and it does so successfully, since no outward sensitivity is involved in the analysis of *regam* or *regar* when they are treated as Present Subjunctive forms. No special provision has to be made, therefore, to exempt the Future Indicative *regam* from the Peripherality Constraint; the fact that it is thus exempt follows directly, I suggest, from the way in which systematic homonymy within inflexional paradigms is to be accounted for. And the fact that, within our proposed framework of constraints, no special provision has to be made to account for the interaction of a constraint on Deviation II (the Peripherality Constraint) and a constraint on Deviation IV (the Systematic Homonymy Claim) provides an element of confirmation for the framework as a whole.

5.1.4 Outward sensitivity

Even if the apparent counterexample in Latin is taken care of, we still cannot say that all pure sensitivity complies with our present version of the Peripherality Constraint. The very facts that we considered earlier, concerning Zulu possessive concords, contain a clear prima facie example of outward sensitivity. The usual Singular prefix for Class 1a/2a is *u*-: *uthisha* 'teacher', *ubaba* 'my father', *udokotela* 'doctor'. But this *u*- is replaced by *ka*- just when the noun acquires a concordial Class property through participating in a possessive construction;[9] and, as Tables 5.18 and 5.19 show, if this concordial property receives an overt realisation (as it does for most Classes), this realisation is more, not less, peripheral than the -*ka*- which is apparently sensitive to it. I will now present two more examples of outward sensitivity, and then point out a shared feature which suggests a suitable way of amending the Peripherality Constraint. To anticipate: the amendment will involve a distinction between sensitivity to individual properties (like 1st Person) and sensitivity to whole categories (like Person).

One of these examples was mentioned as an instance of Deviation II at (112c) in Chapter 1. It involves the realisation of Plural in Hungarian nouns. Here, the usual Plural marker -*k* ~ -*ok* ~ -*ak*[10] is replaced by -*((j)a)i*- when a Personal Possession marker such as -*m* ~ -*om* ~ -*am* 'my' follows (see Table 5.21).

Table 5.21

Base	Unpossessed Plural	With 1st Singular Possessor: Singular	Plural
ruha 'dress'	ruhák	ruhám	ruháim (*not* *ruhákam)
kalap 'hat'	kalapok	kalapom	kalapjaim (*not* *kalapokam)
ház 'house'	házak	házam	házaim (*not* *házakam)

This characteristic of Hungarian — that the Plural suffix on nouns differs in shape according to whether a Possessive suffix follows or not — is evidently ancient and stable, since it is shared with the related but geographically far distant Ugric languages Ostyak and Vogul, which also display a similar variability in the suffix for the Dual, absent in Hungarian (Gulya 1966: 52, 58-63; Kálmán 1976: 29-32).

What I suggest is significant about both these instances of outward sensitivity, by contrast with typical examples of inward sensitivity, is their consistency. The peculiar Latin 2 Sg inflexion -*istī* is found with only one combination of Aspect, Tense, Mood and Voice; likewise, the Turkish 1st Pl suffix -*k* is found in the *di*-Past and not in other Tenses. On the other hand, the realisation -*ka*- for Class 1a/2a Sg in Zulu is found with not just one or two but with all Possessive concords. There is no logical necessity in this; one can perfectly well imagine a pseudo-Zulu identical with actual Zulu except that the Class 7/8 Sg Possessive form is '*sothisha*' (from underlying /sa + uthisha/) rather than the actual *sikathisha* presented in Table 5.18. And when we look at further Hungarian data, we find a similar pattern. Consider the facts about the marking of Number and Personal Possession on Hungarian nouns ((112c) and Table 5.21). In Table 5.21 I gave only examples where the Possessor was 1st Person Singular. Something new emerges if we look at a complete paradigm for Possession, Table 5.22.

Table 5.22

Possessor:			Singular	Plural	
	Sg	1	ruhám 'my suit'	ruháim 'my suits'	(cf. ruhák 'suits')
		2	ruhád	ruháid	
		3	ruhája	ruhái	
	Pl	1	ruhánk	ruháink	
		2	ruhátok	ruháitok	
		3	ruhájuk	ruháik	
	Sg	1	kalapom 'my hat'	kalapjaim 'my hats'	(cf. kalapok 'hats')
		2	kalapod	kalapjaid	
		3	kalapja	kalapjai	
	Pl	1	kalapunk	kalapjaink	
		2	kalapotok	kalapjaitok	
		3	kalapjuk	kalapjaik	

What I want to emphasise here is the fact that, although Plural is realised differently according to whether or not some marker of Possession is present, it is realised in the same way with all such markers. One could easily imagine a fictitious set of forms as in Table 5.23 (where individual fictitious forms are indicated by quotation marks):

Table 5.23

Possessor:	Sg	1	ruhák	kalapok
			ruháim	kalapjaim
		2	'ruhákod'	'kalapokod'
		3	ruhái	kalapjai
	Pl	1	ruháink	kalapjaink
		2	'ruhákotok'	'kalapokotok'
		3	ruháik	kalapjaik

In this fictitious set of forms, it is only with certain Possessors (namely, 1st and 3rd Person ones) that the realisation of Plural differs from its 'unpossessed' realisation. There is nothing implausible, in principle, about inconsistent outward sensitivity of this kind; we have already seen that, in Latin, only four of the six Person–Number combinations are realised differently with the Imperfective and Perfective Present, namely 1st Sg, 2nd Sg and Pl, and 3rd Pl — a clear instance of inconsistent sensitivity inwards. The fact that Hungarian does not display inconsistent sensitivity here could be a mere fact of Hungarian grammar, accidental from a general linguistic point of view. But the parallel with the Zulu state of affairs suggests it may be more than an accident.

Beja, a North Cushitic language of the Sudan and northern Ethiopia, behaves in one respect remarkably like Hungarian. As in Hungarian, there are six Personal Possessive suffixes which may be added to nouns (R.A. Hudson 1974: 123). Beja also has a set of three 'inseparable postpositions' meaning 'in, about', 'like', and 'from, by', which may be added to nouns with Genitive inflexion. Hudson calls these postpositions inseparable because they precede (and are thus, in my terminology, more central than) any Personal Possessive suffixes attached to the same noun. What is interesting about these three 'postpositions' is that, just like the Plural marker in Hungarian, they each have two allomorphs, the choice between them depending on whether a Possessive suffix follows. Thus, 'from, by' may be realised either -́- (that is, by an accent on the preceding vocalic mora) or -s-, the latter occurring if and only if there is a following Possessive suffix (preceded necessarily by a Case–Number suffix, which in this instance will be Accusative). Examples are:[11]

(507) a. ti- ʔoor-t- i-
the-girl-Fem-Gen-*from*
'from the girl'
b. ti- ʔoor-t- ii- s- oo-'k
the-girl-Fem-Gen-*from*-Acc-*your*(Sg)
'from your daughter'

(508) a. ti- huus- aa-t- e-´
the-knife-Pl-Fem- $\begin{Bmatrix} \text{Gen} \\ \text{Pl} \end{Bmatrix}$ -*from*
'from the knives'
b. ti- huus- aa-t- ee- s- ee- n
the-knife-Pl-Fem- $\begin{Bmatrix} \text{Gen} \\ \text{Pl} \end{Bmatrix}$ -*from*-Acc-*our*
'from our knives'

The important point here is that, as in Hungarian, all Possessive suffixes trigger just the same allomorphy.

On the basis of these examples, a promising amendment to our first formulation of the Peripherality Constraint at (505) might be one which does not rule out outward sensitivity altogether but which imposes a requirement of consistency on it. Here is a new version, with the alterations italicised:

(509) PERIPHERALITY CONSTRAINT (second formulation):
The realisation of a property may be sensitive inwards, i.e. to a property realised more centrally in the wordform (that is, closer in linear sequence to the root) but not outwards to *an individual* property realised more peripherally (further from the root). *It may, however, be sensitive outwards consistently to all the properties within a given category.*

This formulation squares with the Zulu, Hungarian and Beja facts cited; all involve outwards sensitivity, but only of the consistent kind permitted by (509).[12] The new formulation is clearly vulnerable to any actual instances of inconsistent outward sensitivity of the kind posited for pseudo-Zulu and pseudo-Hungarian above; but, until such instances are adduced, it may stand as a quite restrictive generalisation about pure sensitivity. Moreover, it has some, at first sight, rather unexpected consequences for syntactic analysis, as we will find in the next section.

5.1.5 Zero realisations and morphosyntactic zeros

The use of zero (particularly 'zero morphemes') in linguistic analysis was a live issue some years ago (Bloch 1947; Haas 1957) and is still not entirely dead (Kastowsky 1980). In connexion with the Peripherality Constraint, the issue arises because of certain aspects of both the Zulu and Hungarian facts already cited and certain further facts in Zulu and Turkish to be introduced presently.

Pure sensitivity, with which we are currently concerned, involves explicitly both a conditioned property (P) and a conditioning property (Q) with a distinct principal exponent. In a Zulu form such as *likathisha* '(Class 5/6 Sg) of the teacher' presented in Table 5.18, the Class 1a/2a Sg marker *-ka-* is clearly distinct from *li-*, the overt Possessive concord for (and principal exponent of) Class 5/6 Sg. But in the form *kathisha*, which occurs at a variety of places in the paradigm in Table 5.18, there is no overt Possessive concord, so that, strictly speaking, the sensitivity is not pure. The question therefore arises how we should interpret the proviso on outward sensitivity in the second formulation of the Peripherality Constraint: should it apply only where there is an overt realisation of the conditioning property, or should it apply whenever any property within the conditioning category is present, irrespective of whether that property has a separate overt realisation? The first interpretation imposes a less severe restriction on exponence than the second. In terms of the Zulu Possessive paradigm for *uthisha*, the first interpretation requires only that *-ka-* should consistently replace *u-* whenever one of the overt Possessive concords listed in Table 5.19, namely *ba-*, *li-*, *si-*, *zi-*, *lu-*, *bu-* or *ku-*, precedes. The second interpretation, however, requires that *ka-* should appear consistently throughout the Possessive paradigm. Clearly, it is desirable to choose the more restrictive interpretation, if possible; and in fact this is possible, so far as the Zulu facts are concerned.

When we look at the marking of Possession in Hungarian nouns, we find that the more restrictive interpretation can be sustained there too. In the paradigm in Table 5.22 there is one Plural form without any overt marking of Possessor, namely 3rd Sg; and here we find the same 'special' Plural suffix *-(a)i* as we find in those Persons with an overt Possessive suffix (*ruhái* 'his/her suits', *kalapjai* 'his/her hats'). So until further evidence forces us to abandon it, it seems reasonable to maintain the more restrictive interpretation.

This decision does, however, have a consequence for the controversy about zero morphemes. Is *kathisha* to be analysed as containing a zero prefix Ø as the exponent of Class 1/2 and so on, preceding (and thus more peripheral than) the prefix *ka-*? At first sight, this may seem arbitrary and artificial. Would it not be more straightforward to say that Class 1/2 Sg is not realised at all in the form *kathisha*, or else that its realisation is fused in *-ka-* with the realisation of *uthisha*'s own Class and Number, 1a/2a Singular? The difficulty with the first of these alternatives is that, if the Possessive concordial property is not realised anywhere in the word-form, that is tantamount to saying that it is morphologically irrelevant, so it is impossible for the realisation of the word's intrinsic Class and Number to be sensitive to it. The difficulty with the second alternative is that it would require us to amend the Peripherality Constraint so as to require consistent sensitivity not only to more peripheral properties within a given category but also to those properties within that category which are realised simultaneously with the conditioned property — a rather unnatural complication of the Constraint and, moreover, one which renders it excessively strong (as we shall see in section 5.1.8 below). The analysis which combines the strongest defensible restriction on outward sensitivity with the most straightforward formulation of the Peripherality Constraint is one which rejects both these alternatives in favour of recognising zero prefixes in Zulu forms such as *kathisha*; and an analogous argument can be constructed in favour of a zero 3rd Sg suffix in Hungarian forms such as *ruhái* and *kalapjai.*

The restrictive (or 'zeros-included') interpretation of the proviso on outward sensitivity has a potential advantage in syntactic analysis, too (although whether it has a practical advantage depends on whether data of the relevant kind present themselves). What I want to suggest is that, if the zeros-included interpretation is correct, then some imaginable combinations of syntactic and morphological behaviour which at first sight may seem quite plausible or innocuous are in fact impossible, and morphological evidence can in principle count in favour of one possible syntactic analysis over another in rather surprising ways.

Assuming the zeros-included interpretation, impossible combinations of morphological and syntactic behaviour would occur in situations in which there is conclusive syntactic evidence in favour of a certain property whose existence the Peripherality Constraint precludes. It is quite easy to devise an imaginary situation where such evidence exists. Let us imagine a language L with, prima facie, three Tenses (Past, Present and Future) limited to 'finite verbs', and a 'sequence of tenses' rule affecting the Tense of verbs in subordinate clauses embedded under certain main-clause verbs in the Past tense. (L might, in fact, resemble English, with its restrictions on Tense in 'reported speech'.) Because of this effect on subordinated verbs, there can be no doubt about the syntactic, as opposed to purely semantic, relevance of the property Past Tense. Let us suppose also, however, that L has two Aspects, Perfective and Imperfective, applicable not only to finite verbs but also to non-finite forms such as infinitives and participles; and that the realisation of the Perfective Aspect is sensitive to its grammatical context as illustrated in (510), which also shows the realisation of the Tenses:

(510) a. Sequence of realisation of categories:
Verb stem + Aspect (+ Tense)
b. Realisation of Aspect:
Imperfective -ba-
Perfective   -ka- in Tensed contexts
              -la- elsewhere
c. Realisation of Tense:
Present -ti
Past   ∅
Future   -mi

There are two points to note here. Firstly, there is no independent overt realisation of Past Tense, so its existence rests solely on the syntactic evidence. Secondly, the property Perfective is sensitive outwards, but this sensitivity is consistent with the zeros-included interpretation of the Peripherality Constraint because it is the same for all members of the category Tense. Consider now, however, a hypothetical language L' which differs from L superficially in only one small respect, namely that the realisation of the Perfective Aspect is as in (511) rather than (510):

(511) Realisation of Aspect:
Perfective -ka- in Present and Future contexts
            -la- elsewhere

The set of Perfective endings in the two languages will include the following respectively:

Table 5.24

	L	L'
Present	-kata	-kata
Future	-kami	-kami
Past	-ka	-la
	etc.	etc.

The zeros-included interpretation of the Peripherality Constraint requires us to analyse the Perfective Past suffix -*ka* in L as -*ka*-Ø, and the suffix -*la* in L' as -*la*-Ø. But under this analysis L' is in breach of the Peripherality Constraint, since different exponents of Perfective (-*ka*- and -*la*-) occur with different members of the more peripheral category Tense. The only way to reconcile the morphological behaviour of L' with the Peripherality Constraint is to posit a category Tense in L' containing only the two properties Present and Future, and no longer including Past. But this alternative runs directly counter to the syntactic facts which we have postulated for both L and L' (including sequence of tenses), which support conclusively the existence of a property Past. A consequence of the zeros-included interpretation, therefore, is that although L, as described, is a possible human language, L' is not, despite the apparently trivial nature of the difference between them.

In actual languages the facts (both morphological and syntactic) are likely to be less clear-cut than in our hypothetical examples, and the choice between competing analyses less obvious. It is this very fact, however, which makes the Peripherality Constraint (incorporating the restrictive, zeros-included, interpretation of the proviso on outward sensitivity) a potentially useful tool in syntactic analysis, as well as a strong generalisation about inflexion. Suppose the syntactician is hesitating between competing analyses, and one of these analyses crucially involves positing a morphosyntactic category C one of whose constituent properties (call it c_1) sometimes or always lacks an independent overt realisation. If some more central morphosyntactic property displays outward sensitivity, it will be of interest to check how this property is realised in those environments where property c_1 is purportedly present. If the realisation when c_1 is present differs from what it is when other properties c_2, c_3 etc. also purportedly belonging to C are present, then something is wrong with either the syntactic analysis in question or with the Peripherality Constraint as formulated.

The examples to which we will now turn, both involving outward sensitivity, point towards the recognition of a different kind of zero, not realisational but rather in the morphosyntactic representation. The Potential Mood in Turkish verbs (which can be glossed by English 'can', 'be able to') is usually realised by a suffix -*ebil*- (Table 5.25 below), to which the full range of Tense markers can be added:

Table 5.25

gel-dím	gel-ebil-dím
'I came'	'I was able to come'
gel-eceğ-im	gel-ebil-eceğ-im
'I will come'	'I will be able to come'
gel-ir-im	gel-ebil-ir-im
'I come (Aorist)'	'I can come'

But when the Negative suffix -*me*-/-*miy*- or the peculiar Negative Aorist forms ((113a) in Chapter 1) follow, the suffix -*ebil*- is replaced by -*e*-, as in Table 5.26.

Table 5.26

gél-me-dim	gel-é-me-dim (*not* *gel-ebíl-me-dim)
'I did not come'	'I could not come'
gél-miy-eceğ-im	gel-é-miy-eceğ-im (*not* *gel-ebíl-miy-eceğ-im)
'I will not come'	'I will not be able to come'
gel-mém	gel-é-mem (*not* *gel-ebíl-mém)
'I do not come (Aorist)'	'I cannot come'

173

So the property Potential is sensitive to the property Negative even though the property Negative is realised more peripherally.[13] Another example of outward sensitivity to the property Negative is provided by Zulu, and has already been mentioned at (111b) and (112a). Briefly, again, the usual Class 1 subject concord prefix on verbs, *u-*, is replaced by *-ka-* in Negative contexts; and the property Negative is generally realised separately by a prefix *a-*, preceding, and thus more peripheral than, the subject concord:

(512) a. u-   géz-   a   izin-   kómishi
         1/2-Sg-Subj wash   Pres-Act   9/10-Pl   cup
         'he is washing cups'
     b. a-   ká-   géz-   i   zin-   komishi[14]
         Neg 1/2-Sg-Subj   wash   Pres-Neg-Act 9/10-Pl   cup
         'he is not washing cups'

There is a problem in reconciling these facts with the Peripherality Constraint which relates to the way we handle the property Negative morphosyntactically.

We have assumed, with Matthews, that morphosyntactic properties (such as Accusative, Future) always belong to categories (such as Case, Tense); the possibility of a free-floating property outside any category is excluded by definition. As for the property Negative, a natural assumption is that it belongs to a category of Polarity which has two members, Negative and Positive. Positive has no clearly identifiable overt affixal realisation in either Turkish or Zulu; but, by analogy with our appeal to zero Possessive affixes in Zulu and Hungarian, we might posit a zero realisation for Positive in Turkish and Zulu verbforms occupying the same position as the overt Negative affix. A form such as *geldím* 'I came' will thus be analysed morphologically as *gel-Ø-dím*, parallel with *gél-me-dim* 'I did not come'; and *gelebildím* 'I was able to come' will be analysed as *gel-ebil-Ø-dim*, parallel with *gel-é-me-dim* 'I could not come' (cf. Tables 5.25 and 5.26). But this analysis immediately brings us into conflict with the Peripherality Constraint. Since both properties in the category Polarity have a realisation that is more peripheral than the realisation of the property Potential, the Peripherality Constraint requires that the property Potential should be sensitive in the same way to both; and, since all Turkish verb-forms without exception are either Negative or Positive, this amounts to saying that Potential can be realised in only one way. But this directly conflicts with the Turkish facts: Potential has two exponents, -*ebil*- and -*é*-. And a similar problem arises in Zulu if we assume that there is a zero prefix for Positive on a verb-form like *ugeza* 'he washes'.

The solution to this difficulty, I suggest, is to reject the assumption that Polarity in Turkish and Zulu is a two-member category. If instead we treat it as a single-member category containing only the property Negative, then the allomorphy that Negative triggers is compatible with the proviso on outward sensitivity in the Peripherality Constraint. In Turkish, the exponent -*é*- for Potential takes the place of -*ebil* in the context of all properties in the more peripheral category Polarity, namely the single property Negative; and in Zulu verbs the Class 1a/2a Sg Subject prefix is realised as -*ka*- instead of *u*- in just the same context. Instead of a realisational zero for Positive in these languages, then, our analysis posits what we might call a morphosyntactic zero; Positive simply does not occur in morphosyntactic representations. Single-member categories may seem odd, and at first sight it may appear preferable to drop our present ban on free-floating properties without any categorial allegiance. But this amounts to an otherwise unmotivated stipulation that the minimum number of properties in any category is two; besides, it will force us to complicate our formulation of the Peripherality Constraint further, so as to permit outward sensitivity to individual properties just when these properties belong to no category. Given that there is no good syntactic or morphological ground for denying the possibility of single-member categories, we can look at the Turkish and Zulu facts, in conjunction with the Peripherality Constraint, as simply confirming that such things exist.

5.1.6 A problem: inconstancy of sequence in realisation

We turn now to a problem in applying the revised Peripherality Constraint which is connected with the sequence of realisation of properties. In Table 5.7 and at (503) and (510) the existence of a heading entitled 'Sequence of realisation of the categories' implies that, whatever combination of properties from the various applicable categories is chosen, their sequence of realisation (or at least that of their principal exponents, if any) will be the same. This is indeed much the most frequent state of affairs, seemingly. If we examine a Latin Active verbal paradigm, we can broadly assign each of the categories Aspect, Tense, Mood, Person and Number to one of three positions, thus:

$$\text{Aspect} + \left\{ \begin{array}{c} \text{Mood} \\ \text{Tense} \end{array} \right\} + \left\{ \begin{array}{c} \text{Person} \\ \text{Number} \end{array} \right\}.$$

There is no combination of properties from these categories which exemplifies a different order of realisation,

$$\text{e.g.} \left\{ \begin{array}{c} \text{Mood} \\ \text{Tense} \end{array} \right\} + \text{Aspect} + \left\{ \begin{array}{c} \text{Person} \\ \text{Number} \end{array} \right\}.$$

On the other hand, in Huave, a language of the Isthmus of Tehuantepec in Mexico, the sequence of realisation of verbal properties such as 1st Person and Past Tense depends partly on the arbitrary conjugation-type to which the verb belongs and partly on the combinations in which they occur, irrespective of conjugation-type (Stairs & Hollenbach 1969). The question for us is: how does this variability affect the operation of our constraint on outward sensitivity? For example, if a property a is sensitive outwards to a property c_1 belonging to a category C, must a have the same exponent when accompanied by c_2 and c_3 also belonging to C even if c_2 and c_3 (unlike c_1) are more central than a? Our present formulation of the Peripherality Constraint imposes its requirement of consistency only where members of the conditioning category are unequivocally further from the root than the sensitive property. The question which arises is whether this formulation is restrictive enough. The discussion here will illustrate some of the considerations involved, although I will not be suggesting a definite answer.

The verbal morphology of Huave involves a considerable amount of sensitivity, including some outward sensitivity. The discussion will be inconclusive, however, partly because the relevant contrasts in order of realisation involve not just permutation of prefixes or suffixes on one side or other of the root but permutation around the root, and partly because of difficulty in identifying principal exponents, since much of the sensitivity involved is not pure. The first set of data that I will present, Table 5.27, consists of some partial Tense paradigms belonging to the most productive conjugation-type; italics are used to highlight the affixes which Stairs & Hollenbach construe as exponents of 1st Person:

Table 5.27

	-*ndeak* 'speak' Indicative:			Subordinate:
	Present	Past	Future	
Person: 1	*sa*-ndeak	t-a-ndeak-*as*	sa-*na*-ndeak	*na*-ndeak 'that I speak'
2	i-ndeak	t-e-ndeak, t-i-ndeak	ap-me-ndeak, ap-mi-ndeak	me-ndeak
3	a-ndeak	t-a-ndeak	ap-ma-ndeak	ma-ndeak

Stairs & Hollenbach analyse the property 1st Person as realised by the prefix *sa-* in the Present Indicative, by *na-* in the Future Indicative and Subordinate, and by the suffix *-as* in the Past Indicative. This realisation seems to involve outward sensitivity, in that the property Future which triggers the realisation *-na-* for 1st Person is realised more peripherally, not more centrally. Since Future is the only Tense with a more peripheral realisation, the fact that it constitutes the sole context for the *-na-* allomorph of 1st Person is compatible with our present version of the Peripherality Constraint, but would seem to argue against tightening it up in such a way as to require consistent realisation of 1st Person in all Tense contexts. But there is a complicating factor. The sensitivity displayed by the 1st Person in the Future is not pure, since the element *sa-*, which Stairs & Hollenbach regard as being, in effect, the exponent of Future only, appears not to occur with any other Person; so in the form *sanadeak* 'I will speak', one could, on the face of it, regard *sa-* as an exponent of 1st Person just as much as *-na-* is.[15]

The best reason for not doing so, and for following Stairs & Hollenbach in locating the realisation of Person in the second of the two prefixes, seems to come from comparing the Future with the Subordinate forms: the former look as if they are derived from the latter by the addition of a prefix (*sa-* or *ap-*), which can therefore perhaps be legitimately regarded as realising only the property Future (albeit in inwardly sensitive fashion).[16] But this analysis at the same time points towards a distinction between Future on the one hand and Present and Past on the other, in that neither Present nor Past has any special morphological connexion with the Subordinate forms of the verb — a distinction which casts some doubt on the validity of the three-member category Tense implied in Table 5.27. The upshot is that, whether or not *-na-* is the sole exponent of 1st

Person in the Future form *sanandeak*, the fact that the 1st Person Past is *tandeakas* rather than, say, **tandeakna* may have no relevance for any constraint on outward sensitivity.

Examination of apparent instances of outward sensitivity in the 2nd and 3rd Person forms is equally inconclusive, even when we bring more data into consideration. One of the minority conjugation-types in Huave is one in which Past Tense and all Person markers are consistently suffixed rather than prefixed. In this conjugation, the forms corresponding to those in Table 5.27 (except for the Subordinate forms, which apparently have no distinct morphological parallel in this type) are given in Table 5.28.

Table 5.28

witïi- 'stand up'

Person:	Present	Past	Future
1	witïi-n	witïi-t-os	ap-witïi-n
2	witïi-r	witïi-t-ear	ap-witïi-r
3	witïi-m	witïi-t	ap-witïi-m

By themselves, the forms in Table 5.28 seem to indicate inward but no outward sensitivity, in that the Personal endings in the Past are different from those in the Present and Future. But two points stand out when we compare Table 5.28 with Table 5.27. Firstly, there is a suffixed -*t*- in the Past Tense in 5.28 which seems to correspond to the prefixed *t*- in 5.27. Secondly, although the realisation of 2nd and 3rd Person always follows that of Past Tense, the fact that both are prefixed in Table 5.27 but suffixed in Table 5.28 means that any sensitivity on the part of 2nd Person to Past Tense will be outward in paradigms of the kind illustrated in Table 5.27 but inward in Table 5.28. A potentially interesting question, then, is whether the realisation of 2nd Person is in fact sensitive outwards in the paradigm in Table 5.27 and, if so, whether the same realisation occurs in 5.28. At first sight, there is indeed outward sensitivity in 5.27, in that 2nd Person has three distinct realisations -*i*-, -*e*- and -*me*-, the choice between which is determined by the more peripheral category Tense; moreover, the affix -*ear* which realises 2nd Person in the Past Tense in 5.28 differs from all of these, and particularly from the -*e*- which appears in the Past Tense in

5.27. But things are not so simple. If the Future Tense -*me*- in 5.27 is explicable as derived from the Subordinate Mood, or if we segment the form *apm-e-* or *ap-m-e-* rather than *ap-me-*,[17] then it is only the alternation between -*e*- and *i*- which is at issue. Here we do indeed seem to have outward sensitivity, and indeed of a kind incompatible with the zeros-included interpretation of the Peripherality Constraint as stated at (509), in that a different realisation occurs in the 'zero-marked' Present Tense from the other Tenses. But the facts themselves are somewhat more complex than so far described, in that forms with -*i*- such as *tindeak* 'you spoke' and *apmindeak* 'you will speak' apparently occur in some idiolects instead of *tendeak* and *apmendeak* (Stairs & Hollenbach 1969: 44 note 11). Stairs & Hollenbach do not say which, if either, of these two alternatives is spreading at the expense of the other, nor whether the Subordinate 2nd Person *mendeak* has a similar variant with -*i*-; but, given the constraints on sensitivity so far proposed, it is tempting to see the -*i*- variants as part of a regularising innovation to remove potentially 'illegal' instances of outward sensitivity.[18] And, finally, if there is after all no outward sensitivity in the 2nd Person forms of the prefix conjugation in Table 5.27, they can have no bearing on the general question of how constraints on outward sensitivity operate when the order of realisation of categories is not constant.

Our discussion of the Huave example has been inconclusive. In view of the comparative rarity of this kind of variation in order and the difficulty of finding data which tell unequivocally in favour of one version or another of the Peripherality Constraint, I will not continue the search for any more definite conclusions here. But I have, I hope, succeeded in illustrating the sort of considerations which will be relevant. Languages which it will be interesting to examine in future from this point of view, I suggest, are Mari (or Cheremiss) and those other Uralic languages in which the markers of Number, Case and Personal Possession on nouns appear in different orders according to the particular combinations involved (Comrie 1981: 120).

5.1.7 A second problem: phonological sensitivity outwards

In section 1.4, I distinguished between grammatically (or morphologically) conditioned allomorphy, which is the type of sensitivity with which we are mainly concerned, and phonologically conditioned allomorphy; and I argued that recognising an alternation as phonologically conditioned need not commit one to any particular view of the phonological representations of the alternants. One illustration of this I drew from the larger and more productive of the verbal conjugation-types in modern Hungarian. There, the two 2nd Person Singular Present Indicative Indefinite inflexions *-(a)sz* and *-ol* were deemed not to be rivals because their distribution depended entirely on phonological characteristics of the verb stem; *-ol* attaches to sibilants and affricates and *-(a)sz* occurs elsewhere. Phonologically conditioned alternations of this kind seem to be especially common in Australian languages; for example, the Ergative affix in Dyirbal has a variety of shapes depending on phonological characteristics of the stem to which it is attached (Dixon 1972: 42), while in Warlpiri (see Table 1.1(e)) it is *-ngku* after disyllabic stems and *-rlu* [-ɭu] after stems of three or more syllables (Dixon 1980: 306)

Establishing the phonological conditions for this kind of alternation has not been particularly important from the point of view of inward sensitivity, because no constraint on sensitivity in this direction has so far been proposed. But with outward sensitivity the position is different. Given that we are exploring the imposition of quite tight restrictions on outward sensitivity, the question arises: are there any instances of prima facie outward sensitivity which do not comply with the Peripherality Constraint but which are explicable in phonological terms? I will first describe two sets of data, in Zulu and Turkish, where this sort of outward phonological sensitivity seems plausible. They do not provide conclusive evidence, however, because an account in terms of straightforward morphological sensitivity consistent with the revised Peripherality Constraint is not self-evidently wrong; but discussion of them will illustrate the sort of considerations that are relevant. I will then mention some facts in Fulfulde which seem to constitute stronger evidence for outward phonological sensitivity.

In Zulu, the Locative inflexion on nouns consists of a prefix *e-, o-* or *ku-* with or without a suffix *-ni,* as shown in Table 5.29 (Doke 1973: 232-9). But when either *e-* or *o-* is preceded by one of a number of prefixes, an *-s-* intervenes, as in (513).

SYNTAGMATIC CONSTRAINTS ON ALLOMORPHY

Table 5.29

		Locative
umfula	'river'	emfuleni
indlu	'house'	endlini
uThukela	'Tugela River'	oThukela
izingubo	'blankets'	ezingutsheni
umuntu	'person'	kumuntu
abantu	'people'	kubantu

(513) a. With Possessive concord:
  emfuleni   indlu yasemfuleni
  'at the river' 'the house at the river'
 b. With Predicative concord:
  endlini   abantu basendlini
  'in the house' 'the people are in the house'
 c. With conjunctive prefix *na-* 'and'
  otshanini nasezingutsheni
  'on the grass and on the blankets'
 d. With *nga-* 'near' and certain other 'adverbial formatives' (in Doke's terminology):
  oThukela   ngasoThukela
  'at the Tugela River' 'near the Tugela River'

The problem is how to characterise the environments in which this -*s*- occurs. Let us assume, to begin with, that the -*s*- 'belongs to' the Locative affix rather than to the element which precedes it. One possible complication is that some of the environments seem to involve proclitic elements rather than inflexions, e.g. (513d). But even supposing that this aspect can be dealt with satisfactorily, the question remains whether the inflexional environments can be analysed exhaustively in terms of morphosyntactic categories; for if the -*s*- occurs after a prefix realising property c_1 in category C but not after the prefixes realising other properties belonging to C, then we have a prima facie counterexample to the Peripherality Constraint. In fact, so far as the Possessive and Predicative concords are concerned (513a, b), the Peripherality Constraint is complied with: the -*se*- and -*so*- alternants of the Locative prefix are found wherever any of these concords (all of which are 'non-zero') precedes. But all these concords share a phonological characteristic with the apparently non-inflexional prefixes of (513c) and

181

(513d): they end in a vowel. It therefore seems plausible to account for the distribution of the Locative alternants with and without -*s*- purely phonologically; the former occur after a vowel within the same 'phonological word', the latter elsewhere. This is the same kind of explanation as Dixon gives for the Ergative -*ngku* and -*rlu* in Warlpiri, the only difference being that the phonological conditioning factor in Zulu is more peripheral, not more central.

The 3rd Person Possessive affix (or 'izafet') of Turkish furnishes a possible example of phonological conditioning in both directions, although, as I shall argue, the outward sensitivity is better accounted for grammatically than phonologically. We will ignore for present purposes the four-fold vowel harmony to which this and many other Turkish derivational and inflexional affixes are subject; to simplify matters, I will use only examples involving the front unrounded vowel *i* [i]. Even with this restriction, we find four alternants of the izafet, as in (514):

(514) a. -*i*: e.g. ev 'house'; ev-*i* 'his house'
rehber 'guide'; telefon rehber-*i*
'telephone directory'

b. -*in*: e.g. ev-*in*-de 'in his house'
Loc
telefon rehber-*in*-i kaybettim
Acc
'I've lost the telephone directory'

c. -*si*: e.g. bahçe 'garden'; bahçe-*si* 'her garden'
cadde 'main road'; İstiklâl Cadde-*si*
'Independence Street'

d. -*sin*: e.g. bahçe-*sin*-e 'for her garden'
Dat
İstiklâl Cadde-*sin*-den geldik
Abl
'We've come from Independence Street'

We can describe this inflexion as consisting of -*i*- preceded or not by -*s*- and followed or not by -*n*-. The question now is: under what conditions do this -*s*- and this -*n*- appear?

Comparing (514a, b) with (514c, d), we notice that the -*s*-

appears with the vowel-final stems *bahçe* and *cadde* but not with the consonant-final ones *ev* and *rehber*. This points to a generalisation which is in fact almost without exception in Turkish. Yet the alternation between -*i(n)*- and -*si(n)*- cannot be explained in terms of any general phonological rules or processes in Turkish such as 'postconsonantal *s*-dropping' or 'intervocalic *s*-insertion'; there are plenty of examples of postconsonatal *s*, both with and without morpheme boundary intervening (e.g. *aksi* 'perverse', *insaf* 'justice', *geliyor-sun* 'you are coming'), and nominal inflexion provides examples of both -*y*- and -*n*- as well as -*s*- serving to separate vowels, depending on the forms concerned (see Table 5.30).

Table 5.30

	ev 'house'	bahçe 'garden'
3rd Sg Poss	ev-i	bahçe-si
Genitive	ev-in	bahçe-nin
Accusative	ev-i	bahçe-yi

The endings -*i(n)* and -*si(n)*, therefore, cannot plausibly be derived from the same phonological representation; rather, they seem to provide another example of phonologically distinct inflexional variants whose distribution is conditioned by phonological factors more central in the word.

It is not so clear whether the distribution of -*(s)i* and -*(s)in* is likewise phonologically governed. The examples in (514b, d) demonstrate that the occurrence of the *n* is not restricted to contexts where a vowel follows. What Lewis (1967: 40) says is that '*n* appears between the suffix of the third person and any case-suffix', that is any of the suffixes listed (in their unrounded front-vowel forms only) in Table 5.31.

Table 5.31

Accusative	-(y)i
Genitive	-(n)in
Dative	-(y)e
Locative	-de / -te
Ablative	-den / -ten

It is certainly true that when -*(s)i(n)*- precedes an element outside this list, such as -*(y)le* 'with', the cliticised version of the postposition *ile*, it is the *n*-less form which appears, e.g. *bahçe-si-yle* 'with his garden' like *bahçe-yle* 'with a garden', not **bahçe-sin-le* like *rehber-le* 'with a guide'. It seems very plausible, therefore, that what we have here is an instance of morphological outward sensitivity, whereby an alternant with -*n*- of the 3rd Sg Poss suffix is chosen just where any overt inflexion of Case follows. This sensitivity complies even with the zeros-included interpretation of the Peripherality Constraint, since there are grounds for not regarding the endingless 'Absolute' or 'Nominative' as a member of the category Case in Turkish alongside the properties listed in Table 5.31, in contrast with the Nominative in Finnish (see section 5.1.8 below).

What may give us pause, however, is the fact that the endings listed in Table 5.31 are also the last items in a Turkish noun which are stressable, and thus, since most Turkish nouns are stressed as near the end as possible, they do generally carry the stress. This means that an alternative account of the distribution of -*(s)i* and -*(s)in* might refer to stress; specifically, that -*(s)in*- is always unstressed and always immediately precedes a stressed syllable. This account loses most of its plausibility, however, when we note what happens with the large minority of nouns which are stressed elsewhere than on the final syllable in the basic form and which retain this non-final stress when carrying Possessive and Case affixes. If the 'stress theory' of -*(s)i* and -*(s)in* were correct, we would expect these nouns to select the *n*-less alternant even when inflected for Case, because the Case-ending immediately following would be unstressed (or at any rate would not bear the primary stress). For example, whereas *bahçé* 'garden' forms *bahçe-sin-dén* 'from his garden', with the final affix stressed, in contrast to *bahçe-si-yle* 'with his garden', we might expect *téyze* 'aunt' to form not only *téyze-si-yle* 'with his aunt' but also **téyze-si-den* 'from his aunt'. But, in fact, *téyze* inflects just like *bahçé*, despite the difference in stress pattern: we find *téyze-sin-den* 'from his aunt' just like *bahçe-sin-dén* 'from his garden'. Without a more thorough examination of Turkish phonology, particularly of secondary stress, it would be unwise to rule out entirely an account of the -*(s)i*/-*(s)in* alternation in terms of phonological conditioning; but for the time being at least the explanation in terms of outward sensitivity to the category Case seems more attractive. My main purpose in discussing these Turkish and Zulu data, however, has not been to reach any definitive conclusion but to illustrate the sort of arguments which might lead one to postulate a kind of outward sensitivity which is phonological rather than morphosyntactic and which is thus outside the scope of the Peripherality Constraint.

Some much less equivocal instances of outward phonological sensitivity can be found in Fulfulde (also known as Fula or Fulani), a language of the Sahel region of west Africa. Verbal morphology in this language is complex, involving a large number of distinct 'Tenses' (where 'Tense' is an ad hoc label subsuming combinations of several categories, including Mood, Voice and Aspect; the details are not important here). Inflected verb-forms (or 'verbal complexes', in the terminology of Arnott (1970) and McIntosh (1984)) generally contain markers of subject and (if transitive) object, and sometimes also an 'anteriority marker'[19] -*no*- or -*noo*- indicating priority in time relative to some other event; what is more, the order in which the subject and object markers appear relative to each other, to Tense affixes and to the anteriority marker varies from one Tense to another and also within Tenses, according to the particular combination of elements in question. What is important for our present purposes, however, is that several suffixes have two alternants, one with a long vowel and one with a short vowel (Arnott 1970: 219, 224-5):

(515) a. Anteriority marker   noo ~ no
       b. Relative Past Passive   aa ~ a
       c. Relative Past Middle   ii ~ i

Examples of these alternations (taken, in fact, not from the Gombe dialect described by Arnott but from the similar Southern Zaria dialect described by McIntosh) are:

(516) a. ᶁume ngad-ay- *noo*- 'on?
          what do- Incompletive-Anterior-you (Pl)
              Active
          'What were you (Pl) going to do?'
       b. ᶁume ngad-ay- *no*- daa?
          what do- Incompletive-Anterior-you (Sg)
          'What were you (Sg) going to do?'

185

(517) a. Tokoye suud́-*aa*- 'on?
            where hide-Passive-you (Pl)
            'Where were you (Pl) hidden?'
       b. Tokoye suud́-*a*- daa?
            where hide-Passive-you (Sg)
            'Where were you (Sg) hidden?'

(518) a. Moye njaaf- *ii*- mi?
            whom forgive-Middle-I
            'Whom did I forgive?'
       b. Moye njaaf- *i*- noo- mi?
            whom forgive-Middle-Anterior-I
            'Whom had I forgiven?'

Now, what determines the distribution of the long and short forms?

The Tense suffixes *aa* ~ *a* and *ii* ~ *i* are subject to a generalisation which Arnott states as follows (1970: 225): 'The *shorter* form occurs regularly when there is a subsequent [i.e. more peripheral] long-vowelled element within the complex ... The *longer* form occurs in all other complexes.' With the Anteriority marker *noo* ~ *no* the situation is apparently more complex, since the choice seems to be partly determined by the Tense (1970: 219); but in Tenses belonging to what Arnott calls 'Group B' (Relative Past and Relative Future) the conditioning factor is exactly the same as for *aa* ~ *a* and *ii* ~ *i*: 'the *short-vowelled* form -*no* is used whenever the [Anteriority marker] *is followed by a long-vowelled element within the complex* [Arnott's emphasis]', while the long-vowelled form is found elsewhere. There seems, in fact, to be a general requirement in both the Gombe and Southern Zaria dialects that not more than one long vowel may occur in any verbal complex after the root, and a kind of suffixal precedence hierarchy determines which vowel will win out when a potential clash arises (McIntosh 1984); but, for us, what matters is that the resolution of some clashes involves the phonological sensitivity of one element to a more peripheral one.

An even more interesting Fulfulde example involves what Arnott (1970: 250) calls the Habitual Imperative Singular suffix, -*atay*, found in forms such as *doggatay* 'keep on running!' *wallatay-mo* 'keep on helping him!'. As the second example illustrates, an object-marking suffix such as 3rd Person

Sg -*mo* may follow the Imperative suffix. Imperative forms may in fact be marked suffixally for all Personal objects except 2nd Person (i.e. reflexive) ones. But when we examine all the possible Habitual Imperative Singular forms with suffixal object marking in the Southern Zaria dialect, we find an apparent instance of outward sensitivity in the 1st Sg form (McIntosh, personal communication) as shown in Table 5.32.

Table 5.32

	wall-atay-ɓe	'keep on helping them!'
	wall-atay-min	'keep on helping us!'
	wall-atay-mo	'keep on helping him!'
but:	wall-at-am	'keep on helping me!'

Clearly, unless this outward sensitivity can be shown to be phonological, it constitutes a counterexample to the Peripherality Constraint, since we observe two forms, -*atay*- and -*at*-, each of which occurs with different members of the one category Personal Object. But there is in fact evidence for calling this sensitivity phonological, not morphological. The suffix -*am* is the only one of the four Personal Object suffixes in Table 5.32 which begins with a vowel; and one finds elsewhere in the Fulfulde verbal system alternations governed by whether the following suffix is consonant-initial or vowel-initial. There is another vowel-initial object suffix, the 2nd Sg marker -*e* (which, as already mentioned, is not found with Imperatives); and both -*am* and -*e*, as realisations of 1st and 2nd Object, are in complementary distribution with consonant-initial alternants, namely -*yam* and -*ma* (or -*maa*) respectively. Which realisation will be chosen for each Person depends on the Tense, realised more centrally; and the Gombe and Southern Zaria dialects seem to differ in the selection which certain Tenses impose. What is important for our present purpose, however, is that several Tenses have special realisations in the presence of the two vowel-initial suffixes. For example, in what Arnott calls the General Future Active Tense, the -*am* and -*e* alternants of 1st and 2nd Sg Object are chosen in the Southern Zaria dialect; and it is precisely with these suffixes that the usual Tense suffix -*ay*- is replaced by a suffix -*Vt*-, the quality of the vowel being determined by that of the following syllable,[20] as in Table 5.33.

Table 5.33

	'o-wall-ay-min	'he will help us'
	'o-wall-ay-'on [-ʔon]	'he will help you (Pl)'
	'o wall-ay-ɓe	'he will help them'
	'o-wall-ay-mo	'he will help him/her'
but:	'o wall-at-am	'he will help me'
	'o-wall-et-e	'he will help you (Sg)'

In this Tense, it is just those two forms in which the Object suffix begins with a vowel that are the 'odd men out'. This fact supports the idea that, both here and in Table 5.32, what the Tense markers are sensitive to is indeed a phonological characteristic of certain of the Object suffixes rather than the morphosyntactic properties which these suffixes realise.[21]

What makes this last Fulfulde example especially interesting is the complexity of the realisation process that it seems to involve. The realisation of the Personal Objects is sensitive inwards to morphosyntactic properties of Tense or Mood; but the realisation of these properties is in turn determined partly phonologically by reference to the shapes of the more peripheral Personal suffixes. All this is quite compatible with the Peripherality Constraint, since only phonological, not morphosyntactic, sensitivity 'outwards' is involved. Behaviour such as this must pose severe problems for theories which treat inflexional affixation as a process of accretion, working outwards from the centre to the periphery (e.g. Kiparsky 1982b; Anderson 1982); but since we are not attempting here to develop a formal framework for inflexional description, we can leave these problems on one side.

5.1.8 The Peripherality Constraint and Deviation III

So far, in accordance with the plan announced at the start of the chapter, we have discussed Deviation II so far as possible in isolation from the other three types of deviation from maximally simple 'one-to-one' morphological patterning. I want to touch now on the interaction between the Peripherality Constraint and Deviation III, and thereby show how the Constraint may be reconciled with some apparent counterevidence from Finnish.

Let us consider again the two Finnish nominal paradigms which we discussed from the point of view of homonymy in section 4.2.6. I set them out again here for convenience.

Table 5.34

	Sg	Pl	Sg	Pl
Nominative	pöytä 'table'	pöydät	tehdas 'factory'	tehtaat
Genitive	pöydän	pöytien	tehtaan	tehtaiden
Partitive	pöytää	pöytiä	tehdasta	tehtaita
Essive	pöytänä	pöytinä	tehtaana	tehtaina
Translative	pöydäksi	pöydiksi	tehtaaksi	tehtaiksi
Inessive	pöydässä	pöydissä	tehtaassa	tehtaissa
Elative	pöydästä	pöydistä	tehtaasta	tehtaista
Illative	pöytään	pöytiin	tehtaaseen	tehtaisiin
Adessive	pöydällä	pöydillä	tehtaalla	tehtailla
Ablative	pöydältä	pöydiltä	tehtaalta	tehtailta
Allative	pöydälle	pöydille	tehtaalle	tehtaille
Abessive	pöydättä	pöydittä	tehtaatta	tehtaitta
Comitative		pöytine[22]		tehtaine
Instructive		pöydin		tehtain

The feature which I want to concentrate on this time is the -*i*- which appears in nearly all Cases of the Plural. In most Cases where Singular and Plural are distinguished (i.e. excluding the Comitative and Instructive), the Plural form differs from the Singular only in having an -*i*- immediately preceding the Case ending, where the Singular has -*a*- or -*ä*- [æ]; and even where the difference is greater than this, as in the Partitive, Illative and (for *tehdas*) Genitive, the -*i*- still appears in the Plural form. There therefore seems good ground for calling -*i*-, in my terminology, a principal exponent of Plural. But the -*i*- is lacking in the Nominative Plural (*pöydät, tehtaat*). Must we then say that this is an instance of outward sensitivity? And, if so, unless we can show that 'Nominative' is not a member of the category to which all the other Cases belong, is this not the sort of outward sensitivity that the Peripherality Constraint is supposed to forbid? The answer that I propose involves distinguishing pure sensitivity from the kind of sensitivity implicit in all instances of overlapping exponence.

In the Nominative Plurals *tehdaat* and *pöydät*, not only do we find no element corresponding to the usual exponent of Plural; there is no element specifically identifiable with the Nominative either, since the Nominative Singular lacks any consistent exponent parallel to, say, the Inessive -*ssa*/-*ssä*, and among the affixes that one might plausibly consider exponents of it (e.g. -*nen*, -*s*), -*t* does not appear. So there is no ground for segmenting the endings of *tehtaat* or *pöydät* into a Plural element and a Nominative element. There are therefore two alternative ways of analysing the inflexion in the forms *tehtaat* and *pöydät*: either (a) it realises just one of the two properties Nominative and Plural, the other being realised by zero, or (b) it realises both properties in overlapping fashion. Let us consider first alternative (a). No one has ever seriously proposed treating the -*t* as a marker of Nominative only, with Plural as zero, and I cannot see any argument in favour of that analysis. On the other hand, it is quite common to find it said in descriptions of Finnish (or of Uralic languages generally) that there is no Nominative 'morpheme' or even, in more abstract terms, no Nominative Case (in contrast, to, say, Latin). Now, if we take 'no Nominative morpheme' to mean in our terms 'no morphosyntactic property Nominative belonging to the category Case', then the Finnish facts are perfectly consistent with the Peripherality Constraint; for then the 'Nominative' forms do not properly speaking belong at all in the Case–Number paradigm presented in Table 5.34, and, once we remove them, we are left with only one principal exponent of Plural, namely -*i*-. If, on the other hand, we take 'no Nominative morpheme' to mean 'no overt realisation of the property Nominative', then we do indeed have a prima facie counterexample to the revised Peripherality Constraint with the restrictive 'zeros-included' interpretation of the proviso on outward sensitivity. This is because we have a property (Plural) which is sensitive outwards to Case and which, though realised in the same way with all 'non-zero' Cases, is realised differently with the one 'zero' Case, namely Nominative.

It seems, then, that, if analysis (a) of the Finnish 'Nominative Plural' is correct under this second interpretation, we have found some evidence against our more restrictive hypothesis on outward sensitivity. But I will argue that it is analysis (b), involving overlapping exponence, which is correct; moreover, that instances of overlapping exponence can and should be treated as irrelevant to the Peripherality Constraint.

When we discussed outward sensitivity in relation to the Hungarian and Zulu data, we assumed tacitly that, if a property such as 'Plural' or 'Class 1a/2a Singular' were realised differently with overt and 'zero' members of some more peripheral category C, the realisation found with 'zero' members would be what one might call the 'ordinary' realisation typical of contexts where no category C property was present. Thus, for the 'zero-prefixed' members of the Possessive paradigm of *u-thisha*, presented in Table 5.18, we discussed the implications of only two realisational possibilities: -*kathisha* (the actual realisation) and *uthisha* itself. We did not discuss any third conceivable realisation — say, **tathisha*. But this was not a careless omission, because the two alternatives that we did discuss are the only ones relevant to pure sensitivity. A hypothetical third prefix such as **ta-*, differing from both the 'ordinary' and the post-prefixal alternants of the Class 1a/2a marker, could no longer be regarded legitimately as an exponent of Class 1a/2a displaying pure sensitivity to a zero-marked Possessive concord located elsewhere in the word-form; rather, we would have to regard it as a simultaneous exponent of both class 1a/2a Sg and of the Possessive concord itself. That is, in a hypothetical form **ta-thisha*, the realisation of 'Class 1a/2a Sg' is sensitive neither to a more peripheral overt property nor to a 'zero-marked' property belonging to a category other members of which are realised more peripherally, but rather to a property which is realised entirely simultaneously with it, neither more peripherally nor more centrally. Consequently, **ta-thisha* does not constitute a counterexample to the Peripherality Constraint, simply because the proviso on outward sensitivity does not 'bite' on it at all.

What is the relevance of all this to our Finnish example? Simply that the Nominative Plurals *tehtaat* and *pöydät* are in relevant respects similar to the hypothetical Zulu form **tathisha*. The -*t* of *tehtaat* is certainly an exponent of Plural; but it must be regarded as an exponent of Nominative too, since it is precisely the property Nominative which triggers the realisation -*t* rather than -*i*-. To say, as analysis (a) requires, that the -*t* realises Plural but not Nominative involves a quite arbitrary discrimination between the two properties which jointly identify the place in the paradigm where the -*t* appears. So here, too, we have a property (Plural) sensitive neither to an overtly marked more peripheral Case nor to zero-marked one, but rather to a Case realised entirely simultaneously with it. This amounts to saying that, if we reject the first version of analysis

(a) (according to which there is no morphosyntactic property 'Nominative' at all in Finnish), we are led inescapably to analysis (b), to which, since it involves completely simultaneous exponence, the condition on outward sensitivity is irrelevant.

I have said enough, I hope, to show that the realisation of Plural in the Finnish paradigms in Table 5.34 is consistent with the revised Peripherality Constraint. But one question that remains, perhaps, is why many Uralic scholars have seemingly preferred something closer to analysis (a) than analysis (b) — have preferred, in fact, to regard the -*t* of *tehtaat* as realising Plural but not Nominative. This is due partly, I think, to a tendency to overemphasise the typological consistency of the Uralic languages (or, casting the net more widely, the Uralic and Altaic languages) in contrast to Indo-European, and partly to a difference in terminology. In highly inflected Indo-European languages, we are used to finding overt morphological realisation of a Nominative Case on many nouns, and also concord involving the Nominative as well as other Cases. In a language such as Turkish, by contrast, there is never any overt realisation of 'Nominative', since in the Singular the 'Nominative' slot is occupied by the bare stem and the Plural suffix is unaffected by Case; morever, there is no Case concord. These constitute, in fact, grounds in Turkish for adopting the first interpretation of our analysis (a) for Finnish — for saying that there is no morphosyntactic property 'Nominative' at all. Among Uralic languages, Hungarian (for example) is more similar to Turkish than to most Indo-European languages in these respects. But to claim that no Uralic language has a Nominative 'morpheme' in the sense of 'property' runs counter to not only the sort of Finnish evidence that we have already discussed but also to syntactic evidence. Finnish Case–Number concord, which operates very much like that of Latin, counts in favour of integrating the 'Nominative' with the rest of the Case category; and even if, unlike Latin, Finnish has no clearly identifiable Nominative Singular 'morphemes' in the sense of suffixes characteristic of that Case, this does not affect the argument for regarding -*t* as overt exponent of the Nominative in the Plural.

In this Finnish example, then, there is no counterevidence to the Peripherality Constraint because the inflexion which might provide this counterevidence — the -*t* of the Nominative Plural — emerges as an overlapping exponent of more than one property (a 'portmanteau morph'). The fact that the Peripherality Constraint does not 'bite' on examples of overlapping exponence follows from the fact that we are deliberately restricting so far any proposed constraints on Deviation II to instances of pure sensitivity. But we have always envisaged the possibility of extending the proposed constraints to more complex types of sensitivity. In order not to preclude the Peripherality Constraint in advance from such extension, therefore, we need to make explicit the fact that the existence of completely overlapping exponence somewhere in the paradigm does not render the paradigm incompatible with the Constraint. We need also to formulate the Constraint in such a way that one piece of overlap does not, as it were, free the rest of the paradigm — more precisely, those parts of it where the sensitivity is pure — from the need to comply with the Constraint. I would like to suggest, therefore, a fairly natural amendment to the formulation of the Peripherality Constraint at (509) and point out some consequences of it. The amended formulation, in which the main alterations are italicised, is:

(519) PERIPHERALITY CONSTRAINT (third formulation):
The realisation of a property P may be sensitive inwards, i.e. to a property realised more centrally in the word-form (that is, closer in linear sequence to the root), but not outwards to an individual property realised more peripherally (further from the root). The realisation of P may, however, be sensitive outwards consistently to *all the independently realised properties within a given category, that is to all those properties within the category with which the realisation of P is not entirely simultaneous.*

One consequence of making explicit in this way the compatibility of simultaneous (or fully overlapping) exponence with the Peripherality Constraint is that our attention is drawn to a new possibility for dealing with any apparent instances of outward sensitivity which are at first sight inconsistent with the Constraint. The most straightforward conclusion to be drawn from any such instances is, of course, that the Peripherality Constraint is simply wrong. But another possibility is that the morphological material which we have analysed as involving outward sensitivity, with one property more peripheral than the other, ought rather to be analysed as a simultaneous exponent of both properties concerned. Of course, it would be a mistake to invoke this alternative solely as a device to 'save' the Peripherality Constraint from disproof, without any independent evidence in favour of the 'portmanteau' solution for the problematic forms. But one can envisage situations where relevant independent evidence might be available. Let us suppose that, in a language with a generally transparent 'agglutinating' morphological structure, some phonological or other innovation has the effect of 'splitting' what was previously a single realisation for some property, in such a way that the distribution of the two new alternants involves outward sensitivity of a kind forbidden by the Peripherality Constraint. If the Constraint is correct, we will predict that the exponence relationships within the paradigm concerned will now be reanalysed in such a way that one or both of the alternants is no longer treated as separable from the more peripheral material to which it has apparently become sensitive — in other words, that it and this more peripheral material are combined into a portmanteau realisation. Once this has happened, we can expect to see a loosening of the ties between the formerly agglutinated 'morphs' which have become absorbed into this portmanteau realisation and the same morphs in environments which can still, consistently with the Peripherality Constraint, be analysed as 'agglutinating' — a loosening which should tend to become manifest 'on the surface' through divergence in shape. It remains to be seen whether there are any 'semi-agglutinative' paradigms, or changes involving them, which can in fact be made sense of on these lines. The constellation of inflexional characteristics needed to trigger off the developments I have predicted is perhaps rather unusual, although one might begin by looking at anomalous instances of overlapping exponence within predominantly agglutinating morphological systems, such as in the Turkish Aorist Negative paradigm (see (113a)). I will not pursue this further here. The main point is that the Peripherality Constraint may in principle have a bearing on (and so be empirically testable in) certain at first sight rather unexpected situations potentially involving Deviation III as well as Deviation II.

5.2 PERIPHERALITY AND OTHER CONSTRAINTS ON ALLOMORPHY

The revival of interest in morphology in the last fifteen years has naturally led to the development of ideas which bear on Deviation II. How do these ideas interact with the Peripherality Constraint and, in particular, can the Peripherality Constraint be derived as a consequence of any current theory about inflexion? My answer to this second question will be no; not necessarily because current theories are wrong, but because they bear on different aspects of inflexional behaviour. Theoretical frameworks have been developed which emphasise variously the structure of morphosyntactic representations, the hierarchical organisation (or internal bracketing) of complex word-forms, and the phonological shape and subcategorisation of individual 'morphemes' (roots and affixes). It seems most likely that no one of these aspects of morphology provides the tools with which to express all the constraints to which inflexional behaviour is subject. At first sight this may seem a pessimistic conclusion; but it does not involve a retreat to the old assumption that all inflexional morphology is idiosyncratic and theoretically uninteresting, merely a recognition that the constraints affecting it are probably numerous and complex.

5.2.1 Adjacency

The Peripherality Constraint has been formulated in terms of the linear order of roots and affixes. By contrast, most generative work on inflexional exponence (as on morphology generally) has emphasised the constituent structure, or bracketing, of complex word-forms (e.g. Siegel (1974; 1978), M. Allen (1979), Pesetsky (1979), Lieber (1981), Williams (1981), Kiparsky (1982b), Selkirk (1982)). We will not be concerned here with the relative merits of these two approaches in general, but with the specific question whether the Peripherality Constraint can be derived from any constraint already formulated in the bracketing approach.

One such constraint, proposed independently by Siegel (1978) and M. Allen (1979), is the Adjacency Condition. This is formulated by M. Allen (1979: 49) as follows:

(520) ADJACENCY CONDITION
No WFR [Word Formation Rule] can involve X and Y, unless Y is uniquely contained in the cycle adjacent to X.

For Y to be in the cycle adjacent to X, Y must be separated by only one layer of embedding from X; so, for example, in the word *undistinguished*, analysed as $[un[[distinguish]_V ed]_A]_A$, *un-* is in a cycle adjacent to *-ed* but not to *distinguish*. The effect of the Adjacency Condition can be illustrated by examples taken from Siegel (1978). The 'ungrammaticality', or impossibility, of words such as *undishonest, *undiscrete seems to point to a principle of English morphology blocking the prefix-sequence *un-dis-*; on the other hand, the existence of words such as *undistinguished, undismayed* seems to run counter to this. But Siegel points out an apparently consistent difference in the constituent structure of the 'good' and the 'bad' words with *un-dis-*, illustrated in (521):

(521) [un [[distinguish] ed] *versus* * [un [dis [honest]]]
[un [[dismay] ed]] *versus* * [un [discrete]]

She suggests that the blocking principle just mentioned (or some more general principle of which it is a consequence) does indeed apply in English morphology, but its application is prevented in words such as *undistinguished* by the Adjacency Condition, for in these words *un-* is more than one cycle away from *dis-*, as is shown by the presence of more than one bracket between these affixes in the word's constituent structure. Clearly, if the Adjacency Condition is correct, its empirical consequences are extensive. As M. Allen (1979: 50) puts it: 'given the Adjacency Condition, it becomes impossible for a WFR to refer to any conceivable property of the base at any possible cyclic depth. Rules which crucially involve the notions 'denominal', 'deverbal' and 'deadjectival' are not allowed within a theory of morphology governed by the Adjacency Condition.' This is because a rule to the effect that some affix Y can attach only to deadjectival nouns, for example, would need to be able to 'look beyond' a nominal bracket to an adjectival bracket embedded within it.

A condition with similar effects has been proposed within the framework of 'lexical morphology and phonology' developed principally by Pesetsky (1979), Kiparsky (1982b) and Mohanan (1982). In this framework the emphasis for the purpose of describing word-internal structure is placed not on cycles but on 'levels' or 'strata', each one associated with largely distinct morphological and phonological processes and potentially extending over several cycles. The distinction between levels plays much the same descriptive role in English as does the distinction in SPE between 'morpheme-boundary' affixes (such as negative *in-* and adjective-forming *-ic*) and 'word-boundary' affixes (such as negative *non-* and Plural-marking *-s*); the former belong to Kiparsky's level 1 and the latter to his levels 2 and 3 respectively. For present purposes, what is important about this framework is the Bracketing Erasure Convention that has been incorporated in it (Mohanan & Mohanan 1984: 577):[23]

(522) BRACKET ERASURE CONVENTION
At the end of a stratum, all internal brackets are erased.

The effect of this convention is to make it impossible for any morphological process to be sensitive to the internal bracketing or labelling of that part of any word-form which is the output of an earlier stratum. Thus, supposing that the addition of a Plural suffix is the first morphological process to apply on stratum n in the derivation of a certain word-form, the shape of that suffix cannot depend on whether the noun is (say) derived from a verb, because this implies a representation $[\ldots[\ldots]_V\ldots]_N$ at the end of stratum n-1 whose internal brackets ($[\ldots]_V$) will be deleted before any process of stratum n gets a chance to apply. The Bracket Erasure Convention thus has some consequences similar to those which M. Allen attributes to the Adjacency Condition.

Some empirical differences between the Bracket Erasure Convention and the Adjacency Condition are discussed by Broselow (1983: 343-4), and there are difficulties in reconciling the Condition with certain inflexional facts (Carstairs 1984b: 112-17).[24] But what concerns us here is how they both interact with the Peripherality Constraint. In one respect, they are stronger than the Constraint, in that they bear on situations where there is both suffixation and prefixation. For the Adjacency Condition this is illustrated in Siegel's discussion of *undistinguished*. By contrast, the Peripherality Constraint says nothing about the mutual sensitivity of properties realised on opposite sides of the root. This may indeed be a deficiency in the Constraint. In the case of properties realised on the same side of the root, linear order will reflect depth of embedding exactly (except where infixation occurs), and it would be quite simple to reformulate the Peripherality Constraint in terms of constituency rather than linear order. But, even if we did this, the major empirical differences would remain.

Consider an inflected word of the following structure, where R is a root, A, B and C are affixes each realising some morphosyntactic property, and the brackets are numbered for ease of reference:

(523) [[[[R]$_1$ A]$_2$B]$_3$C]$_4$

        Stratum 1 Stratum 2

The Adjacency Condition rules out the possibility that C may be sensitive to A, and the Bracket Erasure Convention similarly forbids C to be sensitive to bracket 2; yet neither says anything about the mutual sensitivity of A and B. The Peripherality Constraint, by contrast, imposes no limit on the sensitivity of C to A but permits the property realised by A to be sensitive to B only if that property is consistently realised by A in the context of all members of the category to which B belongs. One could sum up by saying that the Adjacency Condition and Bracket Erasure Convention both relate to depth of sensitivity, whereas the Peripherality Constraint (whether stated in terms of linear order or constituency) relates to direction of sensitivity. Much remains to be investigated here, particularly on the implications of the reformulation of the Peripherality Constraint that I have hinted at. But it seems by no means implausible that inflexional behaviour should be subject to constraints of both kinds. If so, without ruling out the possibility of ultimately deriving both from some overarching general principle, we ought not to be surprised to find that neither kind of constraint is a straightforward consequence of the other.

5.2.2 The Elsewhere Condition

In classical generative phonology of the *Sound Pattern of English* variety, an important distinction is drawn between two types of rule ordering: conjunctive and disjunctive. If two rules are conjunctively ordered, then both may apply to the same form (provided, of course, that their structural descriptions are satisfied); but, if the rules are disjunctively ordered, then the application of one precludes the application of the other (at least on the same cycle). Various criteria have been suggested for determining when two rules are disjunctively ordered. The criteria which are relevant here have the effect of ensuring that, in some sense, rules which are relatively narrow in their application are ordered disjunctively before rules which are relatively general; consequently, if some form satisfies the structural description of both a narrower and a more general rule, it is the narrower rule which will apply, precluding the application of the more general one. Versions of this principle which have been proposed for phonology include Kiparsky's (1973) Elsewhere Condition and Koutsoudas, Sanders & Noll's (1974) Proper Inclusion Precedence Principle. But what is important here is the use which has been made of this idea in morphological theory.[25]

Somewhat different versions of the Elsewhere Condition have been proposed for morphology by Kiparsky (1982b: 8-9) and Anderson (1982: 607), but their effects are similar. According to Kiparsky, it is this Condition which accounts for the fact that a noun which is inherently Plural, such as *cattle*, cannot undergo Plural marking (*cattles), and the fact that we do not encounter 'stacked affixes having the same function', as in *ox-en-s. The empirical predictions that flow from the Condition are quite strong: for example, if among the inflected forms of some word there is some stem allomorph which is peculiar to one particular morphosyntactic property, then that allomorph may not in addition carry an affix realising the same property. This prediction, indeed, seems too strong: for example, the English verb *drive* forms a Past Participle *driven* by adding the fairly common suffix *-en* (cf. *taken, given, spoken*), even though the stem allomorph *driv-* (/drɪv/) to which the *-en* is added is itself peculiar to the Past Participle.[26] What is at issue here, however, is not the validity of the Elsewhere Condition in general but the extent to which its effects overlap with those of the Peripherality Constraint. This amounts to asking to what extent the Elsewhere Condition can be interpreted as a constraint on outward sensitivity.

Consider again the Possessed forms of Plural nouns in

Hungarian, set out in Table 5.22. We analysed these earlier as involving outward sensitivity, inasmuch as Plural has the realisation -*i*- instead of -*k* just when a more peripheral realisation of some Person–Number combination is present: e.g. *ruhá-i-m* 'my suits' versus *ruhá-k* 'suits' (cf. *ruhá-m* 'my suit'). This outward sensitivity is of a kind permitted by the Peripherality Constraint, however, because it is consistent; the same Plural exponent -*i*- occurs with all Possessive Person–Number combinations. Let us now consider two varieties of pseudo-Hungarian in Table 5.35 in which the Peripherality Constraint is violated.

Table 5.35

		Pseudo-Hungarian 1	Pseudo-Hungarian 2
Simple Plural		ruhá-k 'suits'	ruhá-k
Possessor: Sg	1	ruhá-i-m 'my suits'	ruhá-i-m
	2	'ruhá-k-od'	ruhá-i-d
	3	'ruhá-k-a'	'ruhá-k-a'
Pl	1	'ruhá-k-unk'	'ruhá-k-unk'
	2	'ruhá-k-otok'	'ruhá-k-otok'
	3	'ruhá-k-uk'	'ruhá-k-uk'

Both of these are excluded by the Peripherality Constraint, because in both the exponent -*i*- for Plural is found with only some, not all, Possessive suffixes. Pseudo-Hungarian 1 is excluded by the Elsewhere Condition also; since it is only with 1 Sg Possessors that -*i*- occurs as the exponent of Plural, this -*i*- by itself is sufficient to identify the Possessor as 1 Sg ('my'), and any further 1 Sg marking, as with the suffix -*m*, ought not to occur. But the Elsewhere Condition does not rule out Pseudo-Hungarian 2. In this language, the Plural -*i*- suffix occurs with both 1 Sg and 2 Sg Possessors; it therefore does not suffice alone to identify the Possessor, and further marking by means of -*m* and -*d* respectively does not violate the Condition. The crucial difference is that in Pseudo-Hungarian 1 the -*i* suffix is unique to one bundle within the Possession category. All hypothetical instances of outward sensitivity where the sensitive property has a similarly unique exponent are just as effectively banned by the Elsewhere Condition as by the Peripherality Constraint. The Peripherality Constraint makes much stronger predictions, however; for in contexts where there is outward sensitivity it not merely bans uniqueness but also imposes consistency.

On the basis of the discussion so far it may seem that the Elsewhere Condition, so far from rendering the Peripherality Constraint superfluous, might actually be derivable as a consequence of it, at least so far as its role in inflexional morphology is concerned. But this is not so. If it were so, then our English example *driven* would present just as much a problem for the Peripherality Constraint as for the Elsewhere Condition. But in *driven* there is inflexional realisation of only a single morphosyntactic property (or property-bundle), namely Past Participle, so the question of sensitivity (in our sense), whether pure or otherwise, does not arise. So just as there is some conceivable inflexional behaviour which is relevant to the Peripherality Constraint but not to the Elsewhere Condition (such as that of Pseudo-Hungarian 2), so there is some which is relevant to the Condition but not to the Constraint. The fact that both happen to 'bite' on Pseudo-Hungarian 1 emerges as an accidental intersection of two independent principles. Of the four Deviations listed in Chapter 1, the Elsewhere Condition seems in fact more relevant to Deviation I (extended exponence) than to Deviation II; and, although we will mention the Condition again in our discussion of stem allomorphy in Chapter 6 (note 3), a fuller study of the Elsewhere Condition in relation to inflexion belongs to the search for constraints on Deviation I.

5.2.3 The Mirror Principle

Ever since Chomsky's 'Remarks on nominalization' (1970), linguists adhering to the Extended Standard Theory of generative grammar have denied syntactic transformations any role in word-formation and have assumed that the principles governing derivational morphology and compounding operate in the lexicon, which is therefore no longer seen as merely a list of idiosyncrasies. Many generativists would say the same about the realisational side of inflexional morphology; transformations such as Affix Hopping which manipulate bound morphemes are therefore excluded in principle. But this strict divorce between syntax and inflexional morphology has recently been challenged by Baker (1985). Baker examines the interaction between agreement rules and what he calls grammatical function changing rules (GF-rules), such as causative and reflexive, in various languages where these rules have concatenative morphological as well as syntactic effects. In these languages, the earlier a given rule applies in the syntactic derivation of a sentence, the more deeply embedded will its affixal exponent be in the structure of the corresponding word-form. Baker concludes that syntactic and morphological operations of the kind he discusses go hand in hand; to leave all morphological operations to a separate component of the grammar which meshes with the syntax only at one point in the derivation of sentences will leave the observed parallelism unexplained. His main claim is summed up in the Mirror Principle: 'Morphological derivations must directly reflect syntactic derivations (and vice versa).'

The morphological aspect of the Mirror Principle embodies a strong claim about the structural order in which certain morphosyntactic properties must be realised in certain word-forms. This is distinct from the question of the shape of their realisations, which is the concern of the Peripherality Constraint. Nevertheless, some expectations about allomorphy seem to flow naturally from the Mirror Principle. A crucial feature of Baker's account is that GF-rules do not simply manipulate abstract morphosyntactic features such as [+ causative]; they can add phonological material too, such as (in Chamorro) the Causative prefix *na'-*. Moreover, this material gets added 'before' any subsequent syntactic rules apply. We will therefore tend to expect affixes added by GF-rules to assume a definitive shape which is not affected by (or not sensitive to) any subsequent rules; for any widespread exceptions to this would cast doubt on the clear identification, crucial to the Mirror Principle, of certain affixes with certain rules. In short, the Mirror Principle seems at first sight hard to reconcile with the existence of any outward sensitivity.

Certainly there is no way of deriving the Peripherality Constraint in its final formulation as a consequence of the Mirror Principle. As to whether the instances of outward sensitivity that we have observed constitute counterevidence to the Principle, the crucial question is whether outward sensitivity occurs in any of the morphological contexts with which Baker is concerned: those involving GF-rules and agreement rules. No clear instances of outward sensitivity appear in the data that Baker examines. It could be, then, that outward sensitivity is subject to two independent constraints: not only the consistency proviso of the Peripherality Constraint but also, as a direct consequence of the way GF-rules and agreement rules operate, a ban on sensitivity to properties which have not yet been added to the word-form by the appropriate rule. This analysis relies on demonstrating that, in all actual instances of outward sensitivity, the more peripheral properties that trigger the allomorphy are (in some sense) already attached to the word-form, not awaiting attachment by a subsequent rule. To investigate this possibility we need more clear-cut criteria for distinguishing GF-rules from others, and in any case it goes beyond our present task of checking the Peripherality Constraint's independence of other recent proposals. But tentatively we can say that the outlook is promising. None of our instances of nonphonological outward sensitivity involves properties such as Causative, Passive, Reciprocal or Reflexive — properties corresponding to Baker's GF-rules. Person–Number, which triggers outward sensitivity in Hungarian and Zulu, is a category which is traditionally assigned by agreement rules of the kind which Baker sees as interacting with GF-rules; but the properties which we have observed to be sensitive to Person–Number (Plural in Hungarian nouns, lexical Class in Zulu nouns) are not themselves likely to be analysed as the product of either agreement or GF-rules, so there is nothing in the Mirror Principle which would forbid us to delay their realisation until after Person–Number has been attached. I will not attempt to take the matter further here; but we can at least regard as weak corroboration of the Mirror Principle the fact that we have observed no outward sensitivity on the part of the sort of properties that Baker is mainly interested in.

NOTES

1. As to Table 5.1(b), I am assuming that the relationship between verb root and Past Participle in English is inflexional, not derivational. This will probably be denied by those who say that word-forms belonging to different word-classes cannot be members of the same inflexional paradigm (e.g. Siegel 1974: 17); for participles notoriously share many of the syntactic characteristics of adjectives. But my assumption is not crucial to my argument, simply because, as I said in Chapter 1, nothing in my argument hinges on the more fundamental implied assumption that it is possible and useful to distinguish sharply between derivation

and inflexion. If past participles are derived rather than inflected forms, our example simply serves to illustrate that some 'derivational properties' are realised sensitively, just as morphosyntactic properties often are, despite (for example) M. Allen's assertion (1979: 3) that suppletion never occurs in derivational morphology.

2. Only back-vowel versions of the relevant suffixes are given here.

3. I assume here that *parlerions* is not to be segmented *parler-i-ons*, with *-i-* realising a distinct property such as 'Past', realised as [ε] (*-ais*, *-ait*, *-aient*) in most other Persons. With an analysis on those lines, the sensitivity involved might indeed be pure.

4. It is not important to decide whether in this hypothetical example there is no property 'Singular' at all or whether there is such a property, 'realised by zero'.

5. For Turkish, the column headings are taken from Lewis (1967: 136). For Hungarian, they are derived from Bánhidi *et al.* (1965).

6. Vago (1980) accounts for the *-ának* ending of the Conditional, as well as the *-(a)nak* ending of the Present, by means of an *n*-Suppletion rule sensitive to Tense. But he calls this rule 'morpholexical'; there is no motivation in Hungarian for a general process of *n*-Epenthesis which might be called 'phonological' in the usual sense.

7. The Zulu material discussed here is essentially the same as was discussed in section 3.1.1 from the point of view of paradigm economy. However, I will present the essential facts in full again, so that the reader need not refer back constantly to Chapter 3.

8. The alternation between long and short *-e-* in the Future forms in Table 5.9, and the similar alternations affecting both *-a-* and *-e-* in Table 5.20 below, can be accounted for phonologically and therefore do not involve morphological sensitivity.

9. A few Class 1a/2a nouns denoting inanimate objects, such as *ugwayi* 'tobacco', do not replace *u-* by *-ka-* in the possessive construction, at least with some native speakers. It is not yet clear how systematic this maintenance of *u-* is. For our present purposes, its main relevance is in emphasising the lack of any phonological motivation for the *u-* ~ *-ka-* alternation in those nouns which display it.

10. The swung dash here is not meant to imply any decision on whether the choice between the alternants so connected is phonologically or morphologically determined. No decision on that issue is needed for present purposes.

11. The variation in length of the Genitive markers is due to whether a segmental suffix follows: most of them require the long alternant (R.A. Hudson 1974: 113). It can thus probably be regarded as an instance of phonological, not morphological, sensitivity of the kind discussed in section 5.1.7 below.

12. The details of the morphological analysis of the Hungarian Possessive paradigms have been a matter of controversy among Hungarian scholars for decades. Under some analyses, such as that of Mel'čuk (1973), the need to recognise what I call 'outward sensitivity' disappears. Mel'čuk analyses the *-(j)a* of a form such as *kalapja* 'his hat' as a mark not of 3rd Sg Possession but of Possession pure and simple; and this mark, he would claim, appears also in a form such as *kalapjaim*

'my hats', which must therefore be analysed thus:

kalap-ja-   i-   m
hat-   Possessed -Plural-1st Sg

In my terms, the consequence of this analysis is that the realisation of Plural in *kalapjaim* is sensitive not outwards to the presence of the property 1st Sg but inwards to the property Possessed. The snag with this is that Mel'čuk's Possession 'Morpheme' *-(j)a* is often absent in the Plural (at least 'on the surface'), e.g. in our example in Table 5.27: alongside *ruhája* 'her dress' we have *ruháim* 'my dresses' etc., not *ruhájaim etc. But, in any case, no questions are begged if we assume that Mel'čuk's analysis is wrong, since it is only if it is wrong that the Hungarian facts potentially endanger the Peripherality Constraint.

13. There are verb-forms in which the property Negative is realised before (and so more centrally than) the property Potential, e.g. *gel-miy-ebil-dim* 'I was able not to come'. In these forms, the property Potential is outside the scope of the negation, as the English gloss here indicates. This example raises questions about syntagmatic relationships between properties and about word-internal constituency which I will not attempt to tackle here; but it does not affect the relevance to the Peripherality Constraint of examples contained in Tables 5.25 and 5.26.

14. The tonal and prefixal contrast between *izin-kómishi* and *zin-komishi* do not concern us here.

15. Matthews (1972a: 99), in his reanalysis of the Huave facts, makes a similar comment.

16. Matthews (1972a: 113) comments that Stairs & Hollenbach do not succeed in conflating Future-formation with Subordinate-formation. It would be more accurate, I think, to say that they do not explore the possibility. To me, it looks promising.

17. This is not so arbitrary as it may at first seem. Matthews (1972a: 111) argues for treating *-m-* as a second Future marker (morphophonologically obscured in the 1st Person), so that the exponent of 2nd Person is the vowel *-e-* alone.

18. Matthews (1972a: 112) speculates that the spread of the *-i-* variants (if it is occurring) may spring from pressure to, as it were, rectify an exception to the general decline in 'marking relationships' from the top left to bottom right of his Person–Tense matrix at Figure 11. In my terms, this involves attributing the spread of *-i-* to pressure towards reducing sensitivity in general, in a systematic way, rather than towards removing outward sensitivity in particular. His suggestion would be supported if one could find evidence in morphological matrices elsewhere of similar 'clines' in allomorphy or 'marking relationships'. This certainly seems worth investigating.

19. 'Anteriority marker' is McIntosh's term; Arnott uses 'preterite element'.

20. This kind of inward-operating vowel harmony occurs also in a number of forms where the element following the Tense suffix is a subject rather than an object suffix; see Arnott (1970: 59).

21. Arnott states explicitly that in the Gombe dialect the 1st Sg

Object marker in the General Future Active Tense is not the vowel-initial -*am* but the consonant-initial -*yam* (1970: 213). If my suggestion about phonological sensitivity is correct, one would expect the form glossed 'he will help me' in the Gombe dialect to show the 'usual' Tense exponent -*ay*-, not -*at*-. This is apparently correct; Arnott gives '*o-wall-ay-yam* instead of the Southern Zaria '*o-wall-at-am*. A similar difference between the two dialects seems to obtain in the Habitual Singular Imperative. Arnott, unlike McIntosh, mentions no -*atay*- ~ -*at*- alternation of the kind we find in Southern Zaria; and he confirms (personal communication) that in Gombe one would expect to hear *wall-atay-yam* rather than *wall-at-am* for 'keep on helping me!'. The realisation of the relevant Tenses in the two dialects thus seems to involve the same kind of outward phonological sensitivity, but the alternants are differently distributed because the realisations of 1st Sg Object differ in a phonologically relevant manner.

22. See Chapter 4, note 11.

23. This is essentially the same as Kiparsky's (1982b: 11) formulation. In the version originally proposed by Pesetsky (1979), brackets are erased after every cycle, i.e., potentially more than once within a level. To go into the empirical effects of this difference would take us too far afield. Needless to say, the Mohanans' and Kiparsky's strata have nothing to do with those of Lamb's stratificational grammar (Lockwood 1972).

24. Certain Zulu Passive forms which constitute a difficulty for the Adjacency Condition (Carstairs 1984b: 114-15) are in fact compatible with the Bracket Erasure Convention, because the sensitivity in question involves only phonological characteristics, not the constituency or labelling, of the relevant embedded material. They thus illustrate a possibility recognised by Pesetsky (1979, footnote 20).

25. A fuller summary of the various versions of the Elsewhere Condition and a critical discussion of its application to morphology are offered by Janda & Sandoval (1984).

26. This example by itself, of course, does not constitute conclusive counterevidence. One might seek to reconcile it with the Condition by treating the /draɪv ~ drɪv/ alternation as purely phonological, or perhaps by exempting from the Condition any affixal inflexion which is analysed as belonging on the same 'deep' stratum as the stem allomorphy itself. But the example does illustrate the sort of problem that the Elsewhere Condition encounters.

6

Two Questions Concerning Stem Allomorphy

6.1 INTRODUCTION: TYPES OF STEM

In Chapter 5 I proposed the Peripherality Constraint as a general constraint on Deviation II (or rather on those examples of Deviation II which exhibit 'pure' sensitivity). In the second section of this chapter I will explain what the Constraint implies about stem allomorphy, and attempt to show that these implications fit in well with the way stems actually behave. In the third section of the chapter I discuss how stem allomorphy interacts with the Paradigm Economy Principle. In a sense, my conclusions here merely consolidate previous ones, because they amount to showing that stem allomorphy, as observed, does not conflict with either of the two constraints discussed. But the discussion is worthwhile because those conclusions are not self-evident; and, in the course of it, we develop a new and, I hope, more satisfactory notion of 'inflexional distinctness' for the purpose of paradigm economy which will be exploited when we discuss German noun inflexion in Chapter 7.

First, I should make it clear what sort of phenomenon I will be discussing under the label of 'stem allomorphy'. Traditionally, linguists have used the word 'stem' in three rather different senses, which we can call **phonological, realisational** and **morpholexical stems**. These can be exemplified by the following three statements about inflexion in Latin:

(601) *Mensa* 'table' is an *a*-stem noun.

(602) The Perfective stem of *amō* 'love' is *amāv-*.

(603) The stem found in the oblique Singular Cases of *iter* 'journey' is *itiner-*.

In use (601), what is emphasised is one phonological characteristic of the stem which undergoes inflexion, on the basis of which its inflexional behaviour is predictable within the grammar of the language in question. Often it would be more accurate to say 'was formerly predictable'; synchronically, to my mind, it is dubious to analyse all Case–Number forms of *mensa* in Golden Age Latin as derived phonologically from underlying representations consisting of /mensa/ (rather than /mens/) plus some affix. If so, '*a*-stem noun' is synchronically no more than a label for a phonologically unpredictable declension-type, just like 'first-declension noun'. A more secure example of inflexional choice based on stem phonology is that between the two 2nd Singular Indefinite endings -*(a)sz* and -*ol* in Hungarian, which I mentioned first in section 1.4; we might describe those Hungarian verbs of the 'normal' conjugation which choose -*ol* as 'sibilant-stem verbs'. But phonological stem classification of this kind does not, of course, imply any alteration in the shape of the stem, and it is not this sense of 'stem' which will interest us. Nor will we be primarily concerned with realisational stems, as illustrated in (602), where what is emphasised is the morphosyntactic function of some partially inflected form. If P is some morphosyntactic property, we typically speak of X' as being the P-stem of some word X when all and only the forms of X which share the property P use X' as a basis for further inflection. But realisational stem-contrast within inflexional paradigms is perfectly compatible with the maintenance throughout the paradigm of a single invariant 'root' or core. For example, *amō* has distinct Imperfective and Perfective realisational stems *am-* (or *amā-*) and *amāv-* respectively, and we might want to go further and, for example, distinguish within the Perfective between a Present Subjunctive 'stem' *amāver(i)-* and a Past Subjunctive 'stem' *amāviss(e)-*; nevertheless, the whole paradigm of *amō* shares a single invariant root *am-*. *Amō* thus does not display any stem allomorphy of the kind we are concerned with: morpholexical stem contrasts as illustrated in (603).

Where we do find such stem allomorphy is in a noun such as *iter* 'journey'. On the basis of the behaviour of a large number of nouns of the 'third declension', such as *caput* 'head' and *nōmen* 'name' illustrated in Table 6.2, we can distinguish a set of Singular Case endings as in Table 6.1.

Table 6.1

Nom/Voc/Acc	Ø	(i.e. no affixal realisation of Case is separable from the rest of the word-form)
Gen	-is	
Dat	-i	
Abl	-e	

Table 6.2

NVA	caput	nōmen
Gen	capitis	nōminis
Dat	capiti	nōmini
Abl	capite	nōmine

Both nouns in Table 6.2 display not only the set of endings listed in Table 6.1 but also an alternation between two stem-forms, one for the Nominative–Vocative–Accusative and one for the other three Cases. Historically this is due to a purely phonological process of medial vowel weakening, and synchronically it is not implausible to treat it in the same way, even though surface exceptions exist which will contribute to the opacity of the process (e.g. *percutis* 'you strike' rather than *percitis alongside *capitis*). But no such phonological explanation could conceivably account for the morpholexical stem alternation we observe in Table 6.3, either historically or synchronically (except under an extremely powerful phonological theory with generous tolerance for ad hoc 'rules'):

Table 6.3

NVA	iter 'journey'
Gen	itineris
Dat	itineri
Abl	itinere

Here we have inescapably two 'stems' in the sense of use (603): allomorphy affecting the core element which is not phonologically resoluble. It is stem allomorphy of this kind whose relationship with the Peripherality Constraint and the Paradigm Economy Principle will interest us.

6.2 STEM ALLOMORPHY AND THE PERIPHERALITY CONSTRAINT

The Peripherality Constraint imposes limits on outward sensitivity in inflexion. The reason why there are questions to be answered about the relationship between this constraint and stem allomorphy is that, if one stem allomorph is found in one part of the paradigm — that is, with one subset of the morphosyntactic property combinations applicable to the word in question — and another stem allomorph with another subset, then, insofar as those property combinations are realised more peripherally, some outward sensitivity seems to be involved. And, since the stem is by definition the most central part of the word-form, those property combinations will indeed be realised more peripherally in most instances. So in principle, it seems, stem allomorphy ought to obey the Peripherality Constraint; or, to put it another way, stem allomorphy ought to provide an extensive hunting-ground for counter-examples to the Constraint.

Let us continue to assume, for the moment, that all stem allomorphy within inflexional paradigms is relevant to the Peripherality Constraint in this way. Does stem allomorphy in fact obey the Constraint? It is natural to look first at the example in Table 6.3. At first sight, the facts here do seem compatible with it. Where Case has an independent overt realisation, the same allomorph *itiner-* is always found; where it has not, as in the Nominative, Vocative and Accusative, the allomorph *iter* can be regarded as realising Case simultaneously with the root, so 'pure' sensitivity is not involved and the Peripherality Constraint cannot be at issue. But it is easy to find examples which cannot be dealt with so easily. In Tables 6.4 to 6.6 I place side by side parts of the inflexional paradigms of two

Table 6.4

Italian: verbal Present Indicatives:

		tenere 'to hold'	temere 'to fear'
Sg	1	teng-o	tem-o
	2	tien-i	tem-i
	3	tien-e	tem-e
Pl	1	ten-iamo	tem-iamo
	2	ten-ete	tem-ete
	3	teng-ono	tem-ono

Table 6.5

German: verbal Present Indicatives:

		geben 'to give'	beben 'to tremble'
Sg	1	geb-e	beb-e
	2	gib-st	beb-st
	3	gib-t	beb-t
Pl	1	geb-en	beb-en
	2	geb-t	beb-t
	3	geb-en	beb-en

Table 6.6

Sanskrit: nominal Case–Number paradigms:

		rājā 'king'	marut 'wind'
Sg	Nom	rājā	marut-am
	Acc	rājān-am	marut-am
	Instr	rājñ-ā	marut-ā
	Dat	rājñ-e	marut-e
	Abl/Gen	rājñ-aḥ	marut-aḥ
	Loc	rājñ- / rājan- } i	marut-i
	Voc	rāja	marut
Du	NVA	rājān-au	marut-au
	IDAb	rāja-bhyām	marud-bhyām
	GL	rājñ-oḥ	marut-oḥ
Pl	NV	rājān-aḥ	marut-aḥ
	A	rājñ-aḥ	marut-aḥ
	I	rāja-bhiḥ	marud-bhiḥ
	DAb	rāja-bhyaḥ	marud-bhyaḥ
	G	rājñ-ām	marut-ām
	L	rāja-su	marut-su

words in Italian, German and Sanskrit respectively, inflexionally identical except that one involves stem allomorphy and one does not (or at least none which is not explicable by reference to 'transparent' low-level phonological rules).

In all these examples, seemingly, stem alternations can be observed which correlate with the presence or absence of individual properties, not whole categories, realised more peripherally. For example, in the Sanskrit example in Table 6.6, it is trivially obvious that none of the stem allomorphs *rājān-*, *rājñ-*, *rājan-* or *rāja-* is associated with all Cases or all Numbers, for that would require there to be no stem allomorphy at all. Nor is any of them consistently associated with particular Cases or

Numbers, even;[1] for example, *rājān-* is found in the Accusative Singular and Dual but not in the Accusative Plural. Do we, then, have outward sensitivity here of a kind flatly inconsistent with the Peripherality Constraint?

The answer to this question depends on what scope we ascribe to the Constraint: whether it applies merely to the realisation of morphosyntactic properties, or to the realisation of the lexical content of inflected words as well. As formulated in Chapter 5, it applies only to the former; it says nothing about allomorphy in that part of the word-form which 'realises', or expresses, the lexical meaning, except insofar as that part of the word-form may also realise some further morphosyntactic property, distinct from that which conditions the allomorphy. An important question in connexion with the examples contained in Tables 6.4 to 6.6, then, is whether or not the stem allomorphy in the left-hand column realises any such property in a fashion incompatible with the Constraint, i.e. involving inconsistent pure outward sensitivity to an independently realised property (cf. the latest formulation of the Peripherality Constraint at (519)). We will consider the question first in relation to the Sanskrit example in Table 6.6. The answer is straightforward, and has essentially been given already; the morpholexical stems are distributed within the paradigm in such a way that none correlates consistently with any one Number or Gender, so none realises any Number or Gender independently of any affix. Less formally, the affixes which fulfil the entire task of realising all Case–Number combinations in the paradigm of *marut* also fulfil the lion's share of it in the paradigm of *rājā*. Even where the stem allomorphy plays a disambiguating role, as in Acc Pl *rājñ-aḥ* versus Nom Pl *rājān-aḥ*, what we have is extended exponence rather than pure sensitivity; we cannot plausibly identify a principal exponent of either Case or Number in the morpholexical stem or the suffix respectively. The stem allomorphy of *rājā* in Table 6.6 is therefore consistent with the Peripherality Constraint.

One can contrast the nominal stem allomorphy illustrated in Table 6.6 with that found in those Arabic nouns which have 'broken' or 'internal' Plurals (already discussed, from the point of view of homonymy, in Chapter 4). In the Sanskrit example in Table 6.6, the stem alternation between the Acc Sg *rājānam* and the Acc Pl *rājñaḥ* is not what mainly carries the Singular–Plural distinction, since the 'strong' stem *rājān-* is not limited to the Singular and the 'weak' *rājñ-* is not limited to the Plural. But in the following Standard Arabic paradigm in Table 6.7, the stem allomorphy is clearly what carries the distinction of Number.

Table 6.7

		Singular	Plural
Indefinite	Nom	rajul-un 'man'	rijāl-un
	Gen	rajul-in	rijāl-in
	Acc	rajul-an	rijāl-an
		Singular	Plural
Definite	Nom	rajul-u	rijāl-u
	Gen	rajul-i	rijāl-i
	Acc	rajul-a	rijāl-a

This paradigm contrasts with that of nouns such as *muˁallimun* 'teacher' or *ḥayawānun* 'animal', which have so-called 'sound' Plurals sharing a morpholexical stem with the Singular, shown in Table 6.8.

Table 6.8

		Singular	Plural	Singular	Plural
Indef	Nom	muˁallim-un	muˁallim-ūna	ḥayawān-un	ḥayawān-ātun
	Gen	muˁallim-in	muˁallim-ina	ḥayawān-in	ḥayawān-ātin
	Acc	muˁallim-an	muˁallim-ina	ḥayawān-an	ḥayawān-ātin
Def	Nom	muˁallim-u	(as above)	ḥayawān-u	ḥayawān-ātu
	Gen	muˁallim-i		ḥayawān-i	ḥayawān-āti
	Acc	muˁallim-a		ḥayawān-a	ḥayawān-āti

In a form such as *ḥayawānātun* 'animals' (Indef Nom Pl)' it seems reasonable to distinguish a Plural suffix -*āt*- from a Case-Definiteness suffix -*un*. We can thus speak of a contrast between the ways in which *rajulun* and *ḥayawānun* form their Plural realisational stems: the first by internal vowel change, the second by suffixation. If this analysis is correct, then it is no accident, in general linguistic terms, that no Arabic noun displays an alternation in the Plural between 'broken' and 'sound' forms; that is, there is no paradigm on the lines of that in Table 6.9.

TWO QUESTIONS CONCERNING STEM ALLOMORPHY

Table 6.9

	Indefinite Singular	Plural	Definite Singular	Plural
N	rajul-un	'rajul-āt-un'	rajul-u	'rajul-āt-u'
G	rajul-in	rijāl-in	rajul-i	rijāl-i
A	rajul-an	rijāl-an	rajul-a	rijāl-a

Such a paradigm, in contrast to that in Table 6.6, would indeed display outward sensitivity of a kind incompatible with the Peripherality Constraint.

For the Italian and German examples in Tables 6.4 and 6.5, deciding what realises what among the various stems and suffixes is somewhat more complex than for the Sanskrit example. To remind ourselves what to look out for, it may be helpful to keep in mind the realisational pattern involved in the 'illegal' outward sensitivity of the pseudo-Hungarian Plural Possessive paradigm in Table 5.23. In this type of pseudo-Hungarian, Plural is realised inconsistently within the Paradigm by -*k* and -*i*, -*k* occurring with the 2nd Person suffixes and -*i* with the rest. Moreover, Plural is realised independently of Possession inasmuch as both -*i* and -*k* are by themselves unambiguous exponents of Plural, so there is no question here of the kind of overlapping exponence which we observed in the Nominative Plural of Finnish nouns and for which provision was made in the third version of the Peripherality Constraint (see section 5.1.8). We can symbolise the relationship between properties and their exponents in the forms in Table 5.23 *ruháim* 'my suits' and '*ruhákod*' 'your suits' as follows, where a solid line indicates that the inflexion in question is an unambiguous exponent of the property in question while a broken line indicates the sort of indirect exponence of a conditioning property Q that is always inherent in the exponent of the property P which it affects — the sort of exponence that we agreed in section 5.1.1 to ignore for the purpose of investigating pure sensitivity:

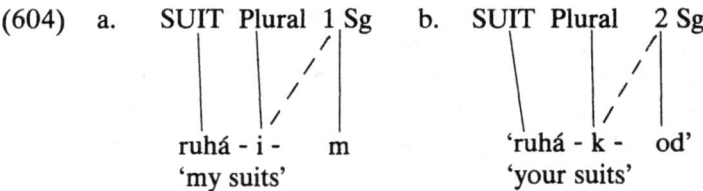

The sloping broken line can be taken here as symbolising outward sensitivity; the absence of a link between Plural and the suffixes *-m* and *-od* indicates that the conditioning possessive properties are realised independently of the conditioned one; and the fact that both *-i-* and *k* appear as exponents of Plural indicates that the outward sensitivity is inconsistent and therefore illegal. Turning now to the Italian Present Indicative forms in Table 6.4, we observe that the verb *tenere*, unlike *temere*, displays three morpholexical stems: *ten-*, *tien-* and *teng-*. *Ten-* and *tien-* can be regarded as phonologically conditioned alternants, the former always unstressed (as in *ten-iamo*, *ten-ete*) and the latter stressed (*tien-i, tien-e*); but no such phonological conditioning can account synchronically for the distribution of *teng-*. Furthermore, *teng-* is restricted to Present forms of the verb, being found only in the Present Indicative and the Present Subjunctive (*teng-a, teng-a, teng-a, ten-iamo, ten-iate, teng-ano*), so it must be acknowledged as an unambiguous exponent of (or realisational stem for) Present Tense. Superficially, then, we have in the forms *tengo* and *tengono* just the sort of 'illegal' outward sensitivity that we found in the pseudo-Hungarian forms *ruháim* and '*ruhákod*', represented diagrammatically at (604). If so, we ought to be able to represent the realisational patterns of, say, *tengo* 'I hold' and *tenete* 'you (Plural) hold' in parallel fashion to (604), thus:[2]

(605) a. HOLD Present 1 Sg   b. HOLD Present 2 Pl

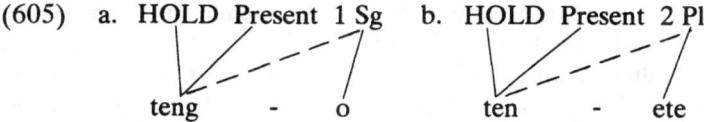

teng   -   o   ten   -   ete

The distribution of the morpholexical stems *teng-* and *ten-/tien-* seems therefore to constitute counterevidence to the Peripherality Constraint.

This argument is invalid, however. The parallel between pseudo-Hungarian and Italian breaks down when we look more closely at the realisational pattern of *ten-ete* (and of other forms with the *ten-/tien-* stem allomorph). The patterns presented in (605) suggest that *teng-* and *tien-/ten-* are both equally unambiguous exponents of Present Tense. But, while this is true of *teng-*, it is not true of *ten-/tien-*. The former, as we have said, is restricted to Present Tense forms, but the latter is found also in the Imperfect (*ten-evo* 'I was holding' etc.) and in certain

215

Preterite forms (*ten-esti* 'you held' etc.). The single solid line connecting Present with *ten-* in (605b) is therefore inadequate as a symbolisation of how Present is realised in the form *tenete*. It is unambiguously realised, in fact, only by the combination of the morpholexical stem *ten-* (versus e.g. Future *terr-ete* 'you will hold') and the suffix *-ete* (versus e.g. Preterite *ten-este* 'you held'). A more accurate symbolisation of the realisational pattern in *ten-ete* would therefore be as follows:

(606)

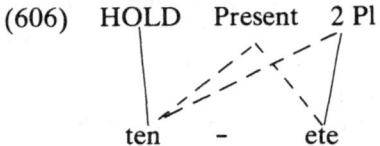

But it is clear from (606) that the realisations of Present and 2 Plural are not independent in the sense required for the Peripherality Constraint to 'bite'. The only property-bundles of the paradigm in Table 6.4 in which Person–Number is independently realised in the necessary sense (i.e. whose exponents play no part in the unambiguous realisation of Present) are 1 Singular and 3 Plural; and since these two bundles share the one morpholexical stem *teng-*, the outward sensitivity involved is of the consistent variety which the Peripherality Constraint permits. All the other property-bundles in Table 6.4 (2 and 3 Singular, 1 and 2 Plural) have realisations overlapping with Present in such a way as to take them outside the scope of the Constraint, just like the Nominative Plural of Finnish nouns. The Italian example in Table 6.4 is therefore quite compatible with the Peripherality Constraint. The relevant aspects of the paradigm in the German material in Table 6.5 are comparable. The morpholexical stem *gib-* can be regarded as an unambiguous exponent of Present, since it occurs only in the Present Indicative and Imperative; yet its ostensible rival, *geb-*, is analogous to Italian *ten-/tien-* in that it occurs outside the Present system, so that the realisational pattern of forms such as 1 Sg *geb-e*, 2 Pl *geb-t* is of the overlapping variety which takes them outside the scope of the Peripherality Constraint.

The sort of verbal stem allomorphy that the Constraint forbids is a pattern where some property (say, some Tense) has not one but two or more morpholexical stems peculiar to it, distributed on the basis of pure sensitivity to more peripheral properties (say, Person–Number bundles). Such a pattern is perfectly imaginable; if it never arises, this finding contributes to the plausibility of the Peripherality Constraint. I will discuss certain sets of forms in Gothic, Old English and Italian, all of which look at first sight as if they may illustrate such a pattern but turn out on closer examination to conform to the Constraint after all.

All the older Germanic languages (Gothic, Old Norse, Old English, Old High German, Old Saxon) display morpholexical stem allomorphy involving ablaut within the Preterite Indicative. Historically, this allomorphy was probably dependent on the position of the accent; but, with the loss of the Indo-European accent in Germanic languages, it lost its phonological conditioning. The sort of allomorphy that remained is illustrated by the paradigms in Gothic and Old English set out in Table 6.10.

Table 6.10

		Gothic: greipan 'to seize'	Old English: grīpan 'to grip'
Preterite:			
Sg	1	graip	grāp
	2	graip-t	grip-e
	3	graip	grāp
Du	1	grip-u	-
	2	grip-uts	-
Pl	1	grip-um	grip-on
	2	grip-uþ	grip-on
	3	grip-un	grip-on

Here we find two morpholexical stems in the Preterite in both Gothic (*graip-*, *grip-*) and Old English (*grāp-*, *grip-*). Now, all these Stems are peculiar to the Preterite in each of the two languages: yet, since the realisation of Person–Number, which determines the choice of stem allomorph, is apparently more peripheral (being located in the ending), 'illegal' outward sensitivity seems to be involved. But emphasis must be placed on the word 'apparently'. Two points about the data in Table 6.10 stand out. Firstly, in Gothic the allomorphy correlates neatly with Number: *graip-* in the Singular, *grip-* in the Dual and Plural. Yet, since Number as such (independent of Person) has

217

no identifiable principal exponent located more peripherally in any of these Gothic forms, the sensitivity to Number apparently displayed by the property Preterite cannot be called 'pure', and the Peripherality Constraint is therefore not contravened; what we see here, rather, is simultaneous exponence of Tense and Number in the stem. Secondly, the Old English distribution of the stem allomorphs is not parallel with that in Gothic. In fact, Old English differs from Gothic in the 2nd Sg in such a way as to disrupt the convenient correlation with Number just mentioned, so that the recognition of 'illegal' outward sensitivity in the Old English 2nd Sg form seems at first sight inescapable. This conclusion is inescapable, however, only if the ending -*e* of the 2nd Sg form *grip-e* (which is not cognate with the -*t* of the corresponding Gothic form *graip-t*) really is a principal exponent of the property-combination 2nd Singular. But it cannot be called such, apparently, because -*e* by itself is not an unambiguous exponent of 2nd Singular anywhere in the paradigm of *grīpan*; rather, we must say that 2nd Sg has no principal exponent in the form *gripe*, being realised equally in the stem and in the ending, so that the Peripherality Constraint is again not violated.[3] Whether solutions on these lines can be sustained for all the Germanic languages remains to be seen. Certainly, cognates of the Old English 2nd Sg ending -*e* (which, in Old English at least, is not a principal exponent) seem to be found in just those Germanic languages which share the Old English rather than the Gothic distribution of stem allomorphs (Krahe 1969: 103, 105); and this fact is promising. But a detailed chronological study would be needed of the changes which took place both in morpholexical stem allomorphy and in endings in order to determine whether the Peripherality Constraint is compatible with these changes and to what extent it may even have helped to motivate them.

I will introduce the Italian example by way of a form of pseudo-Latin. Earlier, I described *amāv-* as the Perfective realisational stem of the Latin verb *amō*. This realisational stem is formed by suffixation. But in several Latin verbs the Perfective realisational stem is distinguished from the Imperfective one by internal differences — by means of a morpholexical stem peculiar to the Perfective.

Examples of Latin Perfective realisational stems involving stem allomorphy in this sense are given in Table 6.11.

Table 6.11

Imperfective	Perfective
faciō 'I make'	fēcī 'I have made'
rumpō 'I break'	rūpī 'I have broken'
agō 'I act'	ēgī 'I have acted'

Compare now the Perfective Present Indicative forms of a verb like *faciō* with those of a verb like *audiō*, whose Perfective stem involves the suffixation of -*v*-, set out in Table 6.12.

Table 6.12

Sg	1	fēc-ī	audī-v-ī
	2	fēc-istī	audī-v-istī
	3	fēc-it	audī-v-it
Pl	1	fēc-imus	audī-v-imus
	2	fēc-istis	audī-v-istis
	3	fēc-erunt	audī-v-erunt

The fact that each verb uses consistently only one Perfective realisational stem ensures compliance with the Peripherality Constraint. By contrast, a logically quite conceivable pseudo-Latin in which *faciō* has two Perfective realisational stems *fēc*- and *facīv*-, distributed as in Table 6.13, is ruled out by the Peripherality Constraint.

Table 6.13

Sg	1	fēc-ī
	2	'facīv-istī'
	3	'facīv-it'
Pl	1	'facīv-imus'
	2	'facīv-istis'
	3	fēc-erunt

But if the stem allomorphy in Table 6.13 is of a kind incompatible with the Peripherality Constraint, and consequently impossible, what about the actual Italian stem allomorphy illustrated in the Italian Preterite Tense-forms in Table 6.14?

Table 6.14

Preterites of:			tenere 'hold' (cf. Table 6.4)	fare 'make' (< Latin facere, cf. Tables 6.12, 6.13)
	Sg	1	tenn-i ['tenni]	fec-i ['fe:tʃ i]
		2	ten-esti [te'nesti]	fac-esti [fa'tʃ esti]
		3	tenn-e ['tenne]	fec-e ['fe:tʃ e]
	Pl	1	ten-emmo [te'nemmo]	fac-emmo [fa'tʃ emmo]
		2	ten-este [te'neste]	fac-este [fa'tʃ este]
		3	tenn-ero ['tennero]	fec-ero ['fe:tʃ ero]

Just as the pseudo-Latin in Table 6.13 is disqualified by the fact that it has two Perfective realisational stems *fēc-* and '*facīv-*', so (at first sight) the Italian Preterite forms ought to be disqualified by the presence of two stem allomorphs *fec-* and *fac-*. But this is not so, because the Italian and Latin forms differ from each other in two crucial respects. Firstly, the Italian stem *fac-* is not an unambiguous exponent of Preterite, since it occurs also in the Imperfect (*fac-evo* 'I was making' etc.), so the realisational pattern for a Preterite form such as *faceste* 'you (Pl) made' is akin to that of the Present form *tenete* in (606) rather than that of *tengo* in (605a). Secondly, the distribution of *fec-* and *fac-*, unlike that of pseudo-Latin *fēc-* and *facīv-*, is phonologically conditioned on the basis of stress. To see this, compare the two columns in Table 6.15 (where pseudo-Latin is stressed according to the usual Latin rule):[4]

Table 6.15

		Italian	Pseudo-Latin
Sg	1	féc-i	féc-ī
	2	fac-ésti	facīv-istī
	3	féc-e	facīv-it
Pl	1	fac-émmo	facīv-imus
	2	fac-éste	facīv-istis
	3	féc-ero	féc-erunt

In Italian, *fec-* is always stressed and *fac-* is unstressed, but no such generalisation can be made about the pseudo-Latin forms. So in Italian, even if the morpholexical stem is an unambiguous exponent of Preterite in *feci, fece* and *fecero*, the sensitivity involved in the choice between the stem allomorphs *fec-* and *fac-* is not morphological but phonological. What we have in Italian is just another instance, this time involving stems, of the phenomenon we observed in affixes in (for example) the Hungarian *-(a)sz/-ol* alternation. The upshot of this discussion is that under no plausible assumption about where the exponence of Preterite can be located in the Italian verb-forms do these verb-forms exhibit 'illegal' outward sensitivity.

Applying the Peripherality Constraint to data involving stem allomorphy is less straightforward than exploring its implications for concatenative affixal inflexion. Probably the next priority in any further development of the Constraint will be a more sophisticated analysis of actual and potential realisational patterns, involving concepts beyond those of pure sensitivity and independent realisation that we have invoked so far. Still, it is reasonably clear what sort of morpholexical stem distribution would unequivocally violate the Peripherality Constraint; and we can take comfort from the fact that we have not encountered any such behaviour so far.

6.3 STEM ALLOMORPHY AND THE PARADIGM ECONOMY PRINCIPLE

In section 3.2.1 I suggested that stem allomorphy could account for some of the prima facie counterevidence to the Paradigm Economy Principle. In this section I will show how this comes about, through a more precise specification of what counts as inflexional distinctness for the purpose of paradigm economy. The practical effect of this refinement is to alter the predictions which flow from the Principle in respect of paradigms containing morpholexical stem allomorphy. This alteration is not merely a weakening, however; some behaviour that would otherwise be forbidden is permitted, but at the same time the non-occurrence of certain types of inflexional pattern, previously a mere accidental gap from the point of view of paradigm economy, now emerges as a consequence of it.

Let us consider again the Italian and German verb forms and the Sanskrit noun forms given in Tables 6.4-6.6. On the left in Table 6.4 we find the Present Indicative of *tenere*, with three morpholexical stems (at least on the surface), while on the left we have *temere*, with only one morpholexical stem. Within the Present Indicative slab, do *tenere* and *temere* conform to the same paradigm or not? Since the suffixal inflexion of the Present Tense of *tenere* and *temere* is identical, this amounts to asking whether the difference in stem behaviour renders them inflexionally distinct. Analogous questions can be asked about *geben* and *beben* in Table 6.5 and about *rājā* and *marut* in Table 6.6. For each of these sets of forms, is a single-paradigm or a multi-paradigm analysis to be preferred? So far, we have assumed that any differences in inflexional behaviour which are not predictable in such a way as to allow the recognition of macroparadigms are signs of paradigmatic distinctness. That assumption imposes the multi-paradigm analysis for the data of Tables 6.4-6.6, because there is synchronically no way of predicting that (for example) *tenere* will show stem allomorphy and *temere* will not. But I will suggest that, for the purposes of identifying paradigms, only affixal inflexion should count, and that the single-paradigm analysis is right.

Although in the data in Tables 6.4-6.6 there is no sign of paradigm mixture, the multiple-paradigm analysis does pose there a problem of a somewhat more subtle kind. Under our present definitions of 'paradigm' and 'macroparadigm', no allowance is made for the possibility of recognising degrees of distinctness (conversely, degrees of similarity) between paradigms; if two words differ in only one macroinflexion out of twenty, they belong to distinct macroparadigms just as much as if they differed in nineteen out of twenty. This is not to say that paradigm resemblance has no psychological reality, or is of no importance in inflexional theory.[5] So far as paradigm economy is concerned, however, once two paradigms are distinguished by distinct inflexions for even a single property-bundle, there is no extra 'cost' or complexity in further differentiation for other bundles. One might express this by saying that the Paradigm Economy Principle tolerates with ease maximal distinctness between paradigms.

So in Italian, if the two-paradigm analysis of *tenere* and *temere* is correct, an opportunity is presented, as it were, for distinctness not only in stem allomorphy but also in the endings. Under this analysis, there would be no extra 'cost' involved if the inflexional patterns were not as in Table 6.4 but as in Table 6.16, for example.

Table 6.16

Pseudo-Italian:	verbal Present Indicatives	
Sg	1	teng-o 'hold'	tem-o 'fear'
	2	tien-i	tem-i
	3	tien-e	tem-e
Pl	1	'ten-emo'	tem-iamo
	2	ten-ete	tem-ete
	3	teng-ono	tem-ono

Here the distinctness extends beyond stem allomorphy to the inflexional endings, namely in the 1st Person Plural, where I have postulated that *tenere* retains the historically 'correct' ending *-emo* (cf. Latin *tenēmus*). Now, as I have said, the fact that the data in Table 6.16 is not what we observe in actual Italian is merely accidental from the point of view of paradigm economy under the two-paradigm analysis. But it is what we will predict if the one-paradigm analysis is correct — in other words, if the stem-allomorphy of *tenere* is ignored for the purpose of paradigm economy. Under this analysis it is quite natural that the differences between the two inflexional patterns should be restricted to the stems; the fact that there are no differences in the endings simply shows that they belong to the same paradigm, and the stem behaviour is, from this point of view, irrelevant.

If we examine more examples, we find that the one-paradigm analysis looks increasingly appropriate. *Tenere* is by no means unique among *-ere* verbs in displaying stem allomorphy in the Present Indicative. Consider Table 6.17.

If we regard stem allomorphy as part of the associated inflexion, it is by no means obvious how many distinct realisations of (say) the 1st Singular we need to recognise, because the stem allomorphy takes different forms. For example, does *piaccio* 'I please' count as displaying a different realisation ('gemination + -o') from *dolgo* ('-g + -o'), and do both in turn differ from *soglio* ('palatalisation + -o')? The more distinct inflexions we posit for this one Person–Number combination, the more distinct paradigms we must recognise, on this assumption; and the more embarrassing it becomes, then, that all the inflexional differences continue to be concentrated in the stems, just as we found when comparing *tenere* and *temere*, and that even when we extend the data thus we do not find any distinct paradigm

223

Table 6.17

Type I: 1st Plural stem = 2nd Plural stem

		rimanere 'remain'	dolere 'hurt'	tacere 'be silent'
Sg	1	rimang-o	dolg-o	tacci-o ['tattʃo]
	2	riman-i	duol-i	tac-i ['ta:tʃi]
	3	riman-e	duol-e	tac-e
Pl	1	riman-iamo	dol-iamo	tac-iamo [ta'tʃa:mo]
	2	riman-ete	dol-ete	tac-ete
	3	rimang-ono	dolg-ono	tacci-ono

Type II: 1st Plural stem = 1st Singular stem

		solere 'be accustomed'	piacere 'please'
Sg	1	sogli-o ['sɔʎʎo]	piacci-o ['pjattʃo]
	2	suol-i	piac-i ['pja:tʃi]
	3	suol-e	piac-e
Pl	1	sogl-iamo [soʎ'ʎa:mo]	piacc-iamo [pjat'tʃa:mo]
	2	sol-ete	piac-ete
	3	sogli-ono ['sɔʎʎono]	piacci-ono

belonging to an -*ere* verb where the opportunity is taken, as it were, to introduce some allomorphy into the endings too.[6]

Let us be as generous as possible towards the multi-paradigm analysis of the data of Tables 6.4 and 6.17 by treating *piaccio*, *dolgo* and *soglio* as all displaying the same realisation of 1st Singular — we could call it 'heavy stem + -*o*'. Any stem-shape different from that which appears in the 1st Singular we will call a 'light' stem. But even on this basis we have to recognise a third 'paradigm', alongside those of *tenere* and *temere* in Table 6.4, namely that of type II verbs in Table 6.17. This is because of the stem allomorph used in the 1st Plural. In *tenere* a light allomorph is used, as in the type I verbs in Table 6.17; but in the type II verbs the heavy allomorph is used. Moreover, the contrast between the type I verb *tacere* and the type II verb *piacere* shows that it is impossible, at least with some verbs, to determine their type on phonological grounds, since these two verbs are phonologically as similar as they could possibly be in all conceivably relevant respects.[7] So, even when we describe stem allomorphy in a fashion deliberately designed to keep down the number of distinct inflexions that we must recognise, we are still forced by the multi-paradigm approach to acknowledge three paradigms among -*ere* verbs, as in Table 6.18.

Table 6.18

		No stem allomorphy (e.g. *temere*)	Stem allomorphy of: type I	type II
Sg	1	-o	H -o	H -o
	2	-i	L -i	L -i
	3	-e	L -e	L -e
Pl	1	-iamo	L -iamo	H -iamo
	2	-ete	L -ete	L -ete
	3	-ono	H -ono	H -ono

where H = heavy stem allomorph
      L = light stem allomorph

We are required to recognise three distinct paradigms here because there are three distinct inflexions for the 1st Plural shown in Table 6.18: *-iamo*, L *-iamo* and H *-iamo*. Now, whereas with only two paradigms (those of *tenere* and *temere*) the concentration of the inflexional differences in the stems might conceivably be put down to accident or coincidence, the addition of a third paradigm with the same set of endings again makes this account look less convincing. It is much more attractive, surely, to say that for the purpose of allocating Italian verbs to paradigms it is the endings alone which count.

There are further examples in Italian of verbs differing in stem behaviour but not in the affixal part of their inflexions. These are found in the 'fourth conjugation' (verbs with an infinitive in *-ire*). Defining 'heavy' and 'light' allomorphs in the same way as we did earlier, we can identify three types, as in Table 6.19.

Table 6.19

		No stem allomorphy (e.g. *partire* 'depart')	Stem allomorphy of: type I (e.g. *salire* 'go up')	type III (e.g. *finire* 'finish')
Sg	1	-o	H -o	H -o
	2	-i	L -i	H -i
	3	-e	L -e	H -e
Pl	1	-iamo	L -iamo	L -iamo
	2	-ite	L -ite	L -ite
	3	-ono	H -ono	H -ono
as in:				
Sg	1	part-o	salg-o	finisc-o
	2	part-i	sal-i	finisc-i
	3	part-e	sal-e	finisc-e
Pl	1	part-iamo	sal-iamo	fin-iamo
	2	part-ite	sal-ite	fin-ite
	3	part-ono	salg-ono	finisc-ono

225

Of these three, only the one labelled 'type III' is new. All but two of its members (*uscire* 'go out', heavy stem *esc-*, and *udire* 'hear', heavy stem *od-*) exhibit the stem-forming suffix *-isc-*.[8] Within type III the choice between heavy and light stem-allomorphs is phonologically determined: the heavy allomorph occurs in just those forms where the stem is stressed. But whether a verb 'goes like' *partire* or *finire* is not phonologically predictable, and a certain number of verbs vacillate between the two (e.g. *assorbire* 'absorb', 1 Sg *assorbisco* or *assorbo*). So, once again, if stem allomorphy is part of inflexion for the purpose of defining paradigms, there is no escaping the recognition of three distinct paradigms; and once again we are left with the embarrassing coincidence that all the paradigmatic differences are concentrated in the stems.

Outside Italian, it is quite easy to find similar examples. In Table 6.6 we have one such in Sanskrit. In *marut* the only stem alternation, that between *marut-* and *marud-*, is attributable to a perfectly general phonological process of voicing assimilation. In *rājā*, on the other hand, things are not so straightforward. The *rājñ- ~ rāja-* alternation is historically due to the syllabification of nasals between consonants, and that treatment may perhaps be synchronically appropriate too. The alternation between *rājā(n)-* and the other stem forms is also phonologically explicable originally; the longer, or 'strong', alternant is found in those forms where the historic Indo-European accent was on the stem, and the shorter, or 'weak' and 'middle', alternants where the accent was on the ending. But by the classical period of Sanskrit literature in the early centuries AD the Indo-European accentual system, still partially maintained in Vedic, had disappeared (Thumb & Hauschild 1958: 208). So from the synchronic point of view the distribution of the 'strong' *rājā(n)-* stem is not phonologically predictable. On this ground, if stem allomorphy is part of inflexion, *marut* and *rājā* must be assigned to different paradigms. But, again, the embarrassing question arises: why are the paradigmatic differences limited to the stems without affecting the endings? As with Italian, we can extend the data further and thereby increase the embarrassment. For example, the noun *panthāḥ* 'road' in Table 6.20, with quite idiosyncratic stem allomorphy, nevertheless displays just the same set of endings as *marut*.

Once again, the embarrassment disappears if we say that this kind of stem allomorphy does not count as inflexion for the pur-

Table 6.20

	Singular	Dual	Plural
NV	panthāḥ	panthān-au	panthān-aḥ
A	panthān-am	panthān-au	path-aḥ
I	path-ā	pathi-bhyām	pathi-bhiḥ
D	path-e	pathi-bhyām	pathi-bhyaḥ
Ab	path-aḥ	pathi-bhyām	pathi-bhyaḥ
G	path-aḥ	path-oḥ	path-ām
L	path-i	path-oḥ	pathi-ṣu

pose of identifying paradigms — in other words, if we adopt the single-paradigm rather than the multi-paradigm analysis of forms such as those in Tables 6.4-6.6.

Although I have argued for the single-paradigm analysis on grounds independent of paradigm economy, its adoption will have important implications there too. Consider the inflexional behaviour of three further Sanskrit nouns, all Neuter, in Table 6.21.

Table 6.21

	Singular	Singular	Singular
NVA	jagat 'world'	nāma 'name'	vāri 'water'
Instr	jagat-ā	nāmn-ā	vāriṇ-ā
Dat	jagat-e	nāmn-e	vāriṇ-e
AbG	jagat-aḥ	nāmn-aḥ	vāriṇ-aḥ
Loc	jagat-i	nāmn- / nāman- } i	vāriṇ-i
	Dual	Dual	Dual
NVA	jagat-ī	nāmn- / nāman- } ī	vāriṇ-ī
IDAb	jagad-bhyām	nāma-bhyām	vāri-bhyām
GL	jagat-oḥ	nāmn-oḥ	vāriṇ-oḥ
	Plural	Plural	Plural
NVA	jagant-i	nāmān-i	vārīn-i
Instr	jagad-bhiḥ	nāma-bhiḥ	vāri-bhiḥ
DAb	jagad-bhyaḥ	nāma-bhyaḥ	vāri-bhyaḥ
Gen	jagat-ām	nāmn-ām	vāriṇ-ām
Loc	jagat-su	nāma-su	vāri-ṣu

The hyphens are inserted in order to draw attention to the inflexional endings to their right. These are the same in all three columns (except for the phonologically predictable substitution of -ṣu for -su in the Loc Pl of *vāri*), and the differences between them are limited to the stems to the left of the hyphens. For example, in the Gen Pl *jagat* exhibits the same stem allomorph as in all other Cases except the NVA Pl, *nāma* exhibits one shared by most Singular Cases but none of the other Plural ones, and the allomorph of the stem of *vāri* is shared only by the NVA Pl. Yet, if affixes alone 'count', these three forms emerge as inflexionally identical. Consequently, if some Sanskrit noun is found which declines partly like *nāma* and partly like *vāri*, then, even if the *nāma*-like and *vāri*-like forms are distributed in such a way that the pattern of mixture cannot be correlated with any fundamental morphosyntactic property contrast such as Singular versus Plural, there will be no question of paradigm mixture and hence no breach of paradigm economy. So the fact that a group of nouns which behave like this does in fact exist in Sanskrit does not constitute counterevidence to the Paradigm Economy Principle, and necessitates no special 'escape clause'. This group consists of *asthi* 'bone', *akṣi* 'eye', *dadhi* 'sour milk' and *sakthi* 'thigh' (Whitney 1889: 122), which decline as in Table 6.22.

Table 6.22

	Singular	Dual	Plural
NVA	asthi	asthn- ⎫ ī asthan- ⎭	asthān-i
I	asthn-ā	asthi-bhyām	asthi-bhiḥ
D	asthn-e	asthi-bhyām	asthi-bhyaḥ
Ab	asthn-aḥ	asthi-bhyām	asthi-bhyaḥ
G	asthn-aḥ	asthn-oḥ	asthn-ām
L	asthn- ⎫ i asthan- ⎭	asthn-oḥ	asthi-ṣu

The boxes in Table 6.22 enclose those forms which resemble *vāri*; the rest 'go like' *nāma*.

The example of *asthi* illustrates how the affix-only approach to identifying paradigms leads to a weakening of the predictions made by the Paradigm Economy Principle in respect of one type of inflexional pattern; for, if stem allomorphy were allowed to contribute to inflexional distinctness, paradigms like that of *asthi* would be predicted not to exist. But in respect of other logically conceivable types of inflexional pattern, the affix-only approach helps to strengthen the Paradigm Economy Principle, in that the Principle now predicts to be impossible some kinds of pattern which would otherwise be compatible with it. Consider two hypothetical nominal paradigms of the shape given in Table 6.23 (where large letters indicate stems, small letters indicate inflexional endings, and stem allomorphs are distinguished by the presence or absence of an apostrophe).

Table 6.23

Case	1	R a	T e
	2	R b	T′f
	3	R c	T g
	4	R d	T′d

These paradigms are clearly distinct. But what happens when we introduce a third inflexional pattern exhibited by a stem S, partially similar to both R and T? One conceivable pattern would be as in Table 6.24.

Table 6.24

Case	1	R a	S a	T e
	2	R b	S′b	T′f
	3	R c	S g	T g
	4	R d	S′d	T′d

Now, does this involve a breach of paradigm economy? If we regard not only affixes but also stem allomorphy as contributing to inflexional distinctness, the answer is no; this is because Case 2 has three distinct realisations, which we can symbolise b, $'b$ and $'f$. But if we adopt the affix-only approach, then the difference in stem allomorphy between Rb and S'b (or, better, the difference in the distribution of distinct stem allomorphs within the declensions of R and S) does not render them inflexionally distinct. Consequently, no Case in Table 6.24 has more than two distinct realisations, and the mixed behaviour of S ('going like' R in Case 1 and T in Case 3) contravenes paradigm economy. If differences in stem allomorphy can render paradigms distinct, therefore, the Paradigm Economy Principle makes no predictions about the examples in Table 6.24; if not, on the other hand, it makes a quite precise prediction, namely that such a pattern could not exist, or, if it did exist, would be under strong pressure to reshape itself into a two-paradigm pattern — most easily, perhaps, by substituting Sc (with the R-type ending) for Sg (with the T-type ending) in Case 3.

It is an open question, of course, whether it is correct to predict the nonexistence of the sort of pattern illustrated in Table 6.24. In more concrete terms, the sort of pattern which would falsify this prediction is illustrated in the pseudo-Italian 'paradigms' in Table 6.25.

Table 6.25

Sg	1	tem-o	teng-o	parl-o 'I speak'
	2	tem-i	tien-i	parl-i
	3	tem-e	tien-e	parl-a
Pl	1	tem-iamo	ten-iamo	parl-iamo
	2	tem-ete	'ten-ate'	parlate
	3	tem-ono	teng-ono	parl-ano

Here, there is no breach of paradigm economy if stem allomorphy is reckoned to contribute to inflexional distinctness, because there are three distinct realisations for 3 Pl (namely -*ono*, H-*ono* and -*ano*); consequently, in the imaginary paradigm in the centre, the pseudo-Italian verb *tenere* is free to choose a 'first conjugation' ending -*ate* in the 2 Pl, like *parlate* 'you speak', instead of choosing -*ete*, like *temete* 'you fear', as the actual Italian verb *tenere* does and as the Paradigm Economy Principle combined with the affix-only approach predicts that it should.

One can summarise the principal claims made so far in this section by saying that, if stem allomorphy is not counted as part of inflexion for the purposes of paradigm economy, then we have a natural explanation for two sets of facts. Firstly, we can explain the failure of the inflexional patterns with and without stem allomorphy in Tables 6.4-6.6 to differ in their endings as well as in their stems, and more precisely the absence of pseudo-Italian versions of the stem-changing verb *tenere* differing from the non-stem-changing verb *temere* in the sorts of ways illustrated in Tables 6.16 and 6.25. Secondly, we can reconcile the Paradigm Economy Principle with the existence of what at first sight seems to be 'illegal' paradigm mixture in Sanskrit nouns like *asthi*, illustrated in Table 6.22. For the purpose of paradigm identification and paradigm economy, then, affixal inflexion plays a special role. But what about non-affixal inflexion of kinds other than stem allomorphy — stress alternation, for example? Is there any evidence that it, too, fails to differentiate paradigms for the purposes of paradigm economy? Tentatively, at least, we can answer yes. In Russian the three Masculine nouns *stol* 'table', *vxod* 'entrance' and *zub* 'tooth' differ in their stress patterns in the Plural as in Table 6.26.

Table 6.26

Nom	stol-ý	vxód-y	zúb-y
Acc	stol-ý	vxód-y	zúb-y
Gen	stol-óv	vxód-ov	zub-óv
Dat	stol-ám	vxód-am	zub-ám
Instr	stol-ámi	vxód-ami	zub-ámi
Loc	stol-áx	vxód-ax	zub-áx

The difference in stress pattern is not associated with any consistent contrast in morphosyntactic or morphosemantic properties, and the behaviour of *zub* is traditionally indicated in dictionaries by citing both the Nom Pl and the Gen Pl forms. There seems no way, within our present framework, to avoid regarding the Plural paradigm of *zub* as 'mixed', the mixture being governed by Case: *zub* 'goes like' *vxod* (i.e. it has stem stress) in the Nom/Acc Plural, but 'goes like' *stol* (i.e. it has ending stress) in the other Plural Cases. The crucial point, however, is that the affixal inflexion of all these three nouns is identical. The stress alternations illustrated show that none of the affixes involved is either intrinsically stressed or intrinsically unstressed, and indeed this lack of specification for stress is shared by all (or nearly all)[9] Russian nominal inflexional affixes; so all (or nearly all) stress alternations within nominal paradigms depend on characteristics (more or less idiosyncratic) of the stem. Consequently, if affixal morphology alone determines paradigm membership, *stol* and *vxod* belong to the same paradigm, and the existence of any declension-type with the same affixes but 'mixed' as regards stress distribution will not offend against paradigm economy. So the fact that such a type exists (illustrated by *zub*) is no embarrassment.

Clearly, more than one 'principal part' will often be needed in order to pin down the inflexional behaviour of words belonging to word-classes which exhibit more than one pattern of morpholexical stem alternation or other kinds of nonaffixal inflexion. For example, Russian dictionaries typically contain careful instructions about how the principal parts cited for nouns are to be used as predictors for stress within the rest of the paradigm, and for some nouns as many as four principal parts are needed. Here, then, is another contribution to solving the problem posed in section 3.2.1: how can proliferation of principal parts be compatible with the Paradigm Economy Principle? Indeed, it may seem that, for some of the examples discussed in section 3.2.4, an explanation in terms of stem allomorphy is just as plausible as one invoking the notion of slabs. For example, the need to cite for the Latin verb *cadere* 'fall' a Perfective principal part *cecidī* 'I have fallen' (cf. Table 3.13(b)) could perhaps be attributed simply to the morpholexical stem alternation *cad-* ~ *cecid-*, without invoking the Slab Codicil and the Perfective–Imperfective contrast. Certainly there is a strong tendency (emphasised by 'natural morphologists' such as Dressler (1977, 1985)) for morpholexical stems to be also realisational stems associated with fundamental morphosyntactic properties, and there are clear historical instances where an unmotivated morpholexical alternation left by phonological changes has acquired a morphosyntactic function and hence a clear realisational status: umlaut in German nouns is a classic example. But the fact that some prima facie breaches of paradigm economy can be accommodated in more than one fashion will not worry us; it would be silly to insist that no two independent explanatory principles should ever have overlapping consequences.[10] Besides, there are clear instances of paradigm mixture which are reconcilable with the Paradigm Economy Principle by means of the Slab Codicil but not by means of the affix-only approach to inflexion, and vice versa. To illustrate the former, we can turn to the three Latin verbs *amāre*, *sonāre* and *terrēre* in Table 3.13(b); each has only one morpholexical stem (*am-*, *son-* and *terr-*), yet their finite forms display paradigm mixture involving the Perfective–Imperfective contrast. To illustrate the latter, we need look no further than the Sanskrit and Italian examples discussed at length in this section.

NOTES

1. It is fortunate for my argument, in fact, that we do not find consistent correlation with Case rather than Number; for that would conflict with some of what is said about 'slabs' in Chapter 3 if (as suggested in Chapter 4) Number is a more 'relevant' or fundamental category than Case.

2. For the sake of simplicity, I ignore in (605) the realisation of the property Indicative.

3. Since the stem allomorph *grip-* is peculiar to the 2 Sg Preterite, the fact that the form also carries a suffix *-e* may violate the Elsewhere Condition (cf. section 5.2.2). But that need not concern us here.

4. The Latin stress rule, to which there are almost no 'surface exceptions', is: stress the penultimate syllable if that syllable is heavy, otherwise the antepenultimate. For more discussion, see e.g. W.S. Allen (1973).

5. Risch's (1977) circular arrangement of the Latin declensions (cf. Carstairs 1984a) seems to presuppose the psychological reality of degrees of similarity between paradigms; and Wurzel (1984) discusses extensively the implications of paradigm resemblance.

6. I am excluding here the highly irregular *avere* 'have' and *sapere* 'know' in which the stem and ending coalesce in most Persons of the Present Indicative. Vincent (1980) adduces diachronic evidence to show that speakers 'analyse' the commonest forms of these verbs as wholes rather than composites of stem plus ending; they are thus autonomous forms, in Bybee's (1985) terminology. The task of investigating the implications of this notion for paradigm economy remains for the future.

7. The contrast between *piacere* and *tacere* in the 1st Plural is confirmed by Garzanti (1963) and Roncari & Brighenti (1940), so seems well established in at least one version of educated standard Italian. Another phonologically similar verb, *giacere* 'lie', seems to vacillate, and on other verbs the authorities differ as to whether the stem used in the 1st Plural is 'light' or 'heavy'.

8. There is a phonological assumption underlying the third column in Table 6.19 which some might question. The stem in *finisco* [fi'nisko] can only be called the same as that in *finisci* [fi'niʃʃi] if we recognise a synchronic rule of velar softening in Italian, or if we regard the distribution of distinct underlying forms /'isk/ and /'iʃʃ/ as phonologically determined. The latter, at least, is very plausible; but even if we deny it, the main point — that the multi-paradigm approach requires three paradigms in Table 6.19 — is unaffected.

9. 'Nearly all', because one might argue that the Nom Pl ending *-a*, when attached to Masculines, is intrinsically stressed (e.g. *professor-á* 'professors', *dom-á* 'houses').

10. On independent but convergent explanatory principles in linguistics, see Sadock (1983).

7

A Case Study: Paradigm Economy in German Nouns

7.1 THE FACTS AND THE PROBLEMS

So far, we have discussed paradigm economy in relation to material from a variety of languages, both Indo-European and non-Indo-European. But this discussion has had a piecemeal character; we have not so far confronted the Paradigm Economy Principle with the inflexional behaviour of an entire word-class in any language. In this chapter, we make good the deficiency by looking in some detail at modern standard German noun inflexion. In a sense, this choice of German is random; since the Paradigm Economy Principle is claimed to have universal validity, it is just as important to confront it with Georgian verbs or Estonian adjectives. But German noun inflexion has three advantages. Firstly, the facts are relatively accessible and well known. Secondly, they have been the subject of two thorough and lucid theoretical studies by Wurzel (1970; 1984), who addresses questions about paradigms which are independent of, and thus in a sense complement, those that we are concerned with here;[1] they have also been discussed (from a different point of view) by Lieber (1981). Thirdly (and most importantly), German nouns present at first sight quite a severe challenge to the Paradigm Economy Principle. As any second-language learner of German will testify, distinct inflexional patterns seem numerous although the affixal resources involved are few. If we want to find solid counterevidence to the Principle, then, German noun inflexion seems a good place to search.

German nouns are inflected for two non-lexically-determined categories: Number (Singular and Plural) and Case

(Nominative, Accusative, Genitive and Dative). There are thus eight morphosyntactic property-bundles to be realised, although this is effectively reduced to six by the fact that the Nominative, Accusative and Genitive Plural are always homonymous within any paradigm. If at the outset we ignore all but the most obvious of the phonological factors which may point towards combining paradigms into macroparadigms, the total number of paradigms that we will need to recognise comes to at least sixteen, corresponding closely to the total of 'some 15' inflexion-classes given by Wurzel (1984: 210). In Table 7.1 I list examples for each, in the usual orthography (where *ä*, *ö*, *ü* represent 'umlauted' or front rounded vowels).

Table 7.1

		I	II	III	IV
Sg	N	Tag 'day'	Ziegel 'brick'	Gast 'guest'	Hand 'hand'
	A	Tag	Ziegel	Gast	Hand
	G	Tag-es	Ziegel-s	Gast-es	Hand
	D	Tag-e	Ziegel	Gast-e	Hand
Pl	NAG	Tag-e	Ziegel	Gäst-e	Händ-e
	D	Tag-en	Ziegel-n	Gäst-en	Händ-en
		V	VI	VII	VIII
Sg	N	Apfel 'apple'	Mutter 'mother'	Mann 'man'	Uhu 'eagle-owl'
	A	Apfel	Mutter	Mann	Uhu
	G	Apfel-s	Mutter	Mann-es	Uhu-s
	D	Apfel	Mutter	Mann-e	Uhu
Pl	NAG	Äpfel	Mütter	Männ-er	Uhu-s
	D	Äpfel-n	Mütter-n	Männ-ern	Uhu-s
		IX	X	XI	XII
Sg	N	Mutti 'mummy'	Bär 'bear'	Rose 'rose'	Dorn 'thorn'
	A	Mutti	Bär-en	Rose	Dorn
	G	Mutti	Bär-en	Rose	Dorn-es
	D	Mutti	Bär-en	Rose	Dorn-e
Pl	NAG	Mutti-s	Bär-en	Rose-n	Dorn-en
	D	Mutti-s	Bär-en	Rose-n	Dorn-en
		XIII	XIV	XV	XVI
Sg	N	Name 'name'	Museum 'museum'	Firma 'firm'	Cello 'cello'
	A	Name-n[2]	Museum	Firma	Cello
	G	Name-ns	Museum-s	Firma	Cello-s
	D	Name-n	Museum	Firma	Cello
Pl	NAG	Name-n	Muse-en	Firm-en	Cell-i
	D	Name-n	Muse-en	Firm-en	Cell-i

The two superficially distinct Genitive endings *-es* and *-s* can straight away be combined as members of one macroinflexion, distributed according to a combination of phonological and stylistic factors, and have implicitly been combined thus in all traditional and pedagogical descriptions of modern German. Broadly speaking, the *-es* alternant may occur only after a stressed syllable; but, as usual, we can leave on one side the question of whether only one phonological representation is involved. The same applies to the endings *-en* and *-n*. On this basis, and exploiting the traditional status of the Genitive Singular and Nominative Plural as principal parts, we can highlight the main characteristics of each paradigm as in Table 7.2.

Table 7.2

		I	II	III	IV	V	VI	VII	VIII	IX	X	XI
Gen	Sg	-s	-s	-s	Ø	-s	Ø	-s	-s	Ø	-n	Ø
Nom	Pl	-e	Ø	¨e	¨e	¨	¨	¨er	-s	-s	-n	-n

		XII	XIII	XIV	XV	XVI
Gen	Sg	-s	-ns	-s	Ø	-s
Nom	Pl	-n	-n	truncation -n	truncation -n	truncation -i

Our next task is to list the inflexional resources available for each property-bundle, bearing in mind our decision in Chapter 6 that only affixal inflexion 'counts' for the purposes of paradigm economy, as in Table 7.3.

Table 7.3

Sg	Nom	Ø
	Acc	Ø, -n
	Gen	Ø, -s, -n
	Dat	Ø, -e, -n
Pl	NAG	Ø, -e, -er, -s, -n, -i
	D	-n, -ern, -s, -i

From this it emerges that the most generously supplied property-bundles are the non-Dative Plural Cases, which have six realisations. The Paradigm Economy Principle therefore seems to predict that there should be no more than six distinct nominal paradigms in German. How can we reconcile this prediction with the total of 16 paradigms illustrated in Table 7.1 — or twelve, if we disregard those four (III, V, XIV and XV) which are distinct from some other paradigm (I, II, XII and XI respectively) by stem allomorphy alone?

The rest of this chapter will be devoted to showing that this reconciliation can indeed be effected, and that the inflexional behaviour of German nouns is therefore compatible with the Principle. The argument will involve macroparadigms, slabs and the affix-only approach to paradigmatic distinctness, and will thus illustrate further the usefulness of these elements of our theoretical 'package'.

7.2 GERMAN NOMINAL MACROPARADIGMS

We have already noted how the traditional analysis ignores the occasional schwa (spelt -*e*-) in the Genitive Singular alternants -*s* and -*es*, and similarly in the -*n* and -*en* of the Dative Plural and other Cases. In this, the macroparadigm concept is implicitly invoked. But there is scope for much wider application of the macroparadigm concept in German, involving not only phonological but also morphosyntactic and even morphosemantic predictability. We can thereby combine the 16 paradigms in Tables 7.1 and 7.2 into a total number of macroparadigms much closer to, or even exactly equivalent to, what the Paradigm Economy Principle requires.

Consider the paradigms I and III (*Tag* and *Gast*) on the one hand and II and V (*Ziegel* and *Apfel*) on the other. Affixally, the inflexion of I and III is identical, so for the purposes of paradigm economy we can classify them as a single paradigm; let us call it I'. For the same reason, we can classify II and V as a single paradigm II'. Now let us compare I' and II'. Their inflexional differences are set out in Table 7.4.

Table 7.4

	I'	II'
Gen Sg	-es	-s
Nom Pl	-e	Ø
Dat Pl	-en	-n

The -*es*/-*s* and -*en*/-*n* alternations have already been mentioned; only the -*s* and -*n* alternants are permitted after an unstressed syllable ending in a sonorant, so the nonexistence of e.g. *Ziegeles and *Äpfelen is phonologically predictable. But the same applies to the -*e*/∅ alternation in the Nom Pl also. In German nouns (unlike adjectives), the Nom Pl ending -*e* never occurs after -*el*, -*en*, -*er*, so that if we posit a single macroparadigm embracing paradigms I′ and II′ (let us call it I″), the distribution of -*e* and ∅ as Nominative Plural allomorphs is phonologically predictable within it. The paradigms IV (*Hand*) and VI (*Mutter*) are related in just the same way; we can combine them into one macroparadigm (call it IV″) on the strength of the fact that the non-Dative Plural Cases lack the suffix -*e* just in the two nouns *Mutter* 'mother' and *Tochter* 'daughter' which end in unstressed -*er*. These two nouns in fact constitute the entire membership of declension-class VI.

It is worth emphasising that the fact that we combine two paradigms into a single macroparadigm for the purposes of paradigm economy need not commit us to regarding them as identical for all purposes. Wurzel (1984), in common with Mayerthaler (1981), attaches considerable weight to typological differences such as that between the *Tag* paradigm (with 'additive' marking for the property Plural) and the *Ziegel* paradigm (with zero marking). It is because of this that Wurzel rejects his earlier (1970) analysis, under which the Plurals of *Tag* and *Ziegel* were inflexionally identical (/tāg + e/, /tsı̄gel + e/) and differed only phonologically in virtue of a schwa-deletion rule. But there is no real inconsistency between Wurzel's current approach and ours. If (as is likely) a variety of independent principles govern both synchronic and diachronic aspects of morphological organisation, it is not surprising that behaviour which counts as similar from the point of view of one principle (e.g. paradigm economy) should count as different from the point of view of another (e.g. 'iconicity' in morphological marking). Tension between phonological and morphological consistency has long been recognised as a factor in morphological change; it is time now to recognise that tension between purely morphological principles may be a factor too.

So far, then, we have set up on the basis of phonological predictability two macroparadigms: I″ (embracing the paradigms I, II, III and V) and IV″ (embracing IV and VI). Our next step will be to combine I″ and IV″ into a single big macroparadigm on the basis of morphosyntactic predictability. This involves taking account of the morphosyntactic category of Gender, which we have not so far mentioned. German has three Genders (Masculine, Feminine and Neuter), which are manifested in nouns, attributive adjectives and determiners. The crucial fact about nominal Gender for present purposes is that all the six paradigms within macroparadigms I" and IV" are restricted to only one or two Genders, as follows in Table 7.5.

Table 7.5

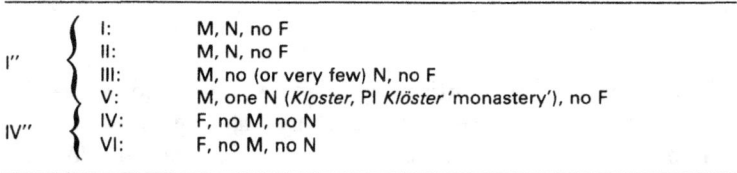

I" {	I:	M, N, no F
	II:	M, N, no F
	III:	M, no (or very few) N, no F
	V:	M, one N (*Kloster*, Pl *Klöster* 'monastery'), no F
IV" {	IV:	F, no M, no N
	VI:	F, no M, no N

It also emerges from Table 7.5 that the macroparadigms as well as the paradigms correlate with Gender; IV" (combining two paradigms which display no overt inflexion in the Singular) contains only Feminines while I" (combining various paradigms with -s in the Genitive Singular) contains no Feminines. We can therefore set up a grand macroparadigm within which inflexional behaviour is determined partly on the basis of phonology and partly on the basis of Gender. In so doing, we are saying in effect that the inflexion of *Hand* (for example) is related to that of *Gast* in just the way that the inflexion of Latin *dominus* was related in section 3.2.2 to that of *bellum*. Invoking traditional terminology, we can call this grand German macroparadigm the Strong macroparadigm.

It is natural to ask at this point whether the distinction between Feminines and non-Feminines has any relevance elsewhere — that is, in what were listed as paradigms VII-XVI in Tables 7.1 and 7.2. The answer is yes. The facts are as set out in Table 7.6.

Again we see a clear division between paradigms which contain only Feminines and ones which contain none. This suggests that we should look for a way of combining inflexionally similar paradigms into macroparadigms on the basis of this Gender distinction. In Table 7.6 as in Table 7.5, the Feminine-only paradigms (IX, XI and XV) turn out to be invariant in the

PARADIGM ECONOMY IN GERMAN NOUNS

Table 7.6

VII:	M, N, no F
VIII:	M, N, no F
IX:	F, no M, no N
X:	M only
XI:	F only
XII:	M, N, no F
XIII:	M, no N (unless we count *Herz* 'heart' with Acc Sg *Herz*, not **Herzen*), no F
XIV:	M, N, no F
XV:	F, no M, no N
XVI:	Italian loanwords only; M, N, no F

Singular, as we can confirm by checking in Table 7.1; so it makes sense to try to combine these paradigms with non-Feminine ones from which they differ inflexionally in the Singular but which they resemble in the Plural. On this basis, we arrive at the following possibilities of combination:

(701) IX (*Mutti*) can be combined with VIII (*Uhu*)
        XI (*Rose*) can be combined with X (*Bär*) or XII (*Dorn*) or XIII (*Name*)
        XV (*Firma*) can be combined with XIV (*Museum*)

There are also two non-Feminine paradigms (VII (*Mann*) and XVI (*Cello*)) with no Feminine analogues; these must therefore (at this stage, at least) constitute macroparadigms on their own. So far as the Feminine paradigms IX and XV are concerned, the Macroparadigm Uniqueness Claim is complied with; for each of the two, there is only one relevantly similar non-Feminine paradigm. There is no problem, therefore, in recognising Gender-based macroparadigms that we can call VIII" (embracing *Uhu* and *Mutti*) and XIV" (embracing *Museum* and *Firma*). The problem posed by XI (*Rose*) will be discussed further when we examine the intricacies of paradigms I, XII and XIII in the next section. Meanwhile, however, let us summarise how far we have reached in our attempt to reconcile the German facts with the Paradigm Economy Principle.

Ignoring for the moment paradigms X-XIII, the macroparadigms we have arrived at and their corresponding affixal macroinflexions are as in Table 7.7.

Table 7.7

Strong (paradigms I-VI):
  Sg Nom   Ø
       Acc   Ø
       Gen   -s *non-F*; Ø F^3
       Dat   -e *as a stylistic option after stressed syllables in non-F nouns; otherwise* Ø
  Pl NAG   Ø *after stems in* -el, -er, -en; -e *elsewhere*
       Dat   Ø *after stems in* -en;[4] -n *elsewhere*
VII (one paradigm only):
  Sg   *as Strong macroparadigm*
  Pl NAG   -er
       Dat   -ern
VIII″ (paradigms VIII, IX):
  Sg Nom   Ø
       Acc   Ø
       Gen   -s *non-F*; Ø *F*
       Dat   Ø
  Pl   -s
XIV″ (paradigms XIV, XV):
  Sg   *as VIII″*
  Pl   -n
XVI (one paradigm only):
  Sg   *as VIII″*
  Pl   -i

The total of five macroparadigms here is consistent with the Paradigm Economy Principle, because there are five distinct macroinflexions for the most generously provided property-bundles (the non-Dative Plural Cases), namely Ø/ -e, -er, -s, -n and -i. If, however, we look at the entire inflexional resources available for these Cases as summarised in Table 7.3, we find that these five macroparadigms have used them all up; there are no further Plural endings left over to legitimise (as it were) the existence of further macroparadigms. Yet we know that four further paradigms (X-XIII) exist. This is the problem that we will tackle in the next section.

7.3 THE WEAK DECLENSION-TYPES

It may be useful to remind ourselves what the four problematic paradigms X-XIII look like by extracting the relevant characteristics from Table 7.2. It will be useful also to see them alongside macroparadigm XIV″, for reasons which will appear shortly:

Table 7.8

		X	XI	XII	XIII	XIV	XV
						_____XIV″_____	
Gen	Sg	-n	Ø	-s	-ns	-s	Ø
Nom	Pl	-n	-n	-n	-n	truncation -n	truncation -n
	e.g.	Bär	Rose	Dorn	Name	Museum	Firma

The first point to note is that, so far as affixal inflexion is concerned, XIV and XV are identical to XII and XI respectively; so, from the point of view of paradigm economy, we are dealing here with not four 'new' paradigms but two, and our success earlier in combining XIV and XV on the basis of Gender may indicate the possibility of further amalgamations. This possibility is enhanced when we notice that the paradigms in Table 7.8 constitute precisely those with *-n* as the non-Dative Plural suffix. The apparent conflict with the Paradigm Economy Principle would be resolved if all the Singular allomorphy in Table 7.8 were predictable on the basis of lexically determined phonological, syntactic or semantic properties, just as we exploited Gender in building up the Strong macroparadigm. This is in fact the solution that we will mainly explore, while taking note of alternative or supplementary analyses involving the Slab Codicil or stem allomorphy.

We have already noted that XIV and XV are restricted to non-Feminines and Feminines respectively; and, referring to the data in Table 7.6, we find that there are further Gender-based restrictions, with XI containing only Feminines and X, XII and XIII containing none. Anticipating somewhat, we can think in terms of a macroparadigm on the lines set out in Table 7.9, embracing all the paradigms X-XV.

Table 7.9

Weak macroparadigm (first statement):
Sg	Nom	Ø
	Acc	Ø *F*; Ø *non-F* ...; -n *non-F* ...
	Gen	Ø *F*; -s *non-F* ...; -n *non-F* ...; -ns *non-F* ...
	Dat	*as Acc*
Pl		-n

If this analysis works, then paradigm XI no longer poses a difficulty for the Macroparadigm Uniqueness Claim, as suggested at (701), since all the paradigms which it resembles in the Plural belong to the same macroparadigm. The analysis will not work, however, unless we can fill in the dots in Table 7.9 in such a way as to account fully for the variety of exponents for the non-Nominative Singular Cases in the non-Feminines. But there is a semantic category whose relevance here has already been recognised by both Wurzel (1970) and Keller (1978), namely Animacy. Wurzel designates paradigm X (*Bär*) [− Strong, + Animate] and paradigm XII (*Dorn*) [− Strong, − Animate]; that is, within a single inflexional class labelled [− Strong], including paradigms X and XII, the incidence of -*n*, -*s* and Ø as Singular endings is predictable on the basis of Animacy. This certainly squares with the fact that class X contains a number of Animates such as *Fürst* 'prince', *Präsident* 'president', *Held* 'hero' and *Ochs* 'ox', while XII contains a number of Inanimates such as *Staat* 'state', *See* 'lake', *Strahl* 'ray' and *Schmerz* 'pain'. Keller, for his part, regards Animacy as relevant to our class XIII (*Name*) as well. Noting that the relevant Neuters (e.g. *Auge* 'eye', *Insekt* 'insect') are almost all in class XII, he adds (1978: 563): 'the masc. nouns divide into three subclasses according to the formation of the gen. sg.: (a) gen. sg. -*en*, only nouns denoting animate beings; (b) gen. sg. -*ens* [as in *Namens*], inanimate nouns ending in -*e*, e.g. *Gedanke* ['thought'], *Name*, *Wille* ['will']; (c) gen. sg. -*es*, nouns ending in a consonant.' Translating Keller's observations into our format, we can fill in the gaps in Table 7.9 as follows in Table 7.10.

Table 7.10

Weak macroparadigm (second statement):
Sg Nom Ø
   Acc   Ø *F, N, M-Inanimate*
         -n *M-Animate*
   Gen   Ø *F*
         -n *M-Animate*
         -ns *M-Inanimate with stem in -e*
         -s *others* (*i.e. N; M-Inanimate with stem not in -e*)
   Dat   *As Acc*
Pl   -n

Keller's claim about the relevance of Animacy to the -*ns*/-*n* alternation has diachronic as well as synchronic support; in sixteenth century German the two endings competed with each other until they sorted themselves out on the basis of Animate -*n* and Inanimate -*ns* for Masculines and Neuters (Keller 1978: 417). Nevertheless, is not quite adequate as a synchronic statement, because there are small groups of nouns which do not fit: (a) some Masculine Animates with Gen Sg in -*s* (i.e. in class XII), e.g. *Vetter* 'cousin', *Professor*; (b) some Masculine Inanimates with Gen Sg in -*n* (i.e. in class X), e.g. *Diamant* 'diamond', *Dividend*; (c) the single Neuter *Herz* 'heart', with Acc Sg *Herz*, Gen Sg *Herzens*, Dat Sg *Herzen*. Groups (a) and (b) can perhaps be dealt with by incorporating more complex phonological conditioning into the statement of macro-inflexional distribution, overriding the Animacy conditions (-*n* after nasal plus obstruent, -*s* after unstressed vowel plus liquid). This yields an apparently extremely complex macroparadigm statement, which I will not attempt to set out in tabular form. But this may be no drawback, for three reasons. Firstly, there is evidence that Germans themselves find the macroparadigm analysis of paradigms X-XIII excessively complicated; even a well educated native speaker can hesitate over (for example) the Gen Sg of *Professor* (*Professors* or *Professoren*?).[5] Secondly, the notion 'slab', discussed in section 3.2.4, can be exploited in the analysis of paradigms X-XV in a way which reduces this complexity significantly. Thirdly, there are signs of a reanalysis of nouns of class XIII (*Name*) on lines which have the effect of removing them from the Weak macroparadigm into the Strong one. We will look at the second and third points in turn.

The bulk of the Masculine Inanimates in the Weak macroparadigm that we have posited, as well as a few Animates like *Professor*, belong to paradigm XII (*Dorn*). An aspect of this paradigm that we have not yet commented on is the fact that it is 'mixed'; in the Singular it is identical to the Strong macroparadigm. From the point of view of our discussion so far, this is an accident; nothing in our theory requires that, when inflexions are distributed within the Weak macroparadigm on the basis of Animacy, one of the resulting paradigms should mimic another macroparadigm exactly. One way of dealing with class XII, then, might be to remove it from the Weak macroparadigm altogether and straightforwardly to invoke the Slab Codicil at (313). If we do so, we say in effect that paradigm XII does indeed constitute an 'extra' paradigm over and above what paradigm economy strictly permits, but it is legitimised on the basis of the fundamental morphosyntactic property contrast of Number. That approach, however, goes to the opposite extreme; it requires us to treat as accidental the very substantial correlation involving Animacy that we have so far observed. What we want, clearly, is a way of capturing both observations. The approach I suggest involves an extension of the theory of paradigms that we have so far developed, but a natural one that remains within its spirit. In setting out the non-Weak macroparadigms in Table 7.7, we have already allowed ourselves to save space by describing the inflexional pattern for the Singular of VII (*Mann*), XIV" (*Museum*) and XVI (*Cello*) as being like that of the Strong macroparadigm (*Tag*) or macroparadigm VIII" (*Uhu*). But it seems reasonable to regard this as more than a mere abbreviatory device. In other words, we should allow for the possibility that a paradigm may consist not of a bare list of inflexions without any intermediate organising principle, but rather of a collection of slabs, each corresponding to a fundamental morphosyntactic property; apart from being implicit in the Slab Codicil, what is essentially this possibility is explicitly recognised by Bybee (e.g. 1985) and Rudes (1980). The notion 'slab' thus has uses independent of the need to account for certain prima facie breaches of paradigm economy.

The immediate relevance of the notion lies in the way it helps to reduce the complexity of the Weak macroparadigm; the grammar of German does not have to specify separately what the Animate–Inanimate contrast entails for each Case or even each Singular Case, since it can simply state that Weak nouns with the appropriate morphosemantic and phonological properties choose the Strong slab for their Singular inflexion. We can thus regard slab organisation and the category of Animacy as cooperating to make the inflexional complexity of a certain class of German nouns more manageable. Slab-based paradigm mixture without any morphosemantic correlation, as implied by straightforward invocation of the Slab Codicil, would suffice by itself to make the German facts consistent with the Paradigm Economy Principle, and so would the recognition of an extremely elaborate macroparadigm whose macroinflexional complexities were unalleviated by any intermediate organisation into slabs; what we actually find, however, is that the two independent factors combine so as to increase the cohesion and (it is reasonable to think) the learnability of an unusually complicated macroparadigm.

The slab concept thus helps to reduce the idiosyncrasies of the *Dorn* class (paradigm XII), but it is of little help with the *Name* class (paradigm XIII). Here, the evidence points instead to an alternative analysis of the boundary between stem and ending. For convenience, in Table 7.11, I will set out in full the standard German paradigm of *Name*, alongside that of the type II noun *Magen* 'stomach'.

Table 7.11

Sg	Nom	Name 'name'	Magen 'stomach'
	Acc	Namen	Magen
	Gen	Namens	Magens
	Dat	Namen	Magen
Pl	NAG	Namen	Magen
	Dat	Namen	Magen

The reason for setting these two types alongside is to help us reconsider the question of where the inflexional differences between them reside. The way in which I originally presented the facts in Tables 7.1-7.2 implies a clear answer: the differences reside at least partly in the endings, because I attributed to *Name* a Gen Sg ending -*ns* distinct from the ending -*s* of type II (exemplified by *Ziegel*). But this begs the important question of where the boundary between stem and ending is to be placed. I assumed earlier that the appropriate 'base' or stem form for all Cases was identical to the Nominative Singular. But for *Name* at least there is a plausible alternative. Wurzel (1970) analyses the Gen Sg *Namens* as underlyingly /nām + n + s/, where between the root /nām/ and the inflexional affix /s/ there intervenes a stem-forming suffix ('Stammbildungselement') /n/. If we do likewise, and once more set the two paradigms of *Name* and *Magen* side by side, the following picture emerges, as set out in Table 7.12. The only inflexional difference between *Name* and *Magen* now lies in their stem allomorphy, which is irrelevant to paradigm economy. Paradigm XIII thus disappears as a distinct paradigm, being subsumed under paradigm II.

Table 7.12

Sg	Nom	Name	Magen
	Acc	Namen	Magen
	Gen	Namen-s	Magen-s
	Dat	Namen-Ø	Magen-Ø
Pl	NAG	Namen-Ø	Magen-Ø
	Dat	Namen-Ø	Magen-Ø

The fact that many nouns (those of our types III-VII) distinguish a Plural stem with umlaut from a Singular stem without shows that stem allomorphy is not foreign to German nominal declension. The account of *Name* just presented involves recognising a further instance of stem allomorphy, this time between the stem for the Nom Sg and the stem for all other Cases. Now, it has often been remarked that stem allomorphy within paradigms — at least, that which has no phonological motivation or clear-cut morphosyntactic function — tends to be reduced over time, albeit under somewhat hazy conditions. If, then, we find evidence for some diachronic change affecting nouns of the *Name* type which can be seen as levelling of stem allomorphy, then our new analysis, under which *Name* belongs to the same paradigm as *Magen*, is supported.

A diachronic change of the appropriate kind would be encroachment of one of the alternants *Name* and *Namen-* on the sphere of the other. And such a diachronic change does in fact seem to be occurring. Apart from *Name*, the commonest nouns which generally or occasionally follow type XIII are *Buchstabe* 'letter of the alphabet', *Friede* 'peace', *Funke* 'spark', *Gedanke* 'thought', *Glaube* 'belief', *Same* 'seed', *Schade* 'harm' and *Wille* 'will'. Yet concerning all these a standard pedagogical work on German grammar (Schulz & Sundermeyer 1964: 103) states: 'Folgende Substantive auf -e haben im Nominativ Singular *eine jüngere Nebenform auf -en* [my emphasis];' and, as my words 'generally or occasionally' imply, usage is by no means consistent. The Appendix to this chapter shows that three reputable dictionaries agree completely on the behaviour of only three of the nine nouns, namely *Gedanke* (which follows type XIII only), *Friede* (which has a variant *Frieden* of type II) and *Name* itself (whose type II variant *Namen* is variously described as 'weniger gut', 'Austrian' or 'rare'). *Funke, Same* and *Wille* are also said by all three dictionaries to have variant Nom Sg forms in *-en*, implying type II behaviour, and *Glaube* is added to the list by one of the three. There is therefore strong evidence for defection from type XIII to type II. There is also weaker evidence for defection to type X; *Buchstabe, Funke, Same, Glaube* and *Wille* are all alleged by at least one dictionary to have type X forms, although on none of them are all three dictionaries unanimous.

Defection from type XIII to type II is just what we will expect, on the assumption that types XIII and II are identical so far as their affixal inflexion is concerned and thus belong to the same paradigm for the purpose of paradigm economy. The relative weakness of the tendency to defect to type X is also to be expected, on this assumption. Superficially, defection to type II and defection to type X both involve a change in only one form (the Nom Sg and the Gen Sg respectively), and so would seem on *a priori* grounds about equally likely, with the latter perhaps marginally preferred because it involves a change in a more 'marked' form (the Genitive) rather than a less 'marked' one (the Nominative). But, according to our present account, defection to type X involves a more thorough-going reanalysis, affecting not only the form which changes 'on the surface' but also the boundary between stem and affix for all but one of the forms which do not change, as in Table 7.13.

Table 7.13

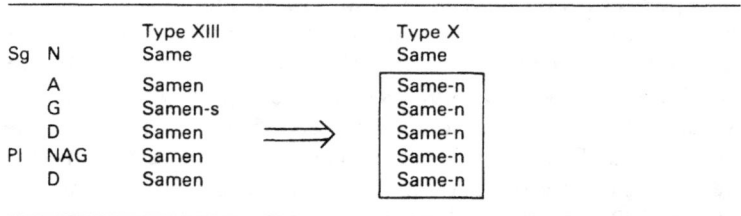

Contrast this with the degree of reanalysis involved in defection to type II, as illustrated in Table 7.14.

Here, it is only the Nom Sg which needs to change either its shape or its analysis. The assumption of a stem-allomorphy reanalysis of type XIII nouns thus suggests a motivation for the shift in progress of type XIII nouns to type II. In this respect, it is superior to the analysis of type XIII as a variant of one massive Weak macroparadigm, as summarised in Table 7.10. If

Table 7.14

		Type XIII	Type II
Sg	N	Same	⎡Samen⎤
	A	Samen	Samen
	G	Samen-s	Samen-s
	D	Samen	Samen
Pl	NAG	Samen	Samen
	D	Samen	Samen

(with an arrow ⟹ between the two paradigms)

type XIII nouns are securely anchored in an 'economical' array of paradigms on the basis of the sort of phonological, morphosyntactic and morphosemantic conditioning that I posited in Table 7.10, then they ought to be subject to no pressure to adopt a new Nominative Singular form. Yet, as we have seen, such pressure does apparently exist. The incorporation of type XIII into the Weak macroparadigm therefore seems in a sense too successful, since it characterises as unproblematic a declension-type which, on the evidence of current linguistic usage, is indeed problematic and subject to 'regularisation' through assimilation to the more numerous declension-type II.

A minor advantage of the stem-allomorphy analysis of type XIII is that it resolves the difficulty posed by the Neuter noun *Herz* 'heart' (see Table 7.6). If we try to fit *Herz* into a single large Weak macroparadigm as specified in Table 7.11, we are at a loss to account for how its inflexion differs from that of other Weak Neuters such as *Insekt* and *Auge*. If, on the other hand, we analyse *Herz* as a Strong (type II) noun with unusual stem allomorphy, then the difficulty disappears. So far as affixal inflexion is concerned, *Herz* is identical with other type II Neuters such as *Laster* 'vice' and all verbal infinitives in *-en* when used as nouns; and the fact that its Nominative Singular stem allomorph extends to the Accusative Singular too, in contrast to *Name* and the other Masculines of type XIII, can be attributed to the usual Indo-European Nom–Acc syncretism of Neuters (see section 4.3.3).

Let us suppose, then, that the assignment of type XIII to the Weak macroparadigm is no longer correct, and that synchronically in modern standard German type XIII is to be regarded as a mere sub-type of type II with unusual stem allomorphy. The fact remains that the Animate–Inanimate correlation of types X and XIII is sufficiently exact to be noticed in Keller's synchronic account, for which paradigm economy is not an issue,[6] and diachronically it contributed to the original stabilisation of type XIII in early modern German. The obvious question then arises: at what point did the macroparadigm analysis become too opaque for all or some native speakers to achieve, so that the stem-allomorphy analysis became preferable? A superficial answer might be: the sort of macroparadigm presented in Table 7.10, with inflexional choice governed by three different sorts of factor (phonological, morphosyntactic and morphosemantic) is too complex to be grasped and internalised. But at what point does a complex analysis become too complex? I will not try to answer this question here. An adequate answer will obviously require a careful study of the inflexional behaviour of the nouns in question over several hundred years and probably also a comparative study of their development in various dialects or *Umgangssprachen.* Whether the detailed results of such a study will tend to support either of our two approaches to reconciling type XIII with the Paradigm Economy Principle remains to be seen. But it is legitimate to claim that our examination of type XIII nouns here does confirm the Paradigm Economy Principle to this extent, that an inflexional pattern which constitutes a prima facie problem for paradigm economy seems to present a problem for speakers of German too; and it would not be surprising to find that different speakers internalised different solutions to it, achieving paradigm economy in different ways.

NOTES

1. For a review of Wurzel (1984), see Carstairs (1985a). Carstairs (1986) discusses German noun inflexion more briefly than here, using Wurzel-style terminology and considering explicitly the relationship between paradigm economy and Wurzel's 'complementary classes'. Apart from Wurzel, my thinking about German owes much to classes on the structure of German conducted by Paul Kiparsky at MIT in 1971, although both the questions addressed and the approach adopted are different.

2. Paradigm XIII is the only one in which the boundary between stem and ending is truly problematic. The implications of this will be discussed in section 7.3.

3. Frans Plank has pointed out (personal communication) that certain Feminine nouns may carry a Genitive -s when they occupy the determiner position within a noun phrase: *Muttis Liebling* 'mummy's darling', *Isoldes Mann* 'Isolde's husband', in contrast to *der Liebling*

seiner Mutti 'his mummy's darling', *der Mann der schönen Isolde* 'the husband of the beautiful Isolde'. But, however this phenomenon is to be described, its generality and the nature of its syntactic conditions show that it does not constitute evidence for a distinct paradigm.

4. Strictly, Ø ought to have been listed as a further exponent of Dat Pl in Table 7.3, and the nouns which exemplify it (such as *Garten* 'garden', *Magen* 'stomach') should have been assigned to an independent paradigm or paradigms in Table 7.1. But, in view of its distribution, this Ø has always been implicitly regarded as a phonologically conditioned variant of *-en/-n*, perhaps from the same phonological source; and in my terms *Garten* and *Magen* unquestionably belong to the Strong macroparadigm (more specifically, to paradigms V and II respectively).

5. Theodora Bynon (personal communication).

6. Wurzel (1970) offers essentially the same synchronic analysis as Keller, despite differences in assumptions and terminology. For him, the *-e* ending of the Nom Sg is a 'Nominativ-Erweiterung' or 'Nominative extension', and the ending *-en* of type X nouns is really a 'Stammbildungselement' or stem-forming element, not a 'Flexiv' or inflexion proper. But his rules of stem-formation and inflexion (1970: 47, 48) cooperate to ensure that all nouns with a Nominative extension acquire a stem-forming *-en* in non-Nominative Cases, but of these only the Inanimates subsequently receive an overt Genitive ending *-s*.

APPENDIX TO CHAPTER 7: INFLEXIONAL VACILLATION AMONG GERMAN NOUNS OF DECLENSION-TYPE XIII (*NAME*)

	Sprach–Brockhaus 1935	Cassels Revised German–English Dictionary 1978	Langenscheidt New Muret–Sanders Encyclopaedic Dictionary 1974
Buchstabe	X	XIII	XIII; -n II 'rare'
Friede	XIII; -n II	XIII; -n II	XIII; -n II
Funke	X; -n II	X; -n II	XIII; -n II
Gedanke	XIII	XIII	XIII
Glaube	XIII	XIII	XIII; -n II 'rare'; X 'rare'
Name	XIII; -n II 'weniger gut'	XIII; -n II 'Austrian'	XIII; -n II 'rare'
Same	X; -n II	XIII; -n II	XIII 'literary'; -n II
Schade	XIII; 'heute meist' -n V	XIII *with umlaut*; -n V	-n V; schade *without* -n *as adjective only*
Wille	XIII; 'seltener' -n II	XIII; -n II 'Austrian'	XIII; -n II 'rare'; X 'rare'

Roman numerals refer to declension-types exemplified in Table 7.1.

8
Next Steps

The aim of this book was to propose and defend certain generalisations about the relationship between morphosyntactic properties and their inflexional exponents. The search for such generalisations was expressed as a search for constraints on deviation from the 'simplest' one-to-one relationship observable in certain 'agglutinating' morphological patterns. Four principal generalisations have in fact been put forward: the Paradigm Economy Principle, the Macroparadigm Uniqueness Claim, the Systematic Homonymy Claim and the Peripherality Constraint. I have also mentioned other recent proposals which seem to bear on this topic: Bybee's 'relevance', Wurzel's 'system congruity', the Adjacency and Elsewhere Conditions, and Baker's 'Mirror Principle'.

In this concluding chapter I want to suggest briefly where one might go from here. A whole host of questions are still to be answered, some of which I have mentioned in the preceding chapters, and different linguists will differ on which are the most important. What I offer here is simply my own opinion on what the most pressing questions at this stage are, classified under five headings:

(a) testing the old generalisations;
(b) establishing new generalisations;
(c) relating the generalisations to each other within a theory of inflexion;
(d) relating the generalisations and the theory to other areas of grammar;
(e) relating the generalisations and the theory to 'external' evidence.

The evidence on which each of my four generalisations is based has been drawn from several languages and language families, but I have clearly examined only a fraction of the actual inflexional behaviour which might conceivably be relevant. An obvious task for the future, then, is to broaden the inquiry by **testing the old generalisations** against more data. At various points I have mentioned aspects of particular languages which ought to be looked at for this purpose. For example, by looking in Fulfulde and Mari, we may hope to glean hints on how, if at all, the Peripherality Constraint can be extended to cover situations where categories are not realised in a constant sequence; and by looking at the history of the older Germanic languages we may hope to test my suggestions about how the Constraint relates to stem allomorphy. On the Systematic Homonymy Claim there is much to be done on determining whether the fundamental distinction between 'systematic' and 'accidental' homonymies is plausible on other grounds; whether, for example, the homonymies we classify as accidental on grounds to do with morphological 'expression' correlate closely with those that would be so classified by someone studying homonymy (or syncretism) primarily from the point of view of morphological 'content' — that is, someone who, like Jakobson or Bierwisch, is interested in those relationships between the properties within a category which are independent of the shapes of their realisations. There is also much to be done in justifying the purported interaction of 'sequencing' and homonymy which I invoked when discussing certain Arabic and Latin facts in sections 4.3.2 and 5.1.3. Finally, in connexion with paradigm economy, there will almost certainly turn out to be instances of 'illegal' paradigm mixture which will need close diachronic examination in order to determine whether they can be reconciled with the Paradigm Economy Principle, on the lines that I have attempted elsewhere for the Latin third declension (Carstairs 1984a). A probable instance of this kind, not previously mentioned, is the *capiō* sub-type of the Latin third conjugation, which 'goes like' the ordinary third-conjugation type of *regō* in some forms and like the fourth conjugation (*audiō*) in others; the fact that this sub-type does not survive as such in any Romance language is encouraging from the point of view of defending the Paradigm Economy Principle, but its history needs to be compared in detail with what the Principle requires or permits at each stage.

In terms of the four deviations mentioned in Chapter 1, we have so far proposed constraints on only two: Deviations II and IV. So in any attempt to **establish new generalisations** there are obvious areas to explore. As various linguists have noted, paradigms which are partly 'fusional' and partly 'agglutinating', in traditional terms, are relatively rare — in other words, paradigms where some combinations of properties are realised simultaneously (exhibiting Deviation III) while other combinations involving the same categories are not. If this rarity is genuine, it may point to a constraint on Deviation III. And Deviation II is almost certainly subject to further constraints not directly involving peripherality, paradigm economy or adjacency.

In keeping with my intention to seek empirically valid generalisations rather than (at this stage) an explanatory theory, I have not made any systematic attempt to **relate the generalisations to each other**. Even so, certain interconnexions have come to light. In the Latin 1st Person Singular Imperfective Future Indicative *regam* 'I will rule', systematic homonymy (in the form of an attraction to the Subjunctive) comes to the rescue of the Peripherality Constraint in a reasonably uncontrived fashion, assuming only a quite natural relationship between 'homonymy rules' and morphological spell-out. Again, assigning macroparadigmatic relevance to the lexically determined property Neuter in the Nominative and Accusative of nouns in Latin and other Indo-European languages has a convenient consequence in that it allows us to call the Nom–Acc homonymy in Neuter nouns systematic (more specifically, a 'syncretism'). And, if it turns out that all inflexional counterexamples to the Adjacency Condition involve not affixes but roots (or morpholexical stems, in the terminology of Chapter 6) (Carstairs 1984b: 86), then an explanation for both this and the failure of stem allomorphy to 'count' for paradigm economy purposes may perhaps be sought in terms of a fundamental distinction between stem allomorphy and other kinds of inflexion, particularly affixation. This, in turn, might help to explain the paradox that in a language such as English relatively 'useful' morphological distinctions of Case and Gender have been lost while a 'useless' distinction between regular *s*-Plural and irregular ablaut-Plural nouns has been stubbornly retained; that is, it might not be accidental that the irregular Plurals all involve stem alternation rather than a range of 'rival' Plural affixes (except for the very marginal -*en* of *oxen* and *children*).

Another set of questions about which I have had little to say concerns the internal structure of morphosyntactic categories — the relationships between the properties which they contain, involving the distinction between more and less 'marked' properties within a given category and possibly involving the decomposition of properties into constituent 'features' or components. This neglect is defensible in the context of an inquiry into exponence relationships specifically; but the fact that so important an aspect of morphological organisation is left untouched by such an inquiry shows clearly that a theory of property–exponent relationships will not constitute a full theory of inflexion. And it is fairly easy, even at this stage, to guess at ways in which a theory of the internal structure of categories might impinge on a theory about constraints on the four deviations of Chapter 1. For example, we might explore whether sensitivity, even of the so far unconstrained 'inward' kind, is equally common among less 'marked' and more 'marked' properties; for example, is the realisation of Instrumental Plural in Russian nouns just as likely to be sensitive, on general grounds, as that of Accusative Singular? On the face of it, the answer seems likely to be no: Instrumental Plural in Russian in fact has only one realisation (-*ami*) whereas Accusative Singular has several, and the same sort of asymmetry is observable in all those languages whose inflexional paradigms display more allomorphy in (to put it crudely) the top left-hand corner than the bottom right-hand corner. Ideas of this kind about the relevance of markedness to morphological exponence have, of course, been put forward before, most famously perhaps by Kurylowicz (1949) as part of an account of 'analogical processes' in linguistic change; the value of Kurylowicz's proposals is weakened, however, by the lack of any coherent synchronic theory of morphology embracing, in my terms, an account of how property–exponent relationships are constrained.[1] Clearly, developing a complete theory of inflexion will require us to explore property–exponent relationships and what one might call 'property–property relationships' side by side.

The task of **relating generalisations about inflexion to other areas of grammar** falls neatly into two, involving phonology on the one hand and syntax and semantics on the other. I have said something about the former in sections 1.4 and 3.1.3, and about the latter in sections 1.1, 4.2.3 and 5.1.5. I have nothing further to say about the relationship with phonology, except to emphasise that a reasonably firmly established account of what is possible and what is not in inflexional exponence will add a useful new ingredient to the debate about phonological representation, and that there are enough instances of inflexion that are phonologically uncontroversial in relevant respects to enable us to contribute to that debate without arguing in a circle. On the syntactic side, one important topic about which I have so far said nothing is the distinction between inflexional affixes and 'clitics', in the sense of Zwicky (1977). There are no universally agreed criteria for distinguishing affixes from clitics synchronically, and affixes are often derivable etymologically from independent words which have undergone cliticisation (for example, the Person−Number endings of the Future and Conditional Tenses in French, or the Passive suffix -*s* in Swedish). Yet, on the face of it, if clitics and affixes get where they are by processes of radically different kinds — for example, by syntactic movement rules and by morphological realisation rules respectively — then we would expect 'core' instances of clitics to have at least some general characteristics that 'core' affixes do not share, and vice versa. Moreover, if we can find any characteristics which clearly belong to one class rather than the other, we will have criteria which may be useful for helping to determine in unclear cases whether something is an affix or a clitic; we can also hope to investigate more fruitfully the diachronic processes whereby clitics change into affixes and, perhaps, affixes into clitics. Is there any sign yet of any such clear characteristics? I suggest that one inflexional characteristic worth examining with this in mind is sensitivity. For an inflexional affix to be sensitive to some lexically or syntactically determined property of its 'host' (or stem) is commonplace; on the other hand, it seems at least unusual for clitics to be sensitive to their hosts as such, other than phonologically (Carstairs 1981c; 1985b). This is not logically necessary; for example, one can perfectly well envisage a language in which object pronouns which are cliticised to verbs vary in shape according to verbal Tense or conjugation-type. If this sort of behaviour is never found, it is at least worth asking whether this indicates a fundamental contrast between inflexional and syntactic organisation.

The final set of pressing questions, I suggest, relates to **'external' evidence for our generalisations**, where by 'external evidence' I mean what Kenstowicz & Kisseberth (1977:

Chapter 1) and Dressler (1977: 7) mean: evidence from psycholinguistics (including aphasia and language acquisition), speech errors, linguistic change and linguistic variation (dialectology and sociolinguistics). I have in various places used arguments from linguistic change, which implies that I share the view, now widely held, that de Saussure's rigid separation of synchrony and diachrony was mistaken, and that comparing the output of the grammars of two historically successive 'états de langue' can yield clues about the framework in which these grammars ought to be written and hence about the synchronic organisation of these grammars themselves — a view whose revival owes much to Kiparsky (1968b) and which has also been argued forcefully by Lightfoot (1979). How much attention one pays to psycholinguistic arguments will depend on how one sees the relationship between the linguist's description of a language system and the psychologist's description of how users of that language acquire, speak and understand it. Debate about this has been long and inconclusive. My own view is that it is at least worth exploring how close the correlation is between (for example) inflexional behaviour that seems complex on 'internal' grounds and behaviour that is acquired late in childhood or that is easily disrupted by speech disorders. Little work has been done on this in the West, although Hooper (1979) has turned to the acquisition of morphology as a source of evidence for morphological generalisations, drawing on some of the work reported by Ferguson and Slobin (1973). But a considerable amount of the work on the acquisition of highly inflected languages that has been published in the Soviet Union and other east European countries will almost certainly turn out to be relevant to the sort of inquiry I am advocating here. This gives the student of inflexional morphology a further reason for learning Russian, beyond the fact that it is itself delightfully complex morphologically.

NOTE

1. For a recent comment on the historical morphologist's continued need for a synchronic theory of morphology, see Andersen (1980: 2).

Bibliography

Aaltio, M.-H. (1964). *Essential Finnish.* London: University of London Press.
Allen, M. (1979). *Morphological Investigations.* University of Connecticut PhD thesis. Ann Arbor: University Microfilms.
Allen, W.S. (1973). *Accent and Rhythm.* Cambridge: Cambridge University Press.
Andersen, H. (1980). Morphological change: towards a typology. In Fisiak (ed.), 1-50.
Anderson, S.R. (1974). *The Organization of Phonology.* New York: Academic Press.
—— (1981). Why phonology isn't 'natural'. *Linguistic Inquiry 12,* 493-539.
—— (1982). Where's morphology? *Linguistic Inquiry 13,* 571-612.
Anderson, S.R. & Kiparsky, P. (eds.). (1973). *A Festschrift for Morris Halle.* New York: Holt Rinehart.
Anttila, R. (1977). *Analogy.* The Hague: Mouton.
Arnott, D.W. (1970). *The Nominal and Verbal Systems of Fula.* Oxford: Oxford University Press.
Aronoff, M. (1976). *Word Formation in Generative Grammar.* (Linguistic Inquiry Monograph No. 1.) Cambridge, Mass.: MIT Press.
Bach, E. & Harms, R.T. (eds.) (1968). *Universals in Linguistic Theory.* New York: Holt Rinehart.
Baker, M. (1985). The Mirror Principle and morphosyntactic explanation. *Linguistic Inquiry 16,* 373-415.
Bally, C. (1944). *Linguistique générale et linguistique française* (2nd edn.). Bern: Francke.
Bánhidi, Z., Jókay, Z. & Szabó, D. (1965). *Learn Hungarian* (4th edn.). Budapest: Tankönyvkiadó.
Bazell, C.E. (1960). A question of syncretism and analogy. *Transactions of the Philological Society,* 1-12.
Bierwisch, M. (1967). Syntactic features in morphology: general problems of so-called pronominal inflection in German. In *To Honour Roman Jakobson: Essays on the Occasion of his Seventieth Birthday,* 239-70. The Hague: Mouton.

Bloch, B. (1947). English verb inflection. *Language* 23, 399-418. Reprinted in RiL I, 243-54.
Bloomfield, L. (1935). *Language* (revised edn.). London: Allen & Unwin.
Broselow, E. (1983). Salish double reduplications: subjacency in morphology. *Natural Language & Linguistic Theory* 1, 317-46.
Bybee [Hooper], J. (1985). *Morphology: A Study of the Relation between Meaning and Form.* (Typological Studies in Language 9.) Amsterdam: John Benjamins.
Bynon, T. (1977). *Historical Linguistics.* Cambridge: Cambridge University Press.
Callow, J.C. (1968). A hierarchical study of neutralization in Kasem. *Journal of Linguistics* 4, 33-45.
Carstairs, A.D. (1981a). Review of Dell (1980). *Linguistics* 18, 943-50.
—— (1981b). *Constraints on Allomorphy in Inflexion:* London University PhD thesis.
—— (1981c). *Notes on Affixes, Clitics and Paradigms.* Bloomington: Indiana University Linguistics Club.
—— (1983). Paradigm economy. *Journal of Linguistics* 19, 115-18.
—— (1984a). Paradigm economy in the Latin third declension. *Transactions of the Philological Society*, 117-37.
—— (1984b). *Constraints on Allomorphy in Inflexion.* (Shortened version of Carstairs 1981b.) Bloomington: Indiana University Linguistics Club.
—— (1984c). Outlines of a constraint on syncretism. *Folia Linguistica* 18, 73-85.
—— (1985a). Review of Wurzel (1984). *Journal of Linguistics* 21, 487-93.
—— (1985b). Diachronic evidence and the affix-clitic distinction. Paper presented at the 7th International Conference on Historical Linguistics, Pavia, September 1985.
—— (1986). Macroclasses and paradigm economy in German nouns. *Zeitschrift fur Phonetik, Sprachwissenschaft und Kommunikationsforschung* 39, 3-11.
Chomsky, N. (1965). *Aspects of the Theory of Syntax.* Cambridge, Mass.: MIT Press.
—— (1970). Remarks on nominalization. In Jacobs, R.A. & Rosenbaum, P.S. (eds.) *Readings in English Transformational Grammar*, 184-221. Waltham: Ginn and Company.
—— (1980). On binding. *Linguistic Inquiry* 11, 1-46.
Chomsky, N. & Halle, M. (1968). *The Sound Pattern of English.* New York: Harper & Row.
Comrie, B. (1978). Genitive-accusatives in Slavic: the rules and their motivation. In Comrie, B. (ed.) *Classification of Grammatical Categories*, 27-42. Edmonton: Linguistic Research Inc.
—— (1981). *Languages of the Soviet Union.* Cambridge: Cambridge University Press.
Comrie, B. & Stone, G. (1978). *The Russian Language Since the Revolution.* Oxford: Oxford University Press.
Davidson, W., Elford, L.W. & Hoijer, H. (1963). Athapaskan

classificatory verbs. In Hoijer, H. (ed.) *Studies in the Athapaskan Languages* (University of California Publications in Linguistics, vol. 29), 30-41. Berkeley: University of California Press.

Dell, F. (1980). *Generative Phonology.* Cambridge: Cambridge University Press.

Dixon, R.M.W. (1972). *The Dyirbal Language of North Queensland.* Cambridge: Cambridge University Press.

—— (1980). *The Languages of Australia.* Cambridge: Cambridge University Press.

Doke, C.M. (1973). *Textbook of Zulu Grammar* (6th edn.). Cape Town: Longman.

Dressler, W.U. (1977). *Grundfragen der Morphonologie.* Vienna: Verlag der Österreichischen Akademie der Wissenschaften.

—— (1985). *Morphonology: The Dynamics of Derivation.* Ann Arbor: Karoma.

Einarsson, S. (1945). *Icelandic.* Baltimore: Johns Hopkins.

Ernout, A. (1953). *Morphologie historique du latin* (3rd edn.). Paris: Klincksieck.

Ferguson, C.A. & Slobin, D.I. (eds.) (1973). *Studies in Child Language Development.* New York: Holt Rinehart.

Fillmore, C.J. (1968). The case for case. In Bach & Harms (eds.), 1-90.

Fisiak, J. (ed.) (1980). *Historical Morphology.* The Hague: Mouton.

Garzanti (1963) = *Dizionario Garzanti della lingua italiana.* Milan: Garzanti.

Gotteri, N. (1981). Neuters, viriles and other objects of wonder: options in the Polish gender system. Paper read at the April 1981 meeting of the Linguistic Association of Great Britain.

Greenberg, J.H. (1963). Some universals of grammar with particular reference to the order of meaningful elements. In Greenberg, J.H. (ed.) *Universals of Language* (2nd edn., 1966), 73-113. Cambridge, Mass.: MIT Press.

Gulya, J. (1966). *Eastern Ostyak Chrestomathy.* Bloomington: Indiana University Press.

Guthrie, M. (1956). Observations on nominal classes in Bantu languages. *Bulletin of the School of Oriental and African Studies* 18, 545-55. Reprinted in Guthrie, M. (1970) *Collected Papers on Bantu Linguistics,* 79-89. Farnborough: Gregg.

Haas, W. (1957). Zero in linguistic description. In *Studies in Linguistic Analysis* (Special Volume of the Philological Society), 33-53. Oxford: Blackwell.

Hakulinen, L. (1957). *Handbuch der finnischen Sprache* (vol. I). Wiesbaden: Horrossowitz. English translation (1961): *The Structure and Development of the Finnish Language.* Bloomington: Indiana University Press.

Halle, M. (1973). Prolegomena to a theory of word-formation. *Linguistic Inquiry* 4, 3-16.

Harms, R.T. (1957). The Finnish genitive plural. *Language* 33, 533-7.

Harris, J.W. (1973). On the order of certain phonological rules in Spanish. In Anderson & Kiparsky (eds.), 59-76.

Harris, M.B. (1978). The interrelationship between phonological and grammatical change. In Fisiak, J. (ed.) *Recent Developments in*

Historical Phonology, 159-72. The Hague: Mouton.
Harris, Z. (1951). *Methods in Structural Linguistics*. (Reprinted as *Structural Linguistics*.) Chicago: Chicago University Press.
Hjelmslev, L. (1935). *La catégorie des cas*. Aarhus: Universitetsforlaget. Reprinted (1972) by Wilhelm Fink Verlag, Munich.
—— (1961). *Prolegomena to a Theory of Language*. Madison: University of Wisconsin Press. Translation of *Omkring sprogteoriens grundlæggelse* (1943). Copenhagen: Munksgard.
Hockett, C.F. (1954). Two models of grammatical description. *Word 10*, 210-31. Reprinted in RiL I, 386-99.
Hooper, J. Bybee (1976). *Introduction to Natural Generative Phonology*. New York: Academic Press.
—— (1979). Child morphology and morphophonemic change. *Linguistics 17*, 21-50. Reprinted in Fisiak (ed.), 157-87.
Huddleston, R. (1975). Homonymy in the English verbal paradigm. *Lingua 37*, 151-76.
Hudson, G. (1975). *Suppletion in the Representation of Alternations*. UCLA PhD thesis. Ann Arbor: University Microfilms.
—— (1980). Automatic alternations in non-transformational phonology. *Language 56*, 94-125.
Hudson, R.A. (1974). A structural sketch of Beja. *African Language Studies 15*, 111-42.
Hyman, L.M. (1975). *Phonology: Theory and Analysis*. New York: Holt Rinehart.
Jakobson, R. (1936). Beitrag zur allgemeinen Kasuslehre. *Travaux du Cercle linguistique de Prague 6*, 240-88. (Page references are to the reprint in RiL II, 51-95.)
Janda, R. (1980). On the decline of declensional systems: the overall loss of OE nominal case inflections and the ME reanalysis of -*es* as *his*. In Traugott *et al.* (eds.), 243-52.
Janda, R. & Sandoval, M. (1984). *"Elsewhere" in Morphology*. Bloomington: Indiana University Linguistics Club.
Joseph, B. & Wallace, R. (1984). Latin morphology: another look. *Linguistic Inquiry 15*, 319-28.
Kálmán, B. (1976). *Wogulische Texte mit einem Glossar*. Budapest: Akadémiai Kiadó.
Kastowsky, D. (1980). Zero in morpholoy: a means of making up for phonological losses. In Fisiak (ed.), 213-50.
Keller, R.E. (1978). *The German Language*. London: Faber & Faber.
Kenstowicz, M. & Kisseberth, C. (1977). *Topics in Phonological Theory*. New York: Academic Press.
—— (1979). *Generative Phonology: Description and Theory*. New York: Academic Press.
King, R.D. (1969). *Historical Linguistics and Generative Grammar*. Englewood Cliffs: Prentice-Hall.
Kiparsky, P. (1968a). How abstract is phonology? Bloomington: Indiana University Linguistics Club. Reprinted in Fujimura, O. (ed.) (1973) *Three Dimensions of Linguistic Theory*, 5-56. Tokyo: TEC Company Ltd. Also in Kiparsky (1982a), 119-63.
—— (1968b). Linguistic universals and linguistic change. In Bach & Harms (eds.), 170-202. Also in Kiparsky (1982a), 13-43.

—— (1971). Historical linguistics. In Dingwall, W.O. (ed.) *A Survey of Linguistic Science* (2nd edn., 1978), 33-57. Stamford, Conn.: Greylock. Also in Kiparsky (1982a), 57-80.
—— (1972). Explanation in phonology. In Peters, S. (ed.) *Goals of Linguistic Theory*, 189-227. Englewood Cliffs: Prentice-Hall. Also in Kiparsky (1982a), 81-118.
—— (1973). "Elsewhere" in phonology. In Anderson & Kiparsky (eds.), 93-106.
—— (1982a). *Explanation in Phonology*. (Publications in Language Sciences 4.) Dordrecht: Foris.
—— (1982b). Lexical morphology and phonology. In Linguistic Society of Korea (ed.) *Linguistics in the Morning Calm* (Selected Papers from SICOL-1981), 1-91. Seoul: Hanshen Publishing Co.
Koutsoudas, A., Sanders, J. & Noll, G. (1974). On the application of phonological rules. *Language 50*, 1-28.
Krahe, H. (1969). *Germanische Sprachwissenschaft II: Formenlehre* (7th edn., revised by W. Meid.) Sammlung Goschen. Berlin: de Gruyter.
Kurylowicz, J. (1949). La nature des procès dits "analogiques". *Acta Linguistica 5*, 121-38. Reprinted in RiL II, 158-74.
Lakoff, R. (1972). Another look at drift. In Stockwell, R.P. & Macauley, R. (eds.) *Linguistic Change and Generative Theory*, 172-98. Bloomington: Indiana University Press.
Lehmann, W.P. (1973). A structural principle of language and its implications. *Language 49*, 47-66.
Leumann, M. (1977). *Lateinische Laut- und Formenlehre* (Handbuch der Altertumswissenschaft Abt. 2, Teil 2, Band 1). Munich: C.H. Beck'sche Verlagsbuchhandlung.
Lewis, G.L. (1967). *Turkish Grammar*. Oxford: Oxford University Press.
Lieber, R. (1981). *On the Organization of the Lexicon*. Bloomington: Indiana University Linguistics Club.
—— (1982). Allomorphy. *Linguistic Analysis 10*, 27-52.
Lightfoot, D.W. (1979). *Principles of Diachronic Syntax*. Cambridge: Cambridge University Press.
Linell, P. (1979). *Psychological Reality in Phonology*. Cambridge: Cambridge University Press.
Lockwood, D.G. (1972). *Introduction to Stratificational Linguistics*. New York: Harcourt Brace Jovanovich.
Lounsbury, F.G. (1953). *Oneida Verb Morphology*. (Yale University Publications in Anthropology 48.) New Haven: Yale University Press.
Martinet, A. (1955). *Économie es changements phonétiques*. Bern: Francke.
Mathesius, V. (1931). Zum Problem der Belastungs- und Kombinationsfähigkeit der Phoneme. *Travaux du Cercle linguistique de Prague 4*, 148-52. Reprinted in Vachek, J. (ed.) (1964) *A Prague School Reader in Linguistics*, 177-82. Bloomington: Indiana University Press.
Matthews, P.H. (1972a). Huave verb morphology: some comments from a non-tagmemic viewpoint. *International Journal of American*

Linguistics 38, 96-118.
—— (1972b). *Inflectional Morphology.* Cambridge: Cambridge University Press.
—— (1974). *Morphology: An Introduction to the Theory of Word-structure.* Cambridge: Cambridge University Press.
Mayerthaler, W. (1981). *Morphologische Natürlichkeit.* Wiesbaden: Athenaion.
McCarthy, J. (1981). A prosodic theory of nonconcatenative morphology. *Linguistic Inquiry* 12, 373-418.
McIntosh, M. (1984). *Fulfulde Syntax and Verbal Morphology.* Boston: KP, in association with the University of Port Harcourt Press.
Meillet, A. (1933). *Esquisse d'une histoire de la langue latine* (3rd edn.). Paris: Hachette.
Meinhof, C. (1948). *Grundzüge einer vergleichenden Grammatik der Bantusprachen* (2nd ed.). Hamburg: Eckardt & Messtorff.
Mel'čuk, I.A. (1973). On the possessive forms of the Hungarian noun. In Kiefer, F. & Ruwet, N. (eds.) *Generative Grammar in Europe,* 315-32. Dordrecht: Reidel.
—— (1976). On suppletion. *Linguistics* 170, 45-90.
Mohanan, K. (1982). *Lexical Phonology.* Bloomington: Indiana University Linguistics Club.
Mohanan, K. & Mohanan, T. (1984). Lexical phonology of the consonant system in Malayalam. *Linguistic Inquiry* 15, 575-602.
Neustupný, J.V. (1978). *Post-structural Approaches to Language.* Tokyo: University of Tokyo Press.
Palmer, F.R. (1962). *The Morphology of the Tigre Noun.* London: Oxford University Press.
Pesetsky, D. (1979). Russian morphology and lexical theory. Unpublished ms, MIT.
Pike, K.L. (1963). Theoretical implications of matrix permutation in Fore (New Guinea). *Anthropological Linguistics* 5.8, 1-23.
—— (1965). Non-linear order and anti-redundancy in German morphological matrices. *Zeitschrift für Mundartforschung* 32, 193-221.
Plank, F. (1979). The functional basis of case systems and declension classes: from Latin to Old French. *Linguistics* 17, 611-40.
—— (1980). Encoding grammatical relations: acceptable and unacceptable non-distinctness. In Fisiak (ed.), 289-325.
—— (1981). *Morphologische (Ir-)Regularitäten: Aspekte der Wortstrukturtheorie.* Tübingen: Gunter Narr Verlag.
—— (to appear). Paradigm size, morphological typology, and universal economy. *Folia Linguistica* 20.
RiL I = Joos, M. (ed.) (1966). *Readings in Linguistics I* (4th edn.). Chicago: University of Chicago Press.
RiL II = Hamp, E.P., Householder, F.W. & Austerlitz, R. (eds.) (1966). *Readings in Linguistics II.* Chicago: University of Chicago Press.
Risch, E. (1977). Das System der lateinischen Deklinationen. *Cahiers Ferdinand de Saussure* 31, 229-45.
Robins, R.H. (1959). In defence of WP. *Transactions of the Philological Society* 116-44.
Roncari, A. & Brighenti, C. (1940). *La lingua italiana insegnata agli*

stranieri. Verona: Mondadori.
Rudes, B.A. (1980). On the nature of verbal suppletion. *Linguistics 18*, 655-76.
Rycroft, D. & Ngcobo, A.B. (1979). *Say It In Zulu.* Teaching material available from the School of Oriental and African Studies, London.
Sadock, J. (1983). The necessary overlapping of grammatical components. In Richardson, J., Marks, M. & Chukerman, A. (eds.) *Papers from the Parasession on the Interplay of Phonology, Morphology and Syntax,* 198-221. Chicago: Chicago Linguistic Society.
Sapir, E. (1921). *Language.* London: Rupert Hart-Davis.
Sauvageot, A. (1949). *Esquisse de la langue finnoise.* Paris: Klincksieck.
—— (1951). *Esquisse de la langue hongroise.* Paris: Klincksieck.
—— (1971). *L'édification de la langue hongroise.* Paris: Klincksieck.
Scalise, S. (1984). *Generative Morphology.* Dordrecht: Foris.
Schulz, H. & Sundermeyer, W. (1964). *Deutsche Sprachlehre fur Ausländer* (25th edn.). Munich: Hueber.
Seiler, H.-J. (1966). Das Paradigma in alter und neuer Sicht. *Kratylos 11*, 190-205.
Selkirk, E.O. (1982). *The Syntax of Words.* Cambridge, Mass.: MIT Press.
Siegel, D.C. (1974). *Topics in English Morphology.* MIT PhD thesis. Published (1979) by Garland, New York.
—— (1978). The Adjacency Constraint and the theory of morphology. *Papers from the North-Eastern Linguistic Society* (NELS) *8*, 189-97.
Sims-Williams, N. (1982). The double system of nominal inflexion in Sogdian. *Transactions of the Philological Society,* 67-76.
Sommer, F. (1948). *Handbuch der lateinischen Laut- und Formenlehre* (2nd and 3rd edn.). Heidelberg: Carl Winter.
Stairs, E.F. & Hollenbach, B.E. (1969). Huave verb morphology. *International Journal of American Linguistics 35*, 38-53.
Thomas-Flinders, T. (ed.) (1981). *Inflectional Morphology: Introduction to the Extended Word-and-Paradigm Theory.* UCLA Occasional Papers #4: Working Papers in Morphology.
Thomason, S.G. (1976). What else happens to opaque rules? *Language 52*, 370-81.
Thumb, A. & Hauschild, R. (1958). *Handbuch des Sanskrit* (3rd edn.) Part I, 1 (Einleitung und Lautlehre). Heidelberg: Carl Winter.
TIL 1957 = *Travaux de l'Institut de Linguistique* (Faculté des Lettres de l'Université de Paris) vol. II: La notion de neutralisation dans la morphologie et le lexique. Paris: Klincksieck.
Traugott, E.C., Labrum, R. & Shepherd, S. (eds.) (1980). *Papers from the 4th International Conference on Historical Linguistics.* Amsterdam: John Benjamins.
Vago, R.M. (1980). *The Sound Pattern of Hungarian.* Washington, D.C.: Georgetown University Press.
Vennemann, T. (1972). Phonetic and conceptual analogy. In Vennemann, T. & Wilbur, T. (eds.) *Schuchardt, the Neogrammarians and the Transformational Theory of Phonological Change,* 181-204. Frankfurt: Athenäum.
—— (1975). An explanation of drift. In Li, C.N. (ed.) *Word Order and*

Word Order Change, 269-305. Austin: University of Texas Press.
Vincent, N. (1980). Words versus morphemes in morphological change: the case of Italian *-iamo*. In Fisiak (ed.), 383-98.
Vogt, H. (1971). *Grammaire de la langue géorgienne*. Oslo: Universitetsforlaget.
Wanner, D. (1972). The derivation of inflexional paradigms in Italian. In Casagrande, J. & Saciuk, B. (eds.) *Generative Studies in Romance Languages*. Rowley, Mass.: Newbury House.
Warburton, I.P. (1973). Modern Greek verb conjugation: inflectional morphology in a transformational grammar. *Lingua 32*, 193-226.
Weinreich, U., Labov, W. & Herzog, M.I. (1968). Empirical foundations for a theory of language change. In Lehmann, W.P. & Malkiel, Y. (eds.) *Directions for Historical Linguistics: A Symposium*, 95-188. Austin: University of Texas Press.
Wheeler, M.W. (1980). Analogy and inflectional affix replacement. In Traugott *et al.* (eds.), 273-84.
Whitney, W.D. (1889). *Sanskrit Grammar* (2nd edn.). Cambridge, Mass.: Harvard University Press.
Williams, E. (1981). On the notions "lexically related" and "head of a word". *Linguistic Inquiry 12*, 245-74.
Wurzel, W.U. (1970). *Studien zur deutschen Lautstruktur*. Berlin: Akademie-Verlag.
—— (1984). *Flexionsmorphologie und Natürlichkeit*. Berlin: Akademie-Verlag.
Zwicky, A. (1977). *On Clitics*. Bloomington: Indiana University Linguistics Club.
—— (1985). How to describe inflection. *Berkeley Linguistic Society Papers 11*, 372-86.

Indexes

INDEX OF LANGUAGES

Afrikaans 5
Arabic 128, 132-6, 143,
  213-14, 253

Beja 167-8

Chamorro 202
Cheremiss *see* Mari
Cherokee 38

Dogrib 40
Dyirbal 3, 42, 45-7, 49, 51, 60,
  62-3, 64, 68, 70, 74-6, 84,
  96, 97-8, 143, 146, 180

English 6, 10, 15, 18-21, 23,
  25, 30, 31-2, 36-8, 40, 95-6,
  97, 106, 143, 148, 196-7,
  199, 201, 203, 254
  see also Old English

Fang 21
Finnish 30, 119-20, 122, 143,
  184, 189-92, 214
French 143, 152, 256
Fula, Fulani *see* Fulfulde
Fulfulde 185-8, 253

Georgian 128, 131-2, 143
German 22, 25, 28, 32, 41, 49,
  65, 83, 88, 89, 93-4, 96, 98,
  102, 123, 139, 143, 211,
  214, 216, 221-2, 232,
  234-51
  see also Old High German
Gothic 217-18
Greek 9, 14, 26, 49, 54, 55,
  58-9, 70, 77, 79, 80, 82-3,
  137-8, 140, 141-2

Hebrew 143
Huave 176-9, 205

Hungarian 9, 15, 21, 22, 30, 31,
  32, 42-4, 47-8, 50, 51, 70,
  75, 80, 83-4, 110, 118-19,
  125, 127, 143, 149, 155-7,
  161, 165-7, 168, 169-70,
  174, 180, 190, 192, 199-201,
  203, 204-5, 208

Icelandic 105, 139
  see also Old Norse
Italian 27, 128-31, 143, 159,
  210-11, 214-16, 218-21,
  221-6, 230, 232, 233

Kasem 88

Latin 2, 3, 7-12, 15, 16, 21, 22,
  24-5, 26, 28-9, 30-1, 32,
  33-4, 35, 37, 38, 40-1, 49,
  55, 58-9, 66-9, 70, 74, 76-7,
  77-9, 80-1, 82, 85, 88, 89,
  93, 98-100, 101, 102-6,
  121-2, 127, 137-8, 141, 144,
  149-52, 154-5, 161, 162-4,
  166, 167, 190, 192, 207-9,
  218-20, 232, 233, 253, 254
Lithuanian 123, 143

Mari 179, 253

Navajo 38

Old English 217-18
Old High German 217
Old Norse 217
Oneida 26
Ostyak 165

Polish 65-6

Russian 10, 49, 60-2, 64, 68,
  74, 84, 85-6, 89, 100-1,

137-8, 142-3, 145, 147,
231-2, 255

Sanskrit 9, 55, 76-7, 142,
211-13, 221-2, 226-8, 230,
232
see also Vedic
Serbo-Croat 84-5
Slovenian 9, 94
Sogdian 22
Spanish 27, 35, 101, 130-1
Swedish 256

Tigre 65
Turkish 16, 21, 22, 79-80, 96,
97, 108, 110, 125, 127,
155-7, 161, 166, 173-5, 180,
182-5, 192, 194, 204

Vedic 142
Vietnamese 2
Vogul 165

Warlpiri 21, 180, 182

Zulu 14, 15, 16, 42, 44-6, 47,
51, 60, 63-6, 68, 70, 74,
84-5, 133, 155, 157-61,
165-7, 168, 169-70, 174-5,
180-2, 190-1, 203, 204, 206

INDEX OF NAMES

Aaltio, M.-H. 120, 139
Allen, M. 4, 195-7, 204
Allen, W.S. 233
Andersen, H. 257
Anderson, S.R. 4, 18, 23, 41,
84, 140, 188, 199
Anttila, R. 22
Arnott, D.W. 185-7, 205, 206
Aronoff, M. 31

Baker, M. 140, 201-3, 252
Bally, C. 22
Bánhidi, Z. 80, 204
Bazell, C.E. 90, 138
Bierwisch, M. 89, 253
Bloch, B. 169
Bloomfield, L. 139
Brighenti, C. 233
Broselow, E. 197
Bybee, J. 19, 41, 56, 80, 85, 86,
121-2, 124, 134, 139, 140,
233, 245, 252, 257
Bynon, T. 251

Callow, J.C. 88
Carstairs, A.D. 23, 55, 84, 99,
138, 139, 144, 145, 197,
206, 233, 250, 253, 254, 256
Chomsky, N. 2, 18-19, 21, 23,
35, 36, 139, 201

Comrie, B. 84, 85, 120
Correard, G. 188

Davidson, W. 38, 40
Dixon, R.M.W. 3, 21, 45-6, 62,
74-5, 84, 86, 96, 145, 180,
182
Doke, C.M. 22, 64, 65, 84, 85,
180
Dressler, W.U. 13, 27, 232, 257

Einarsson, S. 105
Elford, L.W. 38
Ernout, A. 41, 85, 86, 106

Ferguson, C.A. 257
Fillmore, C.J. 3

Gotteri, N. 65
Greenberg, J.H. 121
Gulya, J. 165
Guthrie, M. 21

Haas, W. 169
Hakulinen, L. 120, 139
Halle, M. 18-19, 23, 27, 35
Harms, R.T. 30
Harris, J.W. 27
Harris, M.B. 124, 126

INDEXES

Harris, Z. 26
Hauschild, R. 226
Hjelmslev, L. 89, 120-2, 128, 139
Hockett, C.F. 26
Hoijer, H. 38
Hollenbach, B.E. 176-9, 205
Hooper, J. Bybee: see Bybee, J.
Huddleston, R. 106
Hudson, G. 13, 19-20
Hudson, R.A. 167, 204
Hyman, L.M. 23, 84

Jakobson, R. 89, 100, 253
Janda, R. 41, 145, 206
Jókaj, Z. 80
Joseph, B. 139

Kálmán, B. 165
Kastowsky, D. 169
Keller, R.E. 243-4, 249
Kenstowicz, M. 23, 256
King, R.D. 41
Kiparsky, P. 18, 27, 41, 144, 188, 195, 199, 206, 250, 257
Kisseberth, C. 23, 256
Koutsoudas, A. 199
Krahe, H. 218
Kurylowicz, J. 255

Lakoff, R. 124
Lamb, S.M. 206
Lehmann, W.P. 126
Leumann, M. 41
Lewis, G.L. 79, 183, 204
Lieber, R. 21, 27, 41, 195, 234
Lightfoot, D.W. 126, 257
Linell, P. 23
Lockwood, D.G. 206
Lounsbury, F.G. 26

McCarthy, J. 22
McIntosh, M. 185-7, 205, 206
Martinet, A. 1, 41, 88
Mathesius, V. 41
Matthews, P.H. 2, 4, 14, 15, 21, 26, 149, 205
Mayerthaler, W. 13, 27, 238
Meillet, M. 21
Meinhof, C. 84

Mel'čuk, I.A. 147, 204-5
Mohanan, K. 197, 206
Mohanan, T. 197, 206

Neustupný, J.V. 126
Ngcobo, A.B. 22, 84, 85, 133
Noll, G. 199

Palmer, F.R. 65
Pesetsky, D. 195, 197, 206
Pike, K.L. 22, 88, 110, 112
Plank, F. 4, 88, 90, 250

Risch, E. 85, 223
Robins, R.H. 26
Roncari, A. 233
Rudes, B.A. 86, 245
Rycroft, D. 22, 84, 85, 133

Sadock, J. 233
Sanders, J. 199
Sandoval, M. 206
Sapir, E. 10
Sauvageot, A. 30
Scalise, S. 2, 4, 27
Schulz, H. 247
Seiler, H.-J. 26
Selkirk, E.O. 140, 195
Sherwood, P. 84
Siegel, D.C. 195-7, 203
Sims-Williams, N. 22
Slobin, D.I. 257
Sommer, F. 41
Stairs, E.F. 176-9, 205
Stone, G. 85
Sundermeyer, W. 247
Szabó, D. 80

Thomas-Flinders, T. 140
Thomason, S.G. 94
Thumb, A. 226

Vago, R.M. 139, 145, 204
Vennemann, T. 13, 19, 124
Vincent, N. 233
Vogt, H. 131

Wallace, R. 139
Wanner, D. 27
Warburton, I.P. 140

Weinreich, U. 41
Wheeler, M.W. 22
Whitney, W.D. 228
Williams, E. 27, 89, 139, 195
Wurzel, W.U. 27, 35, 41, 48,
56, 85, 90, 98, 118, 119, 233, 234, 235, 238, 243, 246, 250, 251, 252

Zwicky, A. 90, 139, 140, 156

INDEX OF TOPICS

Definitions and explanations of technical terms are indicated by page-references in bold type.

abstractness, phonological
  18-20
Adjacency Condition 195-8,
  206, 252, 254
agglutinating languages 16,
  125-7, 194, 252
allomorphy 6
  grammatically conditioned
    13, 18-20, 147
  lexically conditioned 18-20,
    147
  phonologically conditioned
    18-21, 44, 46, 47-8, 180,
    185-8, 215, 220-1, 226,
    238, 244, 251
  see also Deviation II, stem
    allomorphy, suppletion
alternation 18, 19, 38, 209, 211
  stress 231
  see also allomorphy
ambiguity 87, 88
analogy 26, 94, 255
autosegmental morphology 22

Bracket Erasure Convention
  197-8, 206

category, morphosyntactic **2**, 17
  internal structure 255
  single-member 175
  see also property
clitics 256
coding, inflexional 13
concord 3, 5
content 1, 5, 17, 87, 89, 153

derivation, contrasted with
inflexion 4-5, 203-4
deviations from one-to-one
  pattern 14-18
  Deviation I **14**
  Deviation II **14**, 15, 25, 87,
    147, 149-52, 164, 188,
    195, 207, 254
  Deviation III **14**, 15, 28,
    107-8, 149, 188-94, 254
  Deviation IV **14**, 16, 25, 87,
    91, 107, 164, 254
diachronic implications 39-40,
  54-5, 88, 95, 124-7, 128-32,
  218, 233, 244, 247, 250,
  253, 257
dominance 120-3, 129, 134
dystaxie 22

Elsewhere Condition 17,
  198-201, 206, 233, 252
exponence
  cumulative 15, 28, 110-14,
    149
  extended 14, 212
  overlapping 15, 149, 193,
    194, 216
  simultaneous 191, 193, 218
exponent, inflexional **6**, 21
  principal **151**, 218
expression 1, 5, 89, 121, 253
external evidence 256-7

formative 6
Free Distribution Characteristic
  29-32
functional yield 29, 41

269

fusional languages 16, 125-7

Gesamtbedeutung 89

homonymy 13, 16, 25, 87-138, 162-4
  lexical 95-6, 101
  systematic 13, 91, 93-102, 253, 254; function 91, 109-14; status 102-6
  see also Deviation IV, syncretism, Systematic Homonymy Claim, takeover
Humboldt's Universal 13

iconicity 238
Independent Distribution Characteristic **33**, 35, 42
Indo-European languages 107, 127-8, 249
inflexion *see* derivation, exponence, realisation
Inflexional Parsimony Hypothesis **31**, 32, 35, 36
isolating languages 2, 17
Item-and-Arrangement 26
'lexical morphology' 196-7

macroinflexion **50-1**, 69, 222, 236
macroparadigm **50**, **69**, 128, 137, 222, 237-41, 254
  uniqueness 70-7
Macroparadigm Uniqueness Claim **76**, 240, 243, 252
markedness 255
matrix
  ideal 22, 112
  optimal 22, 112
  simple 10
Mirror Principle 140, 201-3, 252
morph 6, 154
  discontinuous 13
  portmanteau 13, 193, 194
  replacive 13
  see also zero inflexion
morpheme 6, 21, 26, 190, 195
morphological processes 6, 10

ablaut 6, 10, 22, 254
affixation 6, 21, 58, 221, 230-1, 242, 248, 254
infixation 6
reduplication 6, 10, 21
string-dependent 21

Natural Generative Phonology 19, 147
'natural morphology' 27, 232
neutralisation 87-8
nonlinear phonology 19

observational gap 7, 11, 12
one-to-one pattern 12-13, 252
  see also deviations

paradigm 17, 24-8, 35, 42, **48-9**, 234
  mixture 77, 81, 228, 229, 232, 244, 253
  pressure 26-7
  recent views 26-8
  single versus multiple 222-32
Paradigm Economy Principle 17, **51**, 52-9, 207, 221-32, 234-50, 252, 253
paradigm structure condition 35, 36
paradigmatic dimension *see* Deviations II, IV
pejoration 65-6, 85
Peripherality Constraint 17, **162**, **168**, **193**, 197-8, 199-201, 202-3, 207, 210-21, 252, 254
phonological representation 18, 53-4, 236
polymorphy 22
polysemy 22
principal part 56, 57, 70, 231, 232
productivity 4, 5, 94-5
Proper Inclusion Precedence Principle 199
property
  lexically determined 58, 59-69, 137, 242, 254, 256
  morphosemantic 58, 60-6,

237, 242, 245
morphosyntactic **2**, 6, 17, 58, 237, 239-40, 242, 256

readjustment rules 23
realisation, inflexional **6**, 19, 21
    rules 90
    see also exponence
referral, rules of 90, 139, 140
relevance 86, 121-3, 129, 134, 233, 252

segment transformation 140
    see also sequence of realisation
selectional feature 36
sensitivity 15, 108, 147, 255, 256
    inward 161-2, 255
    outward 165-8, 179-88, 210, 212, 215, 217
    pure **150-1**, 169, 207, 210, 212, 214
sequence of realisation 133-7, 175-9, 253
sequence of tenses 3, 171-2
significant 1, 5
    see also expression
signifié 1, 17
    see also content
slab 58, 77, **81**, 233, 244-5
Slab Codicil **81**, 232, 242
stem
    morpholexical **207-8**, 209, 215, 216-17, 218, 221-2, 229, 232, 254

    phonological **207-8**
    realisational **207-8**, 218-19, 232
stem allomorphy 17, 58, 207-32, 242, 246-9, 253, 254
strict subcategorization feature 36
suppletion 15, 18-20, 23, 38, 147-8
syncretism 27, 88, 89, 92, 93, **115-16**, 123, 133-6, 138, 249, 253, 254
syntactic parsimony 35-40
syntagmatic dimension *see* Deviations I, III
system congruity 118, 120, 252
system-defining structural property 90, 119
Systematic Homonymy Claim 17, **123**, 124-7, 128-38, 163-4, 252, 253

take-over 90, 92, **117**, 123, 134-6, 163

word 1-2
    formation 2, 21
    structure rules 140; *see also* sequence of realisation
Word-and-Paradigm 26

zero inflexion 169-75, 190
    realisational versus morphosyntactic 173

For Product Safety Concerns and Information please contact our EU representative GPSR@taylorandfrancis.com
Taylor & Francis Verlag GmbH, Kaufingerstraße 24, 80331 München, Germany

www.ingramcontent.com/pod-product-compliance
Lightning Source LLC
Chambersburg PA
CBHW071017240426
43661CB00073B/2366